I Love Russia

I Love Russia

REPORTING FROM A LOST COUNTRY

ELENA KOSTYUCHENKO

Translated by BELA SHAYEVICH *and* ILONA YAZHBIN CHAVASSE

PENGUIN PRESS
NEW YORK
2023

PENGUIN PRESS
An imprint of Penguin Random House LLC
penguinrandomhouse.com

Articles were originally published, in Russian, in *Novaya Gazeta*.
The following articles were subsequently published in English as:

"The HBZ" was first published by *Harriman Magazine*, Fall 2018.
"Rust" was first published, in different form, by *n+1*, Issue 42: Vanishing Act, Spring 2022.
"Mykolaiv," was originally published as
"Leave Us Alone: In Mykolaiv," by *n+1* on March 17, 2022.

LIBRARY OF CONGRESS CATALOGING-IN-PUBLICATION DATA
Names: Kostyuchenko, Elena, 1987– author. | Shayevich, Bela, translator. | Chavasse, Ilona Yazhbin, translator.
Title: I love Russia: reporting from a lost country / Elena Kostyuchenko; translated by Bela Shayevich and Ilona Yazhbin Chavasse.
Description: New York: Penguin Press, 2023. | Includes index.
Identifiers: LCCN 2023018497 (print) | LCCN 2023018498 (ebook) | ISBN 9780593655269 (hardcover) | ISBN 9780593655481 (ebook)
Subjects: LCSH: Putin, Vladimir Vladimirovich, 1952—Influence. | Kostyuchenko, Elena, 1987– | Political culture—Russia (Federation) | Social change—Russia (Federation) | Journalism—Political aspects—Russia (Federation) | Freedom of the press—Russia (Federation)—History. | Russia (Federation)—Politics and government. | Russia (Federation)—Social conditions.
Classification: LCC DK510.763 .K6748 2023 (print) | LCC DK510.763 (ebook) |
DDC 947.086/2—dc23/eng/20230520
LC record available at https://lccn.loc.gov/2023018497
LC ebook record available at https://lccn.loc.gov/2023018498

Printed in the United States of America
1st Printing

Designed by Amanda Dewey
Map illustration by Daniel Lagin

To Nugzar Mikeladze

NORWAY
SWEDEN
FINLAND
ESTONIA
LATVIA
LITHUANIA
POLAND
BELARUS
UKRAINE
Kara Sea
Saint Petersburg
Malaya Vishera
Tver
Moscow
Larino
Kostroma
Yaroslavl
Dudinka
Lake Pyasino
Avam River
Kyiv
Odesa
Mykolaiv
Donbas
Crimea
Rostov-on-Don
Ilsky
Volga River
RUSSIA
Raznochinovka
Astrakhan
Beslan
Chechnya
Mesker-Yurt
KAZAKHSTAN

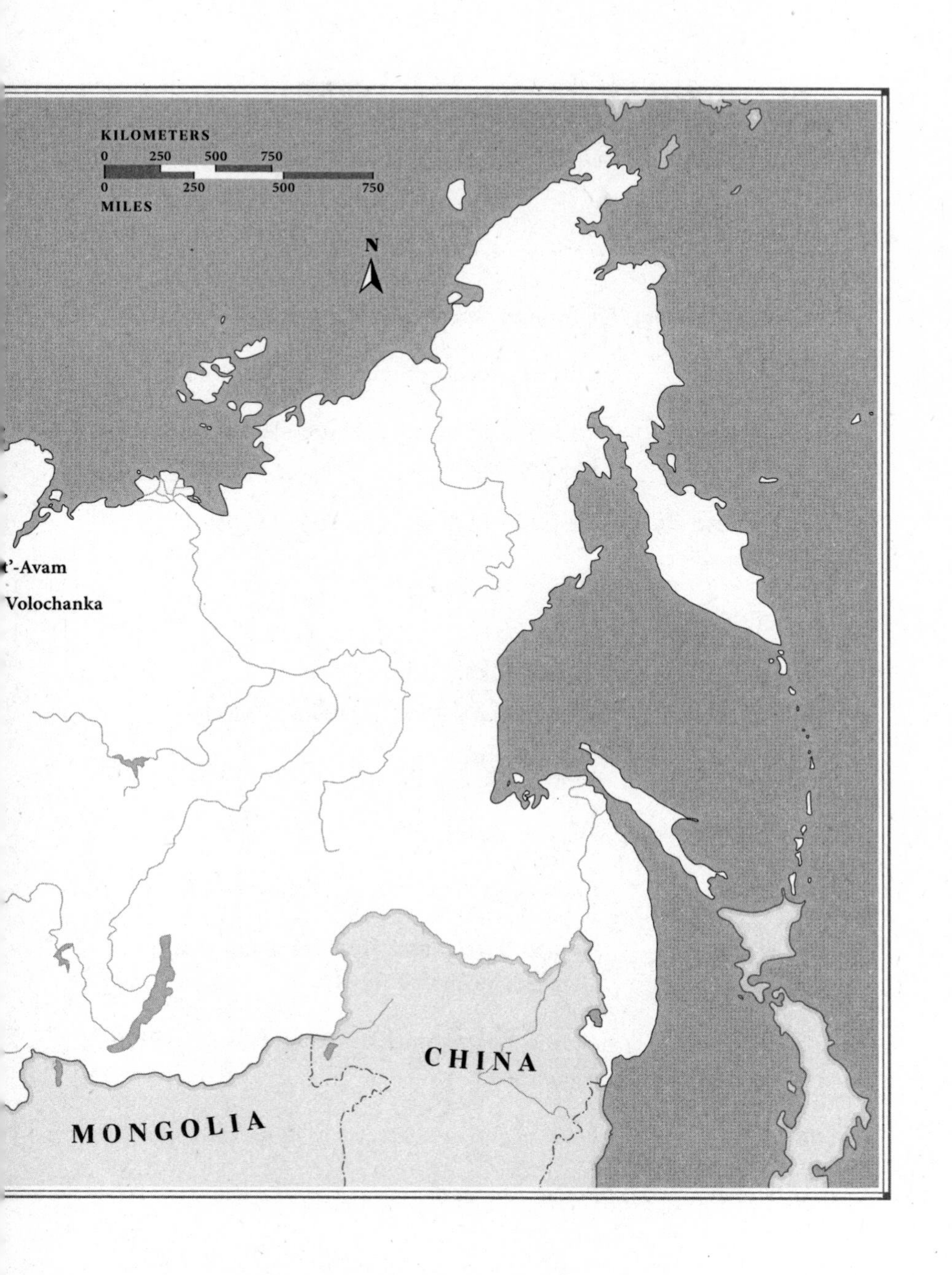
KILOMETERS
0 250 500 750
0 250 500 750
MILES
N
t'-Avam
Volochanka
CHINA
MONGOLIA

DECEMBER 26, 1991	Dissolution of the USSR
JUNE 8, 1991	Chechnya declares independence from Russia
JUNE 12, 1991	Boris Yeltsin elected first president of the Russian Federation
APRIL 1, 1993	First issue of *Novaya Gazeta* is published
DECEMBER 11, 1994– AUGUST 31, 1996	First Russian-Chechen War
AUGUST 7, 1999– APRIL 16, 2009	Second Russian-Chechen War, ending with annexation of Chechnya
AUGUST 9, 1999	Vladimir Putin appointed prime minister
DECEMBER 31, 1999	Yeltsin resigns
MAY 7, 2000	Putin begins first term as president
MAY 12, 2000	*Novaya Gazeta* journalist Igor Domnikov is attacked; he dies on July 16
JULY 3, 2003	*Novaya Gazeta* journalist Yuri Shchekochikhin is murdered
MAY 7, 2004	Putin begins second term as president
SEPTEMBER 1, 2004	Beslan massacre

OCTOBER 7, 2006	*Novaya Gazeta* journalist Anna Politkovskaya is murdered
MAY 7, 2008	Dmitry Medvedev takes office as president, names Putin his prime minister
AUGUST 8, 2008	Russian forces invade Georgia
JANUARY 19, 2009	*Novaya Gazeta*'s Stanislav Markelov and Anastasia Baburova are murdered
JULY 15, 2009	*Novaya Gazeta* journalist Natalia Estemirova is murdered
MAY 7, 2012	Putin begins third term as president
JUNE 11, 2013	The State Duma passes a law restricting all public speech that could be deemed "propaganda of homosexuality"; according to the law LGBTQ+ people are "socially unequal"
MARCH 18, 2014	Russia annexes Crimea
APRIL 7, 2014	War in Donbas begins; Russian troops covertly enter East Ukraine
SEPTEMBER 30, 2015	Russia begins military intervention in Syrian civil war
MAY 7, 2018	Putin begins fourth term as president
FEBRUARY 24, 2022	Russia invades Ukraine

CONTENTS

* *translated by Ilona Yazhbin Chavasse*

I Love Russia

what else:
if night falls
let everyone
close their eyes

if day
breaks
let everyone
open them

◆ FEDOR SVAROVSKY

CHAPTER 1

THE MEN FROM TV

I DON'T REMEMBER MYSELF as an infant, my memories begin from the time I am four, maybe three. I remember the silhouettes bending over me, or maybe I just think I do. I remember my grandma, she died when I was five, which must mean I have memories from when I was younger. Babushka would make fun of me and slap my hand and then laugh. She wasn't always all there, she was sick. When madness came over her, she would get shy and searching. She thought she was living with strangers and would become eager to make us like her. When she regained her senses, she'd turn back into the woman who had for many years been—and remained—the head of the household. She was accustomed to being obeyed and demanded obedience.

I was sick all the time, I'd always get colds. I rarely went out. In my memory, it's always twilight. A new building was slowly rising up in front of our windows, rising to block out the light. In the right corner of the room we lived in, there was a piano for me to grow into. Mama hoped I would one day learn how to play. In the left corner, there was the television. It worked, but the picture was fuzzy, shot through with static, making it look black-and-white.

The television was huge, or it seemed huge to me, with a bulging silver-gray screen made of thick glass. Dust adored it. I would pull up a chair, climb onto it, and brush the screen with my fingers. It felt like touching a moth's wings, ever-so-gently. Mama would say: that's the static.

I waited for evening for my allotted pleasure. That's when *Good Night, Little Ones!* would come on. The puppets, a piglet named Khryusha and a bunny named Stepashka, would talk to each other, and then they would play a cartoon. I loved the hand-drawn animations, but sometimes they'd be stop-motion instead, clay or just dolls. Those seemed like a sad waste of the magic of television. I could play with dolls all by myself.

I noticed that Mama turned on the TV before it was time for *Good Night*. She'd come home from work, hang up her trench coat, and sit down on the couch, still in her shoes. She'd wait a few minutes for her feet to "settle" and then she'd get up and plod over to the TV to turn it on. It'd be a show about grown-ups or news.

I hated the news and didn't understand how anybody could voluntarily watch it. The pictures that broke through the grainy broadcast were mystifying. People yelled, went places, there were identical anchors with identical intonations. I couldn't understand what they said. Mama watched them in silence. She was so tired.

Little by little, I was figuring out what was going on. One day, Mama told me our country used to be called the USSR, but now it was Russia. It had been better in the USSR: there was a lot of food, people were kind to each other. Now things were different. Later, I learned that Mama had been a chemist, but the institute where she had worked no longer paid money,* so she became a cleaning woman and teacher and also washed diapers at my preschool. This was why she was so tired and didn't play with me and didn't hug me as much as I wanted. I asked her whose fault it was that the USSR had turned into Russia. Mama said Yeltsin. Who's

* In the 1990s, during the era of privatization and economic reforms, enterprises stopped paying employees their salaries, systematically, on a massive scale. In 1996, 49.3 percent of workers in Central Russia weren't paid—elsewhere, this number went up to 69 percent. At the same time, there was catastrophic inflation. Just in 1992, prices increased by a factor of twenty-six.

Yeltsin? The president. What is the president? The most important person in the country.

Mama pointed him out to me on the news. The most important person in our country was ugly and old, with a giant head. I didn't understand what he was saying. He mumbled just like my grandma did when she was sick, stretching his words.

I'd watch him and think, It's your fault that my mama is tired. That she drags her feet when she walks like she's old. That she doesn't play with me and doesn't hug me as much as I want. That people used to be kind and live in the USSR, and now we live in Russia, and Russia is worse. When Yeltsin appeared on the screen, I'd furrow my brow and say, Yeltsin is bad. And Mama would smile. I started watching the news with Mama and yelling at Yeltsin just so I could see her smile.

Sometimes Mama's friends from the institute would come over. They'd sit in the kitchen and I would be underfoot. Whenever anyone mentioned Yeltsin, I'd perk up my ears. And then, in the next available pause, I would add, "Yeltsin is bad." The grown-ups laughed. They'd say, "Your little girl is so grown up." The grown-ups told me that Yeltsin was also a drunk. And so I started saying, "Yeltsin is a bad drunk." The grown-ups laughed at this, too.

The older I got, the more I could understand the news. Miners were beating their helmets against a bridge in Moscow.* Mama sent the miners money, she said they were starving. Chechens were fighting with Russians. I was afraid of Chechens, I thought they were all scary bad guys with beards, just like pirates. I wished I could see one of them in real life. Then came the criminals. I never saw them but I would hear them. Sometimes, there would be shooting outside. Mama would say, Stay away from the window.

When I was five, I found out that we were all going to die. Even Mama. A little while later, I realized that Mama might not die of old age sometime in the future, she could die any moment because of the

* In 1998, miners who had stopped being paid blocked roads and protested outside the Parliament in Moscow. They demanded President Yeltsin's resignation.

criminals. I started being scared of the night. Evil came closer at night, darkness opened the door to it. I would get up on the windowsill and stare into the darkness. I believed that my gaze lit Mama's way home and protected her. Sometimes, the terror would overwhelm me. Then I would take out our tin of old buttons and pore through them all like they were treasure. The buttons protected me from the terror a bit.

When I was in third grade, I finally saw the criminals up close. I was taking a shortcut home, through the courtyards, instead of taking the streets. Mama said never to do that, but I was in a hurry. I came upon three men and another one with them, but somehow apart. I remember them wearing black leather trench coats, but I probably made that up. One of the three men was swearing and then another one got out a gun. It was small and very black. I ducked into the nearest building to wait out the shooting. Two gunshots. I waited a little while longer, then peeked out of the doorway. The man who had been standing apart was curled up on the ground. Behind his ear, there was red. I couldn't see the criminals anymore. I made a wide arc around the man, then ran home. I didn't tell Mama. I knew that worrying could make the heart stop, and, with all of my little body, all I wanted was for Mama to live.

The criminals were because of Yeltsin, and so was the darkness outside the window, and all the long evenings waiting for Mama, and how we never had enough money—I knew what money was now, how much it cost. We didn't always have food. When I was nine, I joined a choir, we'd sing in hospitals and Houses of Culture. They paid choir members 30 rubles a concert, 60 for soloists. I wanted to be a soloist. Sixty rubles could get us seven loaves of bread.

I would ask Mama, If the USSR was such a good country, why didn't you stand up for it? Mama would say, We were deceived. Yeltsin lied to us.

I began watching the news with a voracious rage. I was impatient for Yeltsin to die. They would definitely show that on the news.

But: he kept not dying. Other people were dying. There were constantly funerals, coffins upholstered in red were continually being carried out into our courtyard. I would go up to our neighbors and ask, Why did he die? Why did she die? Alcohol poisoning, hanging, shooting, being murdered during a robbery, dying in a hospital that didn't have any drugs or doctors. My mama lived, my gaze protected her. Sometimes I'd bargain with God. I'd tell him, If Mama dies and I go off to live in the forest, what are You gonna do then?

When I was in seventh grade, here is what Yeltsin did. On New Year's Eve, while Mama and I were having our holiday dinner, he came on TV and he said, "I am tired. I'm stepping down." And with that, he stopped being the president. It was a New Year's Eve miracle. Mama cried and laughed and called all her friends and I thought, Finally. Now our new life would begin.

Six months later, there were elections. Vladimir Putin won. Putin was nothing like Yeltsin, he was athletic and young, with clear eyes. The eyes were the only memorable thing on his face. He had a special voice, it always sounded like he was restraining a growl. But when he smiled, everybody around him was very happy.

Mama didn't vote for Putin. She said he was KGB. I knew what KGB agents were, two of them had apartments across the way. They were maniacally suspicious, they drank a lot and weren't friendly. We didn't talk to them much.

On the day of the election, I went out to the courtyard to play. People were coming home from the polling places and asking each other, Did you vote for Putin? Me too. People would ask me about my mother. I would say, No, we're for the communists. Boys from our courtyard told me the communists were all rotting in their graves. We almost got into a fight.

People believed that Putin was going to protect them. Before the elections, buildings were blown up in several cities. We learned the term *terrorist attack*. Men from our building took turns doing night shifts, making sure that nobody wired our house with explosives. Putin said that we simply needed to kill all the terrorists and then the buildings would stop blowing up. He started a new war in Chechnya. I started washing floors. I was almost a grown-up now and I wanted to make some money so that my mother could be less tired. I'd get so tired, I would come home and do exactly what Mama did: go and sit down on the couch with my shoes on until my feet "settled." Mama didn't get mad.

Our television kept getting worse; it became hard to make out the faces in the black-and-white static. I started reading newspapers, we had them at our school library. I got obsessed with them—the pictures didn't change, you could think while you read. I decided to go work at one. The pay was no worse than washing floors. I wrote about bus pass scams, a teen health clinic, the skinheads that had appeared in our city. I was proud I was writing about grown-up things and considered myself a reporter.

Then one day I happened across a copy of *Novaya Gazeta*. I opened it up to a story about Chechnya. It was about a boy who wouldn't let his mother listen to Russian songs on the radio. Russian soldiers had taken his father away and brought him back as a corpse with no nose. The article had the words *cleansing* and *filtration center*. Soldiers killed thirty-six people in the village of Mesker-Yurt. One man (he survived) was crucified, they drove nails through the palms of his hands. The article was signed "Anna Politkovskaya."

I went to the public library and asked to see the collection of *Novaya Gazeta*s. I searched for Politkovskaya's articles. I read them. I'd feel like I was getting a fever, I'd put my hand on my forehead, but it was just clammy and dead. It turned out I didn't know anything about my country. TV had lied to me.

I walked around with this realization for several weeks. I'd read, go pace in the park, and then read more. I wanted to talk to a grown-up about it, but as it turned out, there weren't any around—all of them believed television.

I was angry at *Novaya Gazeta*. It had torn the commonly held truth away from me. I'd never had my own truth before. I am fourteen, I thought, and now I'm like some sort of invalid.

I decided I had to work at *Novaya Gazeta*.

It took me three years, but I made it happen.

PUTIN'S BEEN AT IT FOR A LONG TIME, BUT PICKING MEDVEDEV WAS A HUGE PAIN IN THE ASS

May 8, 2008

The Kremlin has been on high alert since 11 a.m. on May 6 because of the inauguration.* Instead of the usual gaggle of camera-clutching tourists, the cobblestones have been swarming with military men, peculiar people in black suits, tuxedoed musicians, and chorus girls. They're holding the final rehearsals for the parade, and the choir, and the orchestra, too. But most importantly, these rehearsals are for the TV correspondents.

Sixty-nine cameras will be trained on the president as he assumes his new role. They will film from the ground, from the waists and shoulders of cameramen, and from the towers overlooking the square. Channel 1 will be filming from helicopters. After many rounds of negotiations, a Belgian TV crew has been granted permission to mount their cameras to cables strung over the fortress walls.

Rehearsals began at the end of April. The Channel 1 camp by Sobornaya Square has been up for a whole week—some vans, an HQ tent. Inside their tent, they have internet, hot water, salami, and ramen. Men's suits hanging along the walls (anyone caught on camera has to be dressed for the occasion), assorted notices, rehearsal schedules. They've already filmed one hundred hours of the fifty inaugural minutes, from every angle. Putin's procession across the parade, then Medvedev's, the ceremony in the Grand Kremlin Palace, both presidents' reappearances before the crowd, their speeches—again and again and again.

* Russia's constitution does not allow for the president to serve more than two consecutive terms. After completing his first two terms, Vladimir Putin threw his support behind Dmitry Medvedev in the presidential elections of 2008. Medvedev was duly elected president. Putin became prime minister. At the end of Medvedev's term, in 2012, the two men announced a reshuffle. Medvedev would now be prime minister and Putin got to be president once again.

It doesn't seem like the camera choreography should be too complicated. There are just two principal figures. Putin exits one building, then walks to another. He goes up the right-hand staircase of the Grand Kremlin Palace. A short while later, Medvedev's motorcade sets off from the White House and heads to the Kremlin. He enters through a different door. They only meet once they are both inside. After the ceremony, they go down to the soldiers together.

Directors, correspondents, camera operators, editors, guards, and soldiers swarm Sobornaya Square. Nobody wears a badge; after a week of rehearsals, everyone knows one another. The TV people are quick to obey the young men with the transparent earpieces. Everyone—the cameramen, the soldiers, the guards—is constantly on their walkie-talkies. Someone is shouting, "Get the machine gunners behind the sight lines!" Nothing happens.

Nine platoons are going to parade in front of the Grand Kremlin Palace. For now, thirty soldiers representing the front and rear ranks, accompanied by their major general, stride out balletically onto the square, legs straight and toes pointed. The soldiers wear heavy greatcoats—their commander, a dead expression. "Good thing it's cold," says the cameraman standing next to me. "Day before yesterday, one of those boys passed out from the heat in the middle of the rehearsal."

A dozen or so Kremlin street sweepers weave in and out of the ranks. They're all conspicuously Slavic, in handsome green uniforms. There's not a speck of dust to be seen—the cobblestones look like they have been scrubbed—but stubbornly, the sweepers keep on, sweeping between every crack. Periodically, a woman in a business suit shouts at them. "Every last inch of the square better shine!" "Then why didn't they issue us vacuum cleaners?" the sweepers talk back. The woman nods toward the guards. "They wouldn't allow it."

"Sweepers, out! Now! Where are the presidents?" This is Natasha, a slim woman in jeans. She's from the president's office. She is directing the movements of all the cameras.

The "presidents"—the president's bodyguards, doubling as stand-ins—are standing around. Putin is played by a swarthy guy in a raincoat whose only resemblance to the original is his total lack of distinguishing features. "Medvedev" is very young; curly hair, wire in ear, and an exceedingly sly look on his face. "They look nothing like them!" I protest. "It's just the height that matters—down to the inch. So the cameras can hit their marks," Lyosha the technician explains as he puts up a rain shelter for the cameramen. "That Putin's been at it for a long time, but picking Medvedev was a huge pain in the ass."

"Putin—go!" Natasha calls out. The serviceman sets off with a leisurely, presidential gait along the front ranks standing to attention. A camera, attached sideways to its operator's special plastic vest, moves in parallel, behind the row of soldiers. An assistant grips the cameraman by the waist for stability and, step by step, both are backing up, quickly and precisely. "Putin" walks up to the red-carpeted staircase and begins to ascend. The cameraman bends over backward, keeping "Putin" in the center of the frame. "The camera shook! Let's do it again!"

Then they rehearse the post-ceremony departure. The presidents try hard to walk in step, but again everyone is dissatisfied. "Twenty! Twenty paces! Again!" "Are you sure Medvedev should be on Putin's left?" another director asks Natasha. "Maybe we swap them?" "I'm sure. Let's run it again!" Then the directors get in a long argument regarding the placement of the opulent gilded lectern on which the president's speech will be laid out tomorrow. They're arguing over twenty inches, and these, as it turns out, will have a profound effect on the visuals.

Finally, the major general crisply marches up to the stand-ins. He raps out, "Comrade President, the parade in honor of the inauguration of the president of the Russian Federation is assembled." He salutes. "Putin" looks into the nearest camera and moves his lips silently for several minutes. This is the outgoing president's farewell speech. The cameramen film him intently.

While they change over the lighting, the two presidents wait on the staircase, gazing out at the soldiers, looking very important. "Good thing it won't be sunny," says "Putin." "You squint and it makes you look mean. This way you can just look straight ahead. Easy."

"Uh-huh," says "Medvedev."

One of the directors dashes over to explain for the umpteenth time which way everybody is going and when and what camera will be pointed at them. The guards pay the closest attention. They're the ones who will have to relay all these intricacies to the real Putin and Medvedev.

"I hope it's all sinking in," Lyosha grumbles. "Last time, at the economic forum in Saint Petersburg, we also went through all these rehearsals. Made backdrops, filled in an ice rink, guards everywhere, cameras. Putin gets out of the car and they tell him, You walk in front of the cameras like this and like that. He goes, I'm not walking in circles, and crosses right over the ice rink, over the ice. The guards are losing their shit, we're freaking out . . ."

"And what if Putin sneezes?"

Lyosha gives me a blank look.

"Or Medvedev stumbles? Live on the air."

"That is exactly why," Lyosha tells me with pride, "there's always a slight delay in the broadcast with these kinds of events."

So, what have we got here? We're all on tenterhooks, worrying about somebody tripping over a treacherous fold in the carpet, extremists jumping out of the bushes, the president stuttering during his oath, when actually, a happy ending has been preordained all along. What are we all worrying about?

CHAPTER 2

CHILDHOOD ENDS

I WAS AT A FRIEND'S HOUSE when Mama called me and told me she couldn't reach Vanya. Vanya was my adopted younger brother.

I didn't want to leave—it was a summer night, I was being listened to and adored, I had already had half a bottle of wine. I don't remember what I told her, but I know my tone was languid.

I still went.

It was getting light out. I was in a taxi and on the phone with the police. We flew through Moscow, out of the well-groomed historic center into the forest of high-rises on the outskirts. I was shocked at all the trees growing out there—they were huge, rising up to the very top floors.

Vanya lived between Yaroslavl and Kostroma. He worked who the fuck knows where. My sister said that for a while, he'd been sleeping with men for money. They'd traded apartments for the May holidays:* my sister went to Yaroslavl and he went to the apartment that she'd been renting in Moscow and invited his friends.

I went up to his floor. Police crowded the stairwell. They were waiting for first responders to come and open the door.

* May 1 is Labor Day in Russia, and May 9, Victory Day. Both of these are government holidays, and oftentimes they are extended to the intervening days, too.

The first responders arrived and said they wouldn't break it down—the apartment owner had to be present. The owner was an old man who lived at his dacha. We didn't have his phone number.

I told them, My brother's in there. If you don't open the door and something happens to him, I'll put you all behind bars for negligence.

Of course, I didn't really believe anything could have happened to him. But I liked feeling strong, adult, capable of intimidating the cops and first responders.

The men were silent.

Two of Vanya's wasted buddies were hanging around saying dumb shit, both of them a lot older than Vanya. They'd gone out for booze and couldn't get back in. One of them had left his bag in there and kept whining about it.

A first responder went downstairs, assessed the building from the outside, came back and told us that he could attempt to get in through the balcony.

The neighbors let him go through their apartment.

A few minutes passed.

The lock creaked. The first responder came out, looked past me into the stairwell, and said, "Relatives."

I went in.

Vanya lay on the couch, he was very hard. His face was blue green. Next to him there was a bag, a knife, and a container of butane.

His grandmother refused to come. But she demanded that he get buried in her village.

We decided to bury him in Moscow.

I thought, Now I'll have a grave.

They put a lot of makeup on him for the funeral, he was unrecognizable. The bones stuck out of his face, his hair was slicked back. He looks like an opera singer, said Mama.

His cousin came, she had the same face as Vanya, same eyes. She'd also grown up in an orphanage. I never knew that he had a cousin.

He didn't understand fractions. He didn't know how to tell time on an analog clock. He was good at impressions—he got a B in English without knowing a word by simply repeating whatever the teacher said, perfectly. He could sing songs in foreign languages. He loved to dance.

Mama would say, My first grandchild is going to come from my son and not you girls.

The coffin was all white inside.

They stuck a piece of paper with a prayer on it to his forehead.

His friends came up to me and told me that Vanya had been a serious sorcerer. They gave me his handwritten book of spells. There weren't many. I saw his handwriting for the first time—it looked like a child's. Letters of various sizes crowding each other.

I went up to the coffin and laid the book at his feet. There was supposed to be a bag of blessed dirt somewhere in there.

I kept thinking, I'm such an adult now. I'm such an adult now.

Then I had all of these documents to fill out. Then I ran out of documents.

And I was left without a brother.

I never visited his grave again. I simply couldn't.

His photos are on an old computer. He looks so young, sitting there with a beer, smiling placidly, looking straight at the camera. My sister made a video—a slideshow to a song whose chorus went, "And you'll betray me, too."

My sister Sveta is also adopted. Before that, we barely talked. She drank, she stole, she lied, she ran away, she repelled everybody who tried to get close to her. I didn't believe she was planning on living. At Vanya's funeral, she stood there with her face swollen from crying, a giant round head. Her neck couldn't support that head, Sveta kept nodding. She threw dirt on the coffin, then stuck her dirty fingers into her mouth, like a child. She stopped drinking and wandering. She went on to study law and became a photographer. Now she's a smart young woman with too much composure and too much sorrow. It turned out that Vanya saved her life.

THE HZB

May 25, 2011

Katya* is thirteen and pregnant, her ex-boyfriend Gleb is the father. She's almost at six weeks.

"Get an abortion," Maga tells her. "Don't ruin your life, you only have one."

"My mom told me that if I get an abortion she'll send me straight to the orphanage. Or bring me here and push me down an elevator shaft. Make it look like an accident. But Grandma said that if I showed up with a baby she'd kick me out on the street."

Katya lives with her grandma because her mother drinks. She had Katya when she was fifteen; Katya spent the first three years of her life in an orphanage. A story they love to tell in their family is about how when Katya was born, her grandma made Katya's mother sign a document giving her up. But then, on the day Katya's mom turned eighteen, she forced Katya's grandma to sign the paperwork to get Katya back, threatening her with a knife.

"Grandma still regrets it," says Katya, taking a swig of GD.†

"Should you really be drinking?" asks Maga. "It's your first trimester."

"It's retarded anyway. I mean, that would be even better—maybe that way they'll let me give it up. But the best thing would be a miscarriage."

"Drink vodka if you want a miscarriage," a tiny girl named Anya pipes up. "Not GD."

* All names have been changed.
† Grape Day, an alcoholic soda.

"I know a good clinic. Costs fifteen grand to get it done right—it's a lot, mine was twenty-five! But that came with aftercare."

Maga is seventeen, she had an abortion a year ago. Her boyfriend was going off to the army when they found out that Maga was pregnant. "He put the money in front of me and said that if I decided to do that, I should. I thought about it. Who would have even picked me up from the hospital? My mom may be nice, but she said she didn't want to look after some rug rat."

WE'RE ON A BALCONY on the third floor of the Hovrino abandoned hospital. Everyone calls it the HZB. Three interconnected buildings slowly sinking into the ground. Behind us, there are about fifteen people laughing, ages ten to thirty. They're known as stalkers, diggers, suiciders, guards, and ghosts.*

The construction of this enormous hospital complex, intended to hold 1,300 beds, began in 1980, but by 1985, work had stopped. Some people say the funding was cut, others claim that the groundwater had come up and the Likhoborka River, which had been diverted through pipes under the building, flooded the foundation. By the time construction ceased, three ten-story buildings, arranged in the shape of a star, had been built. They even delivered the beds. All that was left to install were the elevators and railings. The unfinished building remained under guard until the beginning of the 1990s. After it stopped having security, the HZB became the neighborhood construction depot. People took literally everything.

Now the HZB is just sinking into the ground. The waterlogged lower levels sit on a layer of permanent ice. It's full of stairs without railings, yawning elevator shafts, and holes in the floor. Ancient layers of dust, broken gravel and cinder blocks, hunks of cement. Water drips down the

* Stalkers are people who seek out abandoned places, named for Andrei Tarkovsky's film *Stalker*. Diggers take part in an urban-exploration subculture called digging. Suiciders are people willing to die, like kamikazes.

support beams. The graffiti covering the walls reads like the collective stream of consciousness: Patriots Suck, Ave Satan, Strogino Rules, confessions of love, poems, swearing, names. While the government shuffled responsibility for the building between its agencies, the HZB filled up with people with nowhere else to go.

THERE'S A BIG CREW hanging out on the third floor. Around fifteen people are out on the balcony, sitting on railings, legs hanging down. At the center of the balcony, there's a table assembled from boards and bricks, overflowing with bags. Another table, a real one, stands by the wall. Some couples are sitting on top of it.

Everyone is passing around two 1.5-liter bottles of GD.

Most of them aren't even fifteen. They know the building like the backs of their hands, they're experts at running from cops down its dark hallways and bringing in tourists for extra cash.

They hang out on the third-floor balcony because it has an excellent view of the "official entrance," a hole in the barbed wire fence.

The hole pulls in goths, impressionable schoolkids, stalkers, college students, paintball players. It's 150 rubles a head to enter; the price of admission includes a tour where the children lead groups through the building recounting the local legends. They introduce themselves as "the junior security team." The head of security is currently Maga. "It used to be cool running around sounding the building out, trying to hear whether there's anyone else in there. Now kids just bring me the money." A few more guards are supposed to come through a bit later: Ratcatcher, Alex Criminal Investigation, and Zheka, the hulk.

To stay out of trouble, the guards share what they make with some of the boys from the Hovrino precinct. Every once in a while, the cops come around to pick up the schoolkids. Guards never chase schoolkids away, they reluctantly share their booze and cigarettes with them, occasionally letting them do their own tours. But if the cops raid the building, it's every man for himself. It's always every man for himself around here.

"JUMPER BLEW 1.26 and Psycho did .09," Katya says. Jumper, a girl with fire-engine-red hair, wrinkles her nose. She's fourteen but still in the seventh grade. After she got caught at the HZB and put on the juvenile delinquent registry, her school held her back a year.

"When you see a cop, you're supposed to scream, 'Look! A dragon!'" says Psycho. "He'll turn around and that's when you run."

"So they pick me and Katya up and put us in the hospital," Jumper continues the tale. "On the fourth day, her folks came and got her, mine showed up on the fifth. By then, I'd fucked up their entire ward!"

"When was that?"

"Around the time when Jenya got the rap."

That's their slang for rape.

The boys are tossing their knives around. Everyone's got one. Most of them are trophies lifted off hapless tourists.

Katya and Psycho play-fight without breaking their embrace. They finally go off "to the fourth floor."

The discussion of Katya's situation continues.

"She's drinking and that's not free. Plus, she buys cigarettes," Maga says. "That's a hundred, one-fifty, rubles a day, but still. I'd lend her the money if she asked. The profits from the tours can all go to her."

"She can go put up flyers," Jumper chimes in.

"I worked at KFC when I was twelve," adds Slam.

"Well aren't you special, Miner?"

Slam got the nickname Miner because of his giant plugs—one and two inches in diameter—which are like tunnels through his earlobes. But he likes his fighter name, Slam, a lot better.

Slam's brother is a champion boxer and fought in Chechnya. He respects him deeply.

"When I was in first grade, I came home with an F and he told me to go do push-ups. At first, it was ten, then it went up to a hundred. If I got tired of push-ups, he said to do squats. When I got tired of squats, it was back to push-ups. He fed me condensed milk to grow my muscles. Everyone beat the shit out of me until fifth grade, but then after that, I was the one beating the shit out of everyone else."

Slam never got around to becoming a better student, but he did become an expert kickboxer. Then he injured his shoulder. He's been out of commission for two years already, and now he's at the HZB.

Slam still talks to his brother, but not to his mom. "She yells at me, I can't stand it."

"I'm a legend here!" Slam screams. "Right, Jumper?"

"He's a legend," Jumper says very seriously.

"Who will stand up for Slam? Jumper?"

"Everyone at the HZB."

"That's riiiiiiight! You heard that? You heard? Because I'm a legend! A legend! I can take anyone!"

To give an example of "an excellent punch," Slam tells the story of how hard he hit his girlfriend from Tver. "Her whole face swole up, the capillaries burst—just from one punch! Man, I haven't been down to see her in a minute. She's probably mad."

"A PATHOLOGIST IS the only kind of doctor who doesn't kill," Shaman explains to the children listening to him.

Shaman is over thirty. He has a bloated red face, greasy hair, and a black leather jacket. He is a father of three and there's a fourth "in the oven." He drinks a lot. He fought in Chechnya, now he runs through the HZB with delirium tremens, brandishing an invisible machine gun. He also "realigns energy fields" by moving his hands in front of people's faces; that's why they call him Shaman.

The guards don't like him that much—he takes a cut of their profits. However, there are always boys hanging around him, learning how to be tour guides. The right to give tours is also something that has to be earned.

A determined posse of stalkers has shown up downstairs—four young men in camo, one of them with a gas mask under his arm. Shaman goes down, trailed by his twelve-year-old boys and Maga. The conversation is what you'd expect. "Who are you?" "This area is restricted and under guard." "Should I call the guards?" "Do you really want to get taken down to the station?" The stalkers readily accept that they'll have to pay these people 150 rubles each to get in. They hand over the cash and ask to be taken to Nemostor, a room on the ground floor, the site of one of the many legends about the HZB.

The story goes that there was once a group of Satanists who'd hang out in the building doing human sacrifices. One day the police, sick of the killing, sealed off the building, kettled the Satanists into the flooded basement, and blew them all up.

"Is it really true that they used grenades?" asks one of the tourists.

"Back in those days, I worked at Hospital 81, in the autopsy room," Shaman begins, after some silence. "The head of my unit was working that shift. He says to me, 'They've brought some people in, already dead. Then they brought in the equipment for organ transplants.' The whole operation was organized by the FSB* . . ."

Nemostor is not very different from other rooms. It's filled with dust, broken gravel, and sunlight from where the windows should be. The walls are covered in pentagrams and paeans to Satan in Old Slavonic and English, with hideous grammar in both. This is where HZB residents usually celebrate New Year's.

"Last time a Satanist came here was 2007," Maga quietly tells me. "Our guys caught him in the basement holding a knife. Jesus Christ! His face was covered in some kind of flour, dark circles under his eyes. Everyone was laughing their asses off and taking pictures. We're like,

* The FSB is Russia's Federal Security Service, the successor to the KGB. According to its charter, the FSB provides "security to the Russian Federation," fights terrorism, and defends the borders. The FSB actively battles "internal enemies"—opposition politicians, independent journalists, activists, anarchists, and religious minorities. Journalists have routinely found proof of FSB associates being involved in rackets, torture, and political killings. The FSB is the most powerful of Russia's law enforcement agencies. From 1998 to 1999, Putin was the director of the FSB.

'What's your name, you freak?" He goes, 'Zinzan.' Zheka punched him a few times and right away he was all, 'I'm Sergey! I'm Sergey!' After they took him in, he had the whole precinct howling."

Satanists are slippery. Sometimes they manage to get in the building and do their makeup once they're already inside. "Then they run around here with their knives. They even caught one with a machete one time."

The standard tour includes Nemostor; the memorial to Edge, a boy who fell down an elevator shaft; the "filmmaker's corridor," which the kids have covered in construction foam and painted so that it looks like the set of a horror film ("These are your brains, these are your intestines, these are your heads"); the roof; and the flooded basement, where "Satanists' bodies can still be found floating around in the water."

We go down into "the negatives," the negative floors of the buildings, to look at the puppy. The puppy died a long time ago, it's just skin and bones. Shaman pokes around in the bones with a stick, lecturing on canine anatomy. The boys film it on a phone. "But its paws are tied together!"

"I even know who tied it up," Maga smirks under her breath.

MAGA WOUND UP at the HZB when she was fifteen. Her boyfriend had died and she spent a month in a mental hospital. "How'd he die? He was murdered. They drained the brake fluid out of his car. He was with his friend. When he realized that he couldn't brake, he drove into a pole on the driver's side. His friend survived. He didn't die right away, either, but when he was in the hospital, the nurse went out for a smoke, and the story gets shady. He was actually headed to see me at our dacha."

Now she is seventeen, but most of the other people at the HZB think that she's actually much older. She has a walkie-talkie hanging from her waist, camouflage, long hair, a watchful gaze, and a peaceful smile. She is all grit. A year ago, when "forty Dagestanis with knives" showed up to the building to fight the residents, Maga fended them off by herself until "reinforcements" arrived.

Maga has even managed to do a year at a medical school. But then she dropped out. "I realized that I don't actually give a shit about other people. I don't care about saving anyone. But a doctor's supposed to take an oath. I'm not the kind of person who takes oaths, anyway. If I do, I'll be just like all those other heartless bitches at the clinics," says Maga.

This summer, Maga is going to apply to study to become a civil servant. She just has to wait until August when she turns eighteen. "I don't want to get my mother involved."

The other kids are empathetically silent. None of them want their parents involved in their vocational futures. Or any other part of their lives. As one of the girls put it, "It's bad enough that they're on my birth certificate."

"My mother's already decided that I'm gonna be a cop. She screams, 'We're not even discussing it!' Drunk bitch. I want to be an archeologist," Liza says. "This summer, I'm going to the Vorontsovka caves."

"She hasn't beaten you in six months! Maybe it'll work out," says Anya. "You used to always come to school covered in bruises."

"I did the math," Liza suddenly says. "And if you count all her miscarriages and abortions, I would have had nine brothers and sisters."

"And then what?"

"Then nothing!"

The boys go off to play. Their game is very simple: you pick a cinder block off the ground—any broken hunk of concrete will do—and try to throw it at another person's head. In many ways, this game is about knowing the space—ambushing from above, jumping out of the dark, coming up on someone from behind. In general, at the HZB, people enjoy simple pleasures. In summer, the girls tan on the roof. The boys poop down the elevator shafts, which requires skill and endurance. Whoever's shit makes the loudest noise at the bottom wins. "One time, they got a tourist," says Maga. "He was this weirdo, all serious. He'd prepared to come here for three weeks, super into the ghosts of the HZB, the spatial anomalies, all that. He ended up getting shat on. He was really upset like, 'The spirits have rejected me.'"

DIMAS STUMBLES OUT onto the balcony, a seventeen-year-old goon, Nychka's little brother. He wails, "Where is she?"

Simka, Dimas's girlfriend, is hiding somewhere. They're in a fight and Dimas is dead set on "punching her lights out." He's drunk out of his mind. Nychka and Slam try holding him back.

"You're not Slam, you're just shit!" Dimas yells, pushing Slam, who falls down, cutting his hand on the broken cement underfoot. Dimas grabs Nychka's throat.

"I'll break you in half."

"And then what?" Nychka asks calmly. "What happens then?"

Dimas releases his sister and leaves. A little while later, he reappears on the roof. We go out onto a wing of the fourth floor, where we can see better. Dimas is walking along the very edge and keeps stretching his feet out over the abyss.

"He's not going to jump," says Nychka, unmoved. "I mean, he's going to jump, but not today and not because of her. He doesn't actually love her."

"But you should have seen that other girl fly off of there!"

Drunken Taya is squirming in the arms of her boyfriend, Tyoma, a serious boy with curly hair. He's trying to hold her down. They're both fifteen.

"Lie down, Taya. Close your eyes and stay still."

"Get off of me, faggot, I am not drunk!"

When Taya was running from the cops the other day, she jumped off the fourth floor.

"How?"

"With a running start," Taya grins, and stares into me. I suddenly realize that she really isn't that drunk.

"She ran another two hundred meters in shock and hid in the

bushes . . . spinal injury, internal injuries . . . Taya, lie down! She fell right into there."

A heap of fallen branches, steel beams, and broken bricks barely covered in weeds.

"It's 'cause she'd rather die than let the cops get her," Tyoma says proudly. "That is just how she is."

Now Dimas is coming back down "to say his goodbyes." He throws a glance around the room, freezes in a cement archway, then lumbers in to hug all the guys and kiss all the girls. He returns to the stairs. No one even attempts to stop him.

He goes back to walking along the edge of the roof, periodically stopping still. I am starting to feel sick.

Simka walks out onto the wing, a petite, sweet-looking sixteen-year-old girl. She and Nychka hurriedly trade a few words, then Nychka calls out, "Dimas! Someone wants to talk to you!"

Dimas comes down. "Who?"

"She does."

"I don't see anyone there." Dimas stares past her. "You know, I was standing on the edge, I even put a foot over, and then I thought, Imagine doing like this because of that slut . . ."

Simka turns around and quickly walks back into the building. "Great job!" Nychka yells at her brother. Dimas runs after her.

They reappear about twenty minutes later.

"You have to apologize to me," Dimas tells Nychka.

"Me?"

"Who was the one screaming, 'Just do it, jump, we're waiting for you on the ground'?"

"Not me!"

"Who said that I don't love her? I do! Say you're sorry."

"Okay, I'm sorry," Nychka mutters.

"I was on the very edge. I was about to do it. But because of this girl—"

Simka presses against him. Her eyes are filled with extraordinary, radiant emptiness.

THE BUILDING ALWAYS gives you a way to die. There'll be two-foot-wide gaps between the floor and the walls on either side of the corridor; stairways with crumbling stairs, sharp metal beams swinging from the ceiling, holes in the walls. Underfoot, broken bricks and twisted rods that will readily trip you. But, most importantly, it has those hollow elevator shafts. They have no walls, they're just holes in the ground that will suddenly open up in the middle of a dark hallway.

HZB residents will gladly recite all the names of people who've fallen down them to their deaths, broken their bones, disappeared. It feels like the closeness of death, the palpable possibility of leaving this life at any moment, through an escape hatch opening right at your feet, is something the residents like. Everyone's slit their wrists at least once. They don't show off their scars. Scars are a sign of failure.

"You take a can, fuck it up with a rock, and you end up with these sharp strips of metal."

"There's no point in slitting your wrists. The scars don't look good on anyone. Someone needs attention and they start doing dumb shit."

"There's this kid here named Fedya. One time, he was like, 'I'm gonna kill myself! I'm gonna kill myself!' And we were like, 'Okay, go for it.' He gets the knife and brings it up to his wrists and then nothing. He didn't have the balls."

"It's all seasonal."

"When everything's fine, no one cares how you are."

"There are friends who it's dangerous to cry in front of."

"I was eight, my dad had died. Heart attack. My mom was like, 'Come here.' I ran away to my room, I didn't want her to see me. I moved my bed in front of the door and slept that way for a month."

"I'm afraid to cry," Anya suddenly says. "More than anything, I'm afraid of crying. I don't know why."

"Come here, I'm going to help you guys make up." Maga takes Dimas and Simka aside.

"This Fen gives you an hour of euphoria. It's fun at the club, you have a good time. Then you start tweaking, but it's not that bad . . ."

They whisper and then go off and come back about ten minutes later.

"Simka, check your nose," Jumper calls out.

Simka sharply inhales, rubs her septum, and turns around.

"She snorted up all the evidence," Dimas laughs.

"Anyway, look," Maga tells them, serious, "I'm giving you 10 baggies and you're bringing back 10 grand. Each bag has a gram. A gram a grand—got it? You can cut it however you want. Check out your clients. If they look like dummies, cut it like you mean it. The most important thing is that no one complain about quality."

They put the baggies, little bubbles of plastic wrap, in their backpacks.

"There will always be enough for you," Maga says. "You don't have to worry about that."

"I'm straight edge," says Slam. "Some people are so surprised when I say that. People say: Wow, you have the world record, you've been sober for four whole days. I don't smoke, I don't—Maga, pat Slam on the back, Slam's sad. Can I get a hug?"

"**I'M IN LOVE WITH HER.** We dated for six months. I used to be hard-core emo, I had the bangs down to my chin. In March, I shaved off my bangs. I wasn't in the building with my best friends for four days. And while I was gone, she fucked around. I get her to come talk to me on a different floor and I ask her, 'Do you want to be with me?' She's like yes. But later on, I see her making out with a disabled guy! A disabled guy!"

The disabled guy is Gosha, and he's standing with his arms around Yen, taking sips of Yaga. He has mild cerebral palsy. When he walks, it looks like he's kind of dancing. Gosha has just run away from a five-day-a-week boarding school that his parents admitted him to. He brags, "They even had barbed wire." Gosha's parents drink, but they're "all right"—they let Gosha have 500 rubles a week from his disability checks.

Yen scornfully squints in the direction of Slam, saying nothing. She's fifteen, extremely beautiful, with an ice-cold gaze. It says "Digger Yen" on her backpack.

Samurai emerges from the depths of the building—a man in a robe, around forty, another HZB legend. He carries a katana.

"I am glad to meet you in this frightening and mysterious place," Samurai says, and then repeats the same thing, but in Cantonese.

He uses the building for meditation and drinking. "It's such a tolerant space, everyone who has a hard time on the outside is accepted here," Samurai says somberly. "It's a utopian world, the world after the apocalypse." He starts doing exercises with his katana. The blade slices through the air.

After shuffling around, Slam goes up to him and asks for the katana. Samurai hands it to him with a bow. He goes up to Yen and draws the sword.

"Do it," Yen says, looking him straight in the eye. "Do it already."

Slam fumbles and gets pulled away from her. They take away the katana.

"You can't even kill," Yen says contemptuously.

Meanwhile, people on the balcony have started talking politics.

VERA WAS THE ONE who started it. She's fifteen, in eighth grade, and refers to everyone in the formal "you."

"Everyone in our class is on the right except for four people," Vera says. "But the school principal's last name is Arakelian. An Armenian. This churka* comes in and fires Russian teachers who've worked there for twenty or thirty years! Her niece walks around like a queen. One time, we were doing cough medicine in class, and she freaked out, screaming 'They're tweakers! They're tweakers!' They tested us every morning for a month after that."

Vera turned to the right under the influence of her older friend Marina. "She's the one who taught me everything about life.

* *Churka*, literally "block of wood," is an offensive term for someone from the Caucasus or Central Asia.

"They come over here from their Chechnya and act like they're in their own house," Vera says, as though she is reciting a script. "They go around with our women. They're from Chechnya, another country!"

"Actually, it's a part of Russia," Anton objects.

There's a brief discussion of the territories in the South. Vera learns that Dagestan and Ingushetia are a part of Russia, and Armenia and Azerbaijan are not. "So what?" asks Jumper. "A churka is a churka."

"One time, Liza and I were running across the street on a red light and there's this khach* sitting in his Volvo," Vera continues. "He sticks his head out of the window and yells, 'Whores!' I mean, he yells it in his own language, but you can tell from the way he said it. I go, 'Sig off!' and Sieg heil! him. We ran away after that! They're animals, you know."

"There's a churka girl in our class. Her name is actually Aishat," says Anya. "Me and her dad have the same birthday, March 28th. It's messed up!"

"Migrant worker, you are through! We are getting rid of you!" Dimas shouts.

"I mean, I get it, the khaches are better than us," Vera suddenly says. "Everyone knows it deep down. That's why people fuck with them. They don't drink, they're all united. Look at us: all our men drink . . . They treat their children different, their families, I see it myself. They have faith. Their God is with them. War is supposed to be cultural, like, we're fighting with what we're made of. One time, I showed up drunk to a Russian test on a Saturday and I got a D. I was so ashamed of myself! That's my own language, Russian! I should know it well enough to get an A."

"In Italy you get a fine just for throwing a wrapper on the ground!" Liza says.

"I'm not saying that there aren't any good churkas. Let them sweep the courtyards, fine. The problem is when they try to walk on their hind legs and put themselves above us . . ."

---

* *Kach,* Armenian for "cross," is a slur for someone from the Caucasus region.

THREE MEN ARE SPOTTED from the balcony. They keep walking past the hole in the fence instead of coming in, inspecting the perimeter. "Are they cops?"

Maga and Dimas go down to assess the situation. We descend through the passages, periodically stopping to listen. When there are five feet left to the ground, Maga jumps and falls over, biting down on her lip, yelping. "I dislocated my kneecap," she hisses. "I have torn tendons."

Maga doesn't want to go to the ER. "Let's just wait for Ratcatcher, he's fixed it before." She calls him, crying into the phone.

Ratcatcher shows up, a strong, bearded, redheaded guy in a biker jacket. He's the most important person in the building, everyone goes up to him to say hello one by one. Little is known about Ratcatcher—he's into role-playing games, he's really smart, he is the one who does the negotiating with the police. In his free time, when he's not "working the building," he is a security guard at a flower shop by the train station. He examines Maga's leg. "You have to go to the ER."

"Fine, let me finish this, and I'll go," Maga says, opening a can of Strike.

"Ooh, give me the tab, I collect them." Liza puts the beer tab onto her string. She has more than a hundred of them, the necklace is almost finished. "Only six aren't from me, I drank the rest myself," she brags.

Ratcatcher goes off to negotiate with Alex, who seems not to have handed over all of the money from his tourists. Alex points the finger at Shaman, and the guards quietly decide to put Shaman through a "morning of long knives" the following day.

THERE'S YELLING UNDER the balcony. Mothers have infiltrated the territory, two blonds in high-heeled boots and bright-colored coats. One of them catches Psycho by the hood. "Get the fuck over here." Psycho breaks free of her and hides behind Liza.

There's a cry from below, "You cunt!"

Finally, one of the blonds grabs on to another one of the kids. "Irina, we're leaving."

We climb up to the roof. Seven stories of stairs without railings, my legs are on fire. It's really warm up there, and only now do we understand how cold it was in the building. We lie down on the sun-warmed moss. Sasha with a Band-Aid on her cheek, Ratcatcher's girlfriend, tells us about the first time she came to the HZB, when she was seven.

"Everything was so different back then. There was a pond over there with little wooden huts all around it. The sunsets were awesome. Now we're surrounded by high-rises. These days, the HZB is practically the shortest building in the whole neighborhood."

An announcement blows in from the direction of the station: trains are arriving. A white dove is circling over the helipad. Behind the helipad, Vera is puking.

"There's actually a superstition that if a dove circles all the way around you, you should make a wish," says Liza. "Although none of that shit ever comes true. I've tried it."

"What did you wish for?"

"To get five grand for my birthday."

Vera comes out from behind the helipad, gets out her phone, and takes a long time to dial a number. She screams into phone, "Why are you freaking out? Like you have never been wasted!"

"I want to cure cancer. That's been my dream since I was twelve," Sasha suddenly says.

We go down to the fourth floor. Yen and some other people are running toward us. "The cops! The cops!" We race through the corridors. Yen hides in a hole in the wall, all the children bound out in different directions.

Only Gosha stays up ahead of us. He has a long stride, his nylon windbreaker balloons out at his sides, his arms pull on the air.

After a turn, we run into total darkness. We slow down and proceed quietly. We can hear Gosha running ahead of us. Suddenly, the footfalls stop. There's a rustling of nylon. We turn our phones on for light. We're one step away from a square hole, surrounded by a four-inch-tall curb. It's an elevator shaft.

Gosha lies four stories beneath us, his face buried in bricks. His long hair completely covers his head. He is not moving.

We can hear shouting going up the floors, "Hovrino police! Don't move, motherfucker!"

They bend over him and turn him over, then ask us to call him an ambulance, it will take longer to come if they radio for it.

"What the fuck are they doing here, huh? Why do they keep fucking getting in here?" a cop says. "Fucking teenyboppers. I'd shoot them all if I could."

An incredibly calm Ratcatcher descends on the scene. He offers to help, he has medical training in "intensive care." The cops decline.

"Which one of the chiefs is coming?" Ratcatcher asks.

Turns out it's someone named Tolya and "you can talk things over with him."

Ratcatcher takes one of the cops aside. They speak quietly, they laugh.

The ambulance and emergency services drive up. They walk toward the shaft, assessing the situation. The woman doctor goes out to smoke with the police. "He's breathing, they're going to transfer him now."

Gosha regains consciousness. He says his name, his date of birth. When they ask him, "What hurts?" he breaks down.

Gosha is loaded onto a stretcher. There's blood coming out of his head, staining the fabric. They carry him through the darkness out to the exit, staying close to the walls to avoid the holes in the floor, lifting him over the rubble.

"How did I fall? How did I fall?" Gosha begins to cry. "I know the building, I couldn't have. I know the building!"

Tyoma, who has been sobbing, climbs out of the darkness. "Gosha, Gosha! That's my friend! Get away, I'll carry him myself!" One of the cops pulls him back, punches him in the face. Tyoma chokes down a scream.

"You gonna keep meowing?"

"No."

"You'll keep your mouth shut?"

"I will."

Mothers wait by the ambulance. They must have been the ones who called the cops. Psycho's mother explains the situation to curious passersby. "I tell him: Misha, get over here. And then this tiny one says to me, 'You are a slut.' Some little skank. I'd break all of their necks."

"Are you going press charges?" a cop double-checks.

"Oh yes I will."

They put us in a car with Tyoma, who is acting tough and smiling defiantly. "I'm gonna tell my dad and he's going to make your life hell." The warrant officer behind the wheel is bursting with rage.

He stops the car outside the station, pulls Tyoma out, and punches him in the chest. The boy's knees buckle. "I can't breathe."

Tyoma is dragged into the precinct and tossed onto a bunk. He tries to stand up, but he's surrounded by mothers, who grab onto his arms. "Calm down! Calm down!" The boy is gasping for breath and tears are spraying out of his eyes.

"You'll all be sorry!"

The warrant officer bends over him, smiling, and suddenly grabs him by the collar, pressing his forehead against Tyoma's bawling face.

"When you're threatening someone, look them in the eyes, you little shit. Look me in the eyes."

"My dad will come . . . ," the boy begins, choking.

The women put their hands over his mouth.

"You're a man. Be quiet, be patient."

The warrant officer notices my attentive gaze and drags me out for a smoke.

"My name is Zhenya Ananiev and I am a warrant officer of the police. Go ahead, file a complaint against me. I have a little shit just like him at home. There's nothing I can do about him, unfortunately. Say one thing to him, try being gentle, he'll look right through you. At least this way I can make an impression on him."

"Like a hundred a year," a detective says lazily. "In summer, we're out there every day. They all keep falling."

"When you have kids of your own and you hit them, you'll understand," Zhenya tells me. "Are you gonna file a complaint against me? I'll start getting ready for my civilian life. I've been the force for fifteen years. You drag a little fuck like him out and he's not breathing."

EVERYONE'S HANGING OUT at the train station. Maga is headed to the ER and they're seeing her off. Drinking, laughing, the kids are glad that they've once again gotten away from the cops.

"He's alive? Well, thank fucking God!" Katya shouts. "The second one down a shaft in a week! Who's next?"

Yen, Gosha's girlfriend, is unperturbed. "I don't love anyone. But I wish it'd been Slam. He was like, 'Don't do tours, there'll be one less little cunt hanging around in the building.' It'd have been better if he'd fallen off the roof, right on his head."

"Or if the cops had taken him instead," Katya adds.

"Exactly."

"No matter who's run the building—the private security company, the cops, us—kids have always fallen down shafts," says Maga. "There's nothing you can do about it." She is also completely calm.

"Shaman, come out at noon tomorrow," Ratcatcher tells him. "We'll come by a little later, and you can get money off tourists."

"Okay."

Slam is running around in circles, yelling. "I'm injured, but it'll heal in a year. Just another year, girls, and that's it! I'll be out of here! Back to the sensei making me run barefoot through snow."

Nine days later, Slam dies, falling down an elevator shaft from the ninth floor.

CHAPTER 3

MOSCOW ISN'T RUSSIA

I MOVED TO MOSCOW when I was fifteen, to a dormitory on Shvernik Street. Two other girls lived in my room. It was very dirty, with tattered wallpaper and GO FUCK YOURSELF scrawled on the ceiling.

At first, I was amazed that you could ride the escalator in the metro as much as you liked, just go in and go up and down. You didn't even have to pay extra.

I made money nannying at a very expensive apartment on Mayakovskaya Square, right in the center, where plaster statues follow you with their empty eyes from the facades of the buildings. I'd walk there, thinking, Holy shit.

I learned how to walk like they do in Moscow, which means very fast, till you're dizzy, without making eye contact with anyone. My feet hurt, my calves grew.

For a long time, Moscow was just the immediate surroundings of the metro stops. There were no smartphones back then—I'd look up directions to where I was going online, then jot them down on a piece of paper.

Moscow had various zones. Downtown, it always felt like I was in a museum. The granite tile sidewalks reminded me of expensive interiors. Down in the metro, I brushed the stone walls, thinking nothing. Farther out on the outskirts, the metro was finished in plastic and the buildings looked much more normal, made of concrete or red brick. The asphalt was cracked and I'd walk around imagining that I was back home in Yaroslavl.

I hadn't really been anywhere else, just Moscow and Yaroslavl. Of course Moscow was richer, it is the capital.

The Kremlin is so red and sweet, you want to lick it. The Red Square around it all flat. I'd walk past the Kremlin to school; I was studying in the journalism department of Moscow State University.

Even the streetlights were different here, bent into curves to look more antique.

I never thought about where the money for all of these luxuries came from, I was simply delighted to find myself in their presence. It was just like when I was younger and got so worked up when the editor in chief of the Yaroslavl newspaper I worked for invited me over. We watched *Indiana Jones* on a flatscreen TV, and then I was given a bouquet made out of sugar. It was a terror and awe to even stir. God forbid if you wanted to go to the bathroom.

Everybody in Moscow was going to nightclubs. Kids from my class went but I never joined them. One of the clubs was called Heaven. It had a bouncer named Pasha who always knew how much your clothes cost. I thought that he must have ESP.

The existence of skirts that cost $300—three times the monthly salary of my mother, a PhD—amazed me like rose-colored whales or elephants who could paint. So many wonders out here in the world. And here I was, living among them.

At a certain point, Moscow decided there weren't enough wonders. It needed more. Urban planners flooded the city. These people believed that if the municipal environment was improved, the rest of life would follow suit. They kicked all the kids' rides out of Gorky Park and made it a place strictly for strolling. They revamped museums and museum cafés, and young people started hanging out at them. It was no longer fashionable to wear $300 skirts—now they had to be straight and simple and cheap, like $100 (exactly as much as my mother made). This was called democratization.

People watched old movies, wore thick, colored glasses, had asymmetrical haircuts. Moscow adjusted itself to these people—they had money or worked for people who did. Moscow changed up its tiling, planted new flowerbeds that looked like wild overgrowths, unveiled innovative cultural spaces. Fresh lighting blossomed on the facades—white, cream, violet, and red—at night, the streets morphed and shimmered like a mirage. Special media and special journalists appeared in order to teach Muscovites how to live as though they were actually in Berlin. Life got too good to criticize.

My work as a journalist took place outside Moscow. I wrote about life outside Moscow. When I would come back from the field, the Muscovites asked, "So what is it like out there, beyond the ring road? Is it scary?"

We would pretend that that was a joke.

But it really was scary out there, beyond the ring road. Life was threadbare. A lot of violence. A lot of Russian roulette—you could end up in jail if a cop didn't like you. Mama was still too shy to ever buy fruit—it's too expensive, what do I need it for—or get clothes at stores—the clothes from the street vendors are perfectly good. I'd come home and take her out to the café and she'd put on lipstick beforehand.

The punchline was that Moscow's luxuries were paid for by money that came from the provinces. That was the first thing that Putin did: he reformed the tax system so that the provinces had to pay Moscow first and then Moscow decided how much to give back to them. It gave back as little as possible. The fancy sidewalks, the streetlights, the cultural spaces—they were not cheap. The tiles I walked on to work were paid for by my mother, the teacher in Yaroslavl.

The older I got, the less this upset me. I had a smartphone now with a taxi app, I no longer went down into the metro. I started admiring the $100 skirts. I liked going to the new cultural spaces and wanted to get an apartment where I could bike to work. I thought that, considering how much I worked and the fact that I wrote about terrifying things, I had the right to a pleasant life. That if anyone did, it was me.

Other Muscovites probably thought the same things about themselves. It became fashionable to be socially conscious, which meant signing up for recurring donations to different charities. For the price of one cup of coffee a month, you could be a good person. That was how Muscovites exculpated themselves from the big, scary Russia that started directly behind their apartment buildings, just a few turns up the road.

Muscovites noticed I'd changed and accepted me as their own. One evening, shortly before Russia began to bomb Kyiv, I was invited to a dinner party. The building was small, with just a few units, right in the city center. A Filipina housekeeper had cooked. A bottle of champagne stood on a side table. The guests were all talking about the news. They called Putin a tsar, which is what people call any beloved curmudgeon. They spoke of oligarchs like they were visionaries, important patrons of important contemporary art. The guests were divided when it came to contemporary art. Names, names, names. Do you know him? I can introduce you. It'd be my pleasure. I ate in silence. I had just gotten back from the Ryazan province, from a village that didn't have roads, where they put out forest fires with buckets of water. The food tasted good.

I think I learned the most important lesson in Moscow: always eat in silence.

That way, you can appreciate the taste.

Russians have a saying, "Moscow isn't Russia and Russia isn't Moscow."

One out of every ten Russians lives in Moscow.

LIFE ON THE SAPSAN WAYSIDE

June 6, 2010

While Sapsans* fly past the station of Chuprianovka, Baba Raya tends to the goats. She has been at it for forty-five years, letting them graze right on the wayside, on the grass growing out of the gravel. There are three nanny goats, all of them Belkas, and two little goat boys, Bunny and Bun-bun. The goats keep going down right to the tracks.

"Don't you worry, I am no fool. I know there's a fine for letting your goats on the tracks. But where else can they graze? In my own vegetable garden? They may have horns, but they're no bags of meat. They're smart ones, these goats of mine," says Baba Raya.

A mechanical voice warns of an oncoming high-speed train. Baba Raya bangs her walking stick on the ground. "Belka, Sapsan! The Sapsan is coming! Get up here! The Sapsan is coming!"

And the goats really do go uphill to wait for the rounded white train to flicker past.

• THE COMMUTER RAIL BETWEEN MOSCOW AND KLIN

8 miles from Moscow, 395 from Saint Petersburg

In Khimki, we waited on an unmoving train for forty minutes.

People sat quietly, nobody getting upset. They didn't even look out the window.

The Sapsan flew by in four seconds flat. But still the commuter train didn't move—ten, fifteen, twenty minutes went by.

* The Sapsan is a high-speed rail that began operating in 2009. It connects Moscow to Saint Petersburg. *Sapsan* means peregrine falcon, which is why people will call them "birdies."

Finally, an old man with a crutch let out a groan and went over to the intercom to talk to the engine driver. He pressed the button. "Are we going or what?"

"We'll go in a minute," the engineer answered.

And with that, the train took off.

Everyone started laughing. "Why didn't we think of that earlier?"

• SHLYUZ

132 miles from Moscow, 271 from Saint Petersburg

Shlyuz is four one-story brick buildings and a train platform. That's it. The village of Lisyi Gory, just over a mile from the station, is not visible through the woods—it feels like Shlyuz is completely cut off from the rest of the world. Which actually isn't far from the truth.

Only one commuter train stops at Shlyuz now, the 8:26 from Bologoye to Tver, for exactly one minute. There are no longer trains going in the direction of Bologoye. Meanwhile, twenty-two commuter rails, sixteen Sapsans, and a dozen express trains rush past the station each day.

"We truly live on the outer limits," says Anna Cheslavovna.

Anna Cheslavovna Matizheva (née Senkevich) looks like a merchant's wife from a Kustodiev painting. She's full-figured, she doesn't wave her hands around, they glide through the air. One hundred percent Polish, when she was young, she never imagined she'd end up in such a deep Russian backwater.

She was born in the city of Lida, in Belarus. She married a soldier in Feodosia, Crimea. "I was swept off my feet by the sea and the stars on his epaulets." When her elder son turned three and her younger son one, she was "completely consumed by pride." She took her children and headed to Moscow. But she didn't quite make it and ended up settling in Shlyuz.

These four brick buildings are known as the barracks. No one remembers what they actually are, not even the people who've lived here the longest. When Anna Cheslavovna first moved into her dungeon, "I was a squatter. I made it legal later." There was a hole in the roof, and the building was heated with a makeshift stove. "When I first moved here, you should have seen how much I wept. Now it isn't so bad." It really isn't. Anna Cheslavovna has plastic windows, three TVs, a washing machine, and a parrot who "says one swear word and one curse word." There is a banya, three cats, two dogs, twelve chickens, "three of them roosters," plum trees, a vegetable garden with beets, beans, and peas, and a man-made pond filled with carp. There's even an absolute luxury: a brick outhouse.

Anna Cheslavovna was an inspector and a "regular track serviceman." She was responsible for the area two miles around but actually serviced over nine. "I'd change out the ties, I'd change out the rails." In the summer, she would make sure that none of the tracks "got out of joint"—when it's hot out, the rails expand in the heat, and a train could fly off them. In 2005, a law was passed "to get all the women off of the railroad itself," and Anna was reassigned to work at the station. She worked in a ticket booth in Tver and as a conductor, but she "wasn't strict enough for the job." So Anna Cheslavovna got hired at the Fourth Municipal Hospital in Tver, delivering food in the surgical ward.

Then the commuter trains seemed to stop noticing Shlyuz. You could walk to Lokotsy, the next station, about two miles down the tracks. But suddenly, it turned out she couldn't walk that far with a slipped disc in her spine and 260/140 blood pressure, even though walking precisely those two miles had been her job for half of her life. Anna Cheslavovna became unemployed.

"If you live here, you have to be willing to do physical labor," Anna Cheslavovna says. "You reap what you sow."

Today, her hometown of Lida and even Feodosia seem like "the stuff of daydreams," irretrievable relics of the past. Her whole life has ended up being tied to the rails.

"I used to think that the railroad was the safest thing in the world. It's not a plane, it's not a car, it's just two pieces of metal and a train," Anna Cheslavovna says. "But actually, it is all very scary."

Listing her former job responsibilities, Anna Cheslavovna casually includes "picking up people who had been cut into pieces."

In her twenty years of service, she "picked up" a good hundred. "People fall asleep on their trains. They'll miss their stop in Likhoslavl and jump out at Shlyuz. They don't wait for the next one, they try to walk back down the tracks. In my experience, if someone has had a little to drink and walks down the tracks, there's a fifty-fifty chance they won't make it home. There are more in the winter: there's snowdrifts along the embankments, people are forced to walk right on the rails. Not all of them will jump aside in time if a train comes."

"It's happened right in front of me, too. A boy runs past my house. I ask, 'Where are you going?' He says, 'Likhoslavl.' I tell him, 'Hold on, the train is about to come, it'll get you home.' He says, 'Bye, lady!' and jumps down onto the tracks. Suddenly, here comes the twenty-four, the Youth Train, and there's just this red rainbow of blood. He's a bag of ground beef. Before the cops got here, the birds were already on him, seagulls, crows. They were already pecking at him. I said to my husband, 'Let's put a sheet over him.' Later, they said he was high. He had no documents, nothing. They buried him with the unidentified dead. His mother and grandmother only found out through a photo they put in the paper."

"Remember this: when a train hits somebody, it doesn't stop," says Anna Cheslavovna. "There's no point. If somebody jumps out onto the tracks right in front of the engine, most often, the driver won't even brake. Because for most trains, they need more than a thousand meters to stop. And if he pulls the emergency brake, the cars might flip over his head. He'll just call the dispatcher. 'A person was run over on such and such mile.' And it's not 'we hit someone,' it's 'got run over.' That's that, the train keeps going."

In 2000, the 182 ran over her son Gena. It happened in front of her. "Gena was running to catch the commuter rail, he ran across the tracks. He thought it was the commuter train crawling toward him, but actually, it was the express." His skull was fractured, his right eye fell out onto his cheek. He had a trepanation, plastic surgery, spent three years going from hospital to hospital. “That’s why they wouldn’t let him into the army and so he never got a profession,” Anna Cheslavovna sighs. Gena now does construction in Moscow. “What he makes, he drinks.”

Four years ago, she lost her eldest son, Petya. He got in a car crash in Moscow, his brakes gave out. “He spent six months trying to recover, but in the end, he still died,” Anna Cheslavovna says, listless. “I thought I was gonna die too, but somehow, I am still here.” When Anna Cheslavovna gets a call in the evening, she still automatically answers, “Hi, Petya.” But then she remembers.

Anna Cheslavovna and her husband and son live in just half of the first house from the direction of Moscow. The local madwoman, Ninka, Nina Ivanovna Smirnova, lives in the other half. Her parents used to be railway engineers, now they are dead. Ninka is alone.

She wears a gray trench, which might be a raincoat, or maybe a robe, and a pink scarf wrapped round her head. When she was a child, she had a bad case of meningitis. Now she yells at the passing trains. “What do they want? Why do they go? We oughta blow up the rails! Bomb them! Hang them and judge them!”

Ninka’s half feels like a separate building. It’s musty, there are piles of rags in every corner, the floor is covered in shredded newspapers. There’s a hoard of jars: Ninka collects them and washes them out. The ceiling is covered in gray stains—there used to be a working stove in here, but she doesn’t use it anymore. Ninka doesn’t have firewood so she sleeps in her clothes. Piles of newspapers on the table, in the cabinet, under her bed. Whenever Ninka gets her 6,200-ruble pension, she goes out to Likhoslavl and buys all the newspapers in the kiosk. “She’ll spend around 700 rubles. A friend of mine works in that kiosk, she can’t be happier when she sees Ninka coming,” Anna Cheslavovna says. “The crosswords, the sports papers—she’ll take it all.”

There are also three fresh, very beautiful, thoughtfully composed bouquets on the table. Ninka devotes all her free time to gathering flowers.

Ninka doesn't go to bed before two. "I wander! I stroll! I watch them all!"

"Sometimes, you'll be sleeping and she'll start banging on your window with a bottle," Anna Cheslavovna complains. "I say, 'Fuck! Ninka, fuck off, I have a headache!' And she goes, 'Let me in, I want to talk.' So I have to let her in. Or else she totally loses it."

Ninka spends hours watching Shlyuz's other residents: the gypsy* children. The gypsies take up the two buildings on the other side of the platform. In one of the houses, it's Grandpa Nikolai and his Russian wife, Nadia. In the other one, a large family: Lena the gypsy, her husband, Sasha, and their seven children ranging from twenty months to seventeen years old.

"Sasha, Masha, Kolya, Sveta," Lena begins listing them off. "Darn it, there are a lot of them!"

She stands with her hands on her hips in the doorway while her grubby, unbelievably beautiful children are hanging down from the banisters, swinging on fences, running around in tall grass. The Rusakovs don't have a vegetable patch or a garden or livestock. Their property is overgrown with mugwort and nettles.

"What do we eat? We hack it. My husband does construction, I work in people's gardens. Plus we get four grand in child support. That's our whole family business."

The children gather mushrooms and brushwood, berries and scrap metal. None of them go to school. "What school could they possibly go to if there is only one train a day!" Lena exclaims.

She's not telling the whole truth: the Rusakovs only moved here from the Novgorod district a year ago, and there was a school there. It's just that "that's not really our way. I only went up to fourth grade. I teach them myself a bit." The little Rusakovs don't know how to read or write. Except Masha, the eldest, who knows how to write her last name. The entire side of the building is covered in chalk: Masha is practicing.

* This family is Russian Roma people. They call themselves gypsies. The text and translation preserve this term.

They have a TV, it teaches the children almost everything about life outside Shlyuz. The older ones have also been to Likhoslavl. No one has been to Moscow. "I don't have time to take them for rides!" Lena laughs.

They have no phone. There was a cell phone, but it got lost. Two weeks ago, when the youngest one got a fever, they had to run to Cheslavovna to call an ambulance. The ambulance agreed to drive up to the turn. Lena raced there, over the tracks, then another mile, with her little boy in her arms.

Anna Cheslavovna tries to keep her distance from them. First of all, "they are dirty." Second, they dug her potatoes up out of her garden. Third of all, "I slaughtered a piglet, salted the meat and canned it. They stole one of my fucking jars!"

Here's how it happened: Cheslavovna had left her cellar door open. And it's not your average cellar, it's a veritable treasure trove filled with many years' worth of stores. "I used to buy peaches off of the southern trains, cherries, plus things I grow—you should taste my lecho, my mushrooms. I used to make two hundred jars in a summer." One day, Anna Cheslavovna came home from work, and her husband said, "Someone just whizzed past me out of the cellar. They had a jar." "So I went straight to the gypsies. I open the door, and there they all are, sitting around the jar. There was like ten pounds of meat in there. All that was left was the stuff at the very bottom. They didn't even have any bread, they didn't have anything, they were just eating the meat by itself! With nothing!" Anna Cheslavovna's anger seems boundless. "I started screaming but then that daddy of theirs, that Sasha, picked up a shovel and almost bashed my skull in. I lost it, I called the cops, I'm lucky enough to have friends on the force! None of them come around bothering me after that. Only once in a while, they'll ask for a few of my mushrooms."

The evening entertainment at the Shlyuz station is watching the Sapsans fly by. People come out for it half an hour early. Everyone—Anna Cheslavovna, Ninka, Lena and her kids, Grandpa Nikolai and his wife, Nadia—is there. They immediately rip branches off of the lilac bushes, which have gone feral, to make wreaths to protect themselves from the mosquitoes, "those noxious bastards."

Tonight, instead of the Sapsan, it's some monster with a red face.

"Is it a switcher?" seven-year-old Kolya suggests.

"No way, are you stupid? It's an inspection locomotive," Sveta corrects him.

Grandpa Nikolai, a real character of an old gypsy with a Belomor cigarette in his teeth, brags, "I'm rich in grandkids. I got thirty of them. I used to have four sons, though there are only two left. And a daughter. A good family. A real family. A big one." Nikolai worked as a railway inspector for sixteen years, now he looks after the kids. "Who can look after them! Those little demons just love jumping all over the tracks!" The demons giggle.

Shlyuz watches two Sapsans pass by in silence. Masha fidgets with the string around her neck. It has a cross on it and an earring. Afterward, they have another smoke and watch the last of the birdies go by. There goes the one to Moscow.

"I wouldn't live in that Moscow of theirs if they paid me," Lena suddenly says. "Every day they got all that . . . you know . . . bustle."

"And we weren't meant to," says Nikolai.

"We weren't meant to," Lena agrees.

• KALASHNIKOVO STATION

143 miles from Moscow, 260 from Saint Petersburg

"21:03. The Sapsan's gone by," Vanya says into the radio. "Just a few more, then I can go to bed."

Vanya's official job title is Cerberus.

Being a Cerberus isn't easy. Everyone hates them. It's not because they protect the birdies—it's how much they make doing it, by local standards. A Cerberus earns 1,300 rubles a shift. "I will work fifteen days on, fifteen days off, and easily get 20 grand every two weeks," Vanya says. "Where else could I make that much?"

Vanya is from Tambov. He was in the army, then he worked as a security guard for 10 grand a month, and then he got lucky: he was recruited to Moscow, and from there, they sent him to Kalashnikovo to guard the Sapsans.

"The work isn't hard, but it's dreary," says Vanya. "You let each of the birdies through, report the time over the radio to the next station, and monitor the situation before and after it passes. No one has thrown any rocks here yet, but people have tried running in front of the train. You're supposed to restrain them by force or convince them to wait for the train to pass."

The Cerberuses live right here at the station, in train cars on turnout tracks. They have no water or electricity. They are "more or less used to" the mosquitoes. They wash in the Kalashnikovo bathhouse and get hot water from the station cashiers.

"I have to suffer for fifteen days at a time, but then I get to go home," Vanya smiles.

Although there is no one waiting for him at home. He doesn't have a wife or kids.

"I haven't actually figured out what all this money is for," Vanya confesses. "But having a job is a luxury, you can't turn it down. Maybe someday, I'll become a traveler. Last year, I went to Ukraine, to the sea. I liked it, I could go again. I've never been to Saint Petersburg. Is it really true that the girls go around in sunglasses during the White Nights?"

Ulyana, a cashier, steps out of the station. She silently pours some sunflower seeds into the Cerberus's hand. She stands next to him, and they start munching on them together.

"Are you complaining again?" Ulyana teases the Cerberus. "It's just a sin for you to complain, you overfed ass!"

They laugh.

Ulyana lives in the village of Gristvyanka—you won't it find on any map, except maybe a military one. Every day, she has to "march" seven miles to the station and seven miles home. "It's amazing exercise,"

Ulyana says. "In the winter, I weighed 230 pounds, now I'm down to 160—pretty good!"

Ulyana actually has two degrees: a vocational one as an "economic worker in the field of forestry" and a college diploma for "cultural worker." However, being a cashier pays better.

"I looked in Tver, in Kalashnikovo, in Likhoslavl. Youth theaters, Houses of Culture, Palaces of Culture, concert halls. The ceiling for my profession is 5,000 rubles a month," Ulyana says, sardonic and angry. "They were hiring a director at the Tver Dramatic. Forty-three hundred a month. At the Kalashnikovo Palace of Culture, they told me that they wouldn't go over 5 grand under any circumstances. I asked, 'Am I allowed to have a second job? No? Well then goodbye!'"

As a cashier, Ulyana makes "almost twelve." And although she tries to convince herself that it's a good job and "it doesn't hurt," of course it hurts.

"It was something I consciously pursued, being a cultural worker. I was in school for six years, I wrote a good thesis. I read so many books. But our country has a greater demand for cashiers," Ulyana laughs. "Next year, I'm going to try to get into VGIK* for screenwriting."

Other job opportunities in the seven-mile radius around Ulyana's house include the sawmill and the light bulb factory. "The Ministry of Defense funded it for a long time because it's easy to convert the light bulb machinery to making grenades. But recently somebody bought the factory and started doing whatever he wants with it. You'd only work there if you had no self-respect."

Kalashnikovo has a population of 4,700. "The locals live off of their vegetable gardens," Vanya explains. "Then they cut down the forest—some people have permits, others do it off the books. They poach, which is to say that they hunt. It's not for fun, they don't put pelts on their walls or sell meat at the market. One moose is 220 pounds of meat. That'll feed a family for the whole winter."

* Russia's most famous film school, located in Moscow.

Boars, bears, and even lynx live in the forests around Kalashnikovo. "Two years ago, an old woman from Fedoskino went out for mushrooms. And never came back," Ulyana tells us to spook us. "They found her all eaten up. But they never did find her head." In the winter—it's rare, but it happens—arctic owls will fly through.

The only sight rarer than the owls is the local police (they usually hide out at the precinct). "Today we spotted two of them on the platform," Ulyana says. "The girls all ran out from behind their registers to get a good look."

The town square is less than five minutes' walk from the station. There are a few benches, a grassy lawn.

The same old statue of Lenin.

The locals explain that he's not exactly same old. The chest of Kalashnikovo's Lenin bears a welding scar. A month ago, some guy tried to sell the leader for scrap.

"He tried to saw off the top half of the statue and it fell down on him," a tipsy woman named Alena explains, holding her two-year-old niece on her hip. It's the little girl's birthday. "Lenin tore open his stomach and spleen. He's still in Tver, in the hospital. Lenin got fixed up just a few days ago. They welded him back together and gave him a fresh coat of silver paint."

For the three weeks before that, the leader's lower half stood covered up in a bedsheet.

The Palace of Culture is also named after Lenin. People are hanging out around each of its columns. A group of heavily made-up girls are fanning themselves with birch bundles, the mosquitoes are getting them. The entrances to the Palace of Culture are heavily littered with empty bottles.

The youth in Kalashnikovo have yet another amusement. It's called cards of fire. That's when somebody who loses at cards has to set a building on fire.

"These days, the Kalashnikovo fire department is practically the best trained in the district," Ulyana says.

Further on, there's the school (the building is 120 years old), and then the "newer" school, which is only 75. Then the burned-out carcass of the old hospital, overgrown with purple flowers. Ulyana says that every election season begins with promises to rebuild the hospital. No one has gotten past the foundation. People from Kalashnikovo go to the hospital in Tver, forty miles away.

The emergency care center is across from the ruins of the hospital. You can still get emergency care. Two nannies in white kerchiefs are laughing, leaning over the fence. An old lady is standing around here, too, Galina Mikhailovna, age seventy-three. Galina Mikhailovna heard that they're going to open a nursing home in the emergency care center soon, and she's come to "get in line." "I'm alone and I'm not very strong, there's no one to take care of me, so I'm just going to come here. As soon as I finish digging up my potatoes, I'm coming."

Kalashnikovo ends. The forest road begins, which will soon, per Ulyana, turn into "impassible overgrowth." It's time for Ulyana to go back to work; I have to walk four miles to the village of Bukhalovo.

I try to give Ulyana my number so that she'll have somewhere to stay when she comes to apply to VGIK, but she doesn't want it. "I'll be fine. You know, I have no business in that Moscow of yours. You're supposed to go around begging, hustling, owing people things. That's what they say on TV, 'Connections, connections, connections.' I'm probably too proud for that. I want to be a fish in my own pond out here. I'll have a house with solar panels and plumbing, horses and dogs, and an SUV. I know that you have to work hard for that."

"I work a lot. I'm twenty-six and I work all the time," Ulyana says. "But I'd probably have to live in another country if I really wanted all that."

Then Ulyana explains that if I see a bear, I should "get a big stick, put your hands up, and wave them over your head so that it'll think that it's facing a really big animal. Then it will probably just go away." She adds, "Whatever you do, don't scream. Animals find screaming extremely irritating." She takes her exit.

• BUKHALOVO PASS

146 miles from Moscow, 257 from Saint Petersburg

It took almost two hours to walk from the town of Kalashnikovo to the village of Bukhalovo.

The forest road, which started out fine, became worse with each step, before turning into a meadow and disappearing entirely. After that, the path was only marked by sporadic but deep indentations apparently left there by trucks. I had to walk fast or else my feet would sink into the ground. I was chased along by clouds of mosquitoes. The insects infested my nostrils and ears and easily penetrated my canvas sneakers. I could only look down at my feet, to make sure not to twist my ankles or slip in the mud. After I fell in a ditch and got up to my knees in water, finding a dry place to step no longer mattered. I lost all sense of time and just marched, marched, marched. The road once again turned into the forest.

By the time I reached Bukhalovo, it was almost night. Two cell phone towers and a sole lamppost stood over its two rows of wooden houses. Next to the lamppost, there was a tractor, rusted and covered in mud, grown over with weeds.

There are sixty-five houses in Bukhalovo. It is hard to believe, but there used to be a livestock-breeding collective farm here, a school, a store, a club, and a medical center. Back then, there was also, of course, a road.

Now the only connection between the village and the rest of the world is the railroad. All of the Spirovo, Akademichesky, Vyshnevolotsky, and Bologoye commuter trains used to stop here. Ever since the advent of the Sapsan, the number of dailies that stop at the station has been cut in half. Now they've canceled the first morning train and all of the evening trains in the direction of Bologoye.

The administration of the village council of the Krasnodarsk Village-Type Settlement, which Bukhalovo is a part of, is located in the village of

Berdichevo. They will show up in Bukhalovo once every couple of years on a tractor—bearing a ballot box, for elections. Two years ago, the enraged local drunks chased the "guy with a box" through the village, and the administration has not shown its face in Bukhalovo since.

On May 30, Auntie Valya—Valentina Mikhailovna Alekseeva—retired. For thirty-nine years, she worked as a maintenance repairwoman at the Tver Cotton and Paper Mill, and that was enough. She decided to throw a party for the whole village. They sent someone out to the train station for victuals, set the tables, sat down, and then suddenly, her stove collapsed.

"It was like a bomb going off!" Auntie Valya laughs. "Then the dust came down. . . . We all coughed it out, and then there we were, all gray, and all of the food was covered in rubble."

They still haven't fixed the stove. Construction materials can only be brought to the village by commuter rail. "How many more years do we have to rely on these commuter trains?" locals demand.

Groceries also only arrive on the dailies. There used to be a grocery truck that would somehow or other make it out to the village. An intrepid Dagestani named Ragim would drive his jeep to Bukhalovo from Kalashnikovo, a trip that took four or five hours. He even ended up carving out something like a track for himself. But the logging trucks broke it up again. Fed up, Ragim said that fixing his truck after every trip "cost more than I make here selling you food." And with that, he stopped coming.

Now the only "grocery" sold in the village is moonshine: diluted antifreeze.

By city standards, there is simply no platform. And of course, the most difficult thing is getting up into the train. "Your hands, your chin—you'll use whatever you got to get up those steps, as long as you can make it in," Auntie Valya says. "If you're lucky, they'll be young men smoking in the vestibules—they'll grab you by your scruff and pull you up. Old women are usually also boosted from behind. They can't raise their legs up that high anymore." Attempts to drag the old women into the commuter train inevitably end in outs: "They'll fall down and land on their backs just like beetles, waving their arms around."

The villagers can tell when the Sapsan is coming from the static on their TVs. They get two channels here—Channel 1 and Channel 2. "If a war breaks out, we will know about it," Bulakhovites say gravely.

The only thing anyone really watches is the medical talk show *Malakhov+*, and they religiously take down the recipes. With an anxious expression, the host will explain, "The next person we'll meet believes that a cocktail of pilewort and coltsfoot helped him get over an incurable stomach ulcer." The last time a doctor came to the village was two years ago. "We all got together at this babushka's house and the doctor saw everyone. She took everyone's blood pressure and wrote out prescriptions." If someone gets sick in the village, they're loaded into the "cow cart"—a wheelbarrow usually used for manure—and taken down to the station. There, they are put on the first passing train, where they ask the engineer to call over the intercom for an ambulance at the next major station. The engineers know their route; they will call.

Once, Auntie Valya broke her leg jumping off of the train into the ditch. "It was the last train," she says. "I had to wait until morning. Overnight, my leg swelled up so much, I couldn't even get it into my rubber boot. They put me in the cow cart in my white trench coat. I sat in the vestibule until Tver like a hobo. That's where the ambulance picked me up."

If the sick person can't be transported, they must resort to the most extreme measure: treatment by phone.

Three years ago, Anatoly Streltsov had a stroke. "He had a bad headache, so he got in bed," says his wife, Valya. "I went up to him and I saw that his eyes had rolled back in his head and his chin had gone out of joint." Valya called the ambulance. The doctor on duty spent a long time asking about the symptoms before coming to her conclusion: he couldn't be transported. She recommended they gather up all the medications they had in the village. The ones that could more or less help were Corvalol, korinfar, Adelphan, furosemide, and Enap. They got lucky. The doctor told them the dosage and asked them to call back every half hour. A day later, again, over the phone, the doctor decided that they could "attempt transporting" the patient. And so Anatoly was taken to Spirovo—in the usual way, on the first train that passed by. He survived.

In the village, the Streltsovs are basically oligarchs. They own the only horse, Venus, and an open wagon. They can get to Kalashnikovo on their own.

That's how the Streltsovs took Anna Kruzhanova, who didn't make the train on time, to Kalashnikovo. She was already dead. Her relatives had to beg them—usually, corpses leave Bukhalovo on those same trains, in those same vestibules.

◆ LEONTIEVO

182 miles from Moscow, 221 from Saint Petersburg

The Sapsans pass by Leontievo very quietly, they practically crawl. They are repairing the tracks to Moscow—seventeen men in orange jumpsuits are cutting the rails apart. Afterward, with the ties still on them, a special machine that looks like a spider picks them up and throws them off to the side; then they clear the old gravel with an excavator and put down fresh gravel, and new rails are laid. They're working fast: First of all, they have to be done by two to let the trains through. Second of all, the chef, Kolya, is making pilaf today, and everyone already knows that there are only going to be fourteen pieces of chicken in it.

On January 12, a thirty-five-year-old unemployed Leontievo man, Mikhail Samartsev, threw a block of ice at a passing Sapsan. He hit it, breaking a window in the sixth car. The Russian Railroad assessed the damage at 120,000 rubles.

"I don't believe that he was the one who did it," says his mother, Nina Fedorovna. "The cops just picked up a group of drunk men from the station. He was the only one who didn't have his passport, so they pinned everything on him."

Nina Fedorovna lives in the village of Solnechny, across the tracks from Leontievo. She is a teacher. Her third-grade class has eight students. Her husband, Vladimir, excuses himself and goes off to work on the vegetable patch. In order to feed themselves, the Samartsevs grow potatoes and keep sheep.

"Misha stole everything from us," Nina Fedorovna complains. "The colander—how much metal is in that?—even the colander. All of the frying pans. And then he comes over and asks me to give him something to eat. I tell him, 'What am I supposed to warm up your food on?' My husband blames me, but is it really my fault? Look at my daughter, Lena. I raised them together."

Lena is the Samartsevs' pride and joy. She graduated from Tver State University with a degree in biology "with an ecological bent." She was always interested in philosophy. "Aristotle and Kant are her favorites." She's gone to conferences, speaks Italian, writes poems and fiction.

Lena works in Valday, as a bookkeeper in a biological research station. In her free time, she translates the poems of a young Italian poet named Marcello Menni and publishes them online.

> Perhaps, it is best not to fight,
> and leave hope behind
> in the misty expanses . . .

Nina Fedorovna looks for a picture of Misha. The most recent one is ten years old. "Maybe he just wasn't strong enough?" she says, trying to account for his life. "I mean, not strong enough to live. He studied to be a glassblower. He wanted to work at the Red May factory—it's near here, that's where they made the stars for the Kremlin. Then they shut it down. That's when he started drinking. But you can't give up like that. Or maybe everyone is supposed to have different amounts of strength?"

When Nina Fedorovna can't find the strength anymore, she thinks about the class that graduated last year. "There were twenty-two of them, and they were all so wonderful, such great friends, so kind. Two of them went on to the high school!" But when she starts remembering the children who've passed through her classroom, she can't stop. "It's happened to me. First, the boy stopped coming to school. Allegedly because his mother couldn't afford some of the fees. Then they found him frozen in the hayloft. The next year, two children were burned alive, a brother and sister, nine and seven. Their mother, my downstairs neighbor, started picking up guys on the highway. One day, she left, but there wasn't any power, so she lit a kerosene lamp for the kids. . . . Now she drinks.

"How are you supposed to understand life after things like that happen?" Nina Fedorovna wonders. "Some people are saved and some aren't. Why? Now I believe in the moiras, the blind Greek women. They weave people's fates out of whatever's at hand and cut the thread whenever they want. That's the only way I can understand anything anymore."

"I don't believe that Misha can get back on his feet," Nina Fedorovna says. She's been crying for a long time now without noticing it. "If I, the mother, am saying, 'Here, take this rope' . . . "

Young, healthy men are getting drunk by the store. They are drinking through Zhenya's paycheck. Zhenya works on the railroad as a woodcutter—he chops down the trees that grow within fifty feet of the tracks. If he can cut down two hundred square feet a day (that's ten to twelve hours of work), by the end of the month, he can make an unheard-of 40 grand. That's what they're drinking their way through.

Zhenya comes up and makes a request. "Tell the people in Moscow they're fags!" Zhenya has a few bones to pick with the government. First of all, he's an orphan and he's supposed to get an apartment, but he never got one and lives in a wooden house with his grandma and grandpa instead. Secondly, Yushkova, the head of the administration of the rural settlement, allowed both of Leontievo's bathhouses to get shut down. "Where are our old people supposed to wash themselves now?" Zhenya screams, fairly drunk. "Where am I supposed to wash myself?

Meanwhile, that whore Yushkova has a private house on a lake!" (I checked it out later—the house isn't as nice as you'd think. It's a very old wooden structure, and there is no lake.)

"I'm skipping out on the army! And I'm not ashamed that I'm skipping out on the army! I personally don't owe this country—nothing!"

Zhenya takes me over to meet his friend Anton.

Anton Abdulkhlanov is sitting on a bench with his grandmother, Lidia Victorovna. Anton fought in both Chechen wars and can continue the conversation about the army.

"Mozdok, Khankala, Alkhan-Yurt, Komsomolskoe, Chervlenoe," Anton calmly lists.

"My brother went off to fight in Chechnya!" Zhenya yells. "One time, he was in a bad mood, so he nailed his wife to the wall. He drove forks through her hands and feet and had her up on the wall! It's all fucking Putin! He can't defend his people!"

"Two contusions, four wounds, two of them from shrapnel and two from bullets," Anton continues.

"I need a tank! I'll crush that Yushkova's administration building into splinters!" Zhenya wails. "And then it's the Kremlin! I don't care if they put me in jail, I'm going to kill Putin! And Medvedev! Why can't our old people wash themselves!"

"Yes, it's true, dearie, there's nowhere to wash. I warm up the water in the trough and then rub myself down," Lidia Victorovna starts in. "They ought to get rid of that Yushkova and put someone good in her place!" And with that, she begins crying and making small crosses over herself.

"Cut it out, Gran. Let's not get upset," Anton consoles her, putting his arm around her shoulders.

"Fucking assholes are running this country!" Zhenya yells.

It doesn't occur to Zhenya or Anton—two strong men—or any of their friends getting wasted in front of the store that they could just build a bathhouse themselves or hire contractors. What's worse is that it also doesn't occur to Lidia Victorovna to ask her grandson to do it.

◆ **THE SAPSAN**

Passing through Uglovka

236 miles from Moscow, 167 from Saint Petersburg

It's not nearly as fast as they said it would be, or as it seemed from outside. The average speed is 118 miles an hour, it only went up to 138 once. The seats have soft headrests, large, panoramic windows, *Dark Planet* playing on the TVs. You can listen to music on the headphones. The conductors wear handsome gray uniforms, badges with their names and a flag, most often the British flag. The flag designates a language they speak. If you go up to one and ask, "Do you speak English?" they'll answer, "A little bit."

Coffee costs 50 rubles and lunch is almost 500.

Smoking is not allowed, so people jump out on the rare one-minute stops and greedily take a few drags. Vendors in trays immediately rush the passengers, plying their wares: smoked eels, wooden spoons from Khokhloma, salted fish, sunflower seeds, vodka, apricots. The conductors are anxious and begin shouting, "Ladies and gentlemen, the train is about to leave the station!" But one passenger always manages to buy a porcelain bell or a bream.

The conversations:

"We were supposed to take seventy-five people a week. That was the assignment. I was like, 'What kind of bullshit is that? Transporting drillers without any helicopters . . .'"

"If you want insurance, we can provide it, at whatever percent you need."

"Hello, my dear Victor Ivanovich!"

A child, "Four plus four . . . eight plus six . . . twelve plus seven . . . thirty plus seven . . ."

"It'll be a breakthrough in Russian shipbuilding: a ship that takes ten hours on just its stern propellers to get all the way to . . ."

"To be perfectly honest, the show wasn't very impressive, plus there was that political subtext."

"You're on your own for now, but when I finish up with these gentlemen, please come back."

A very expensively dressed and well-heeled pregnant woman is lazily clacking away on her glistening Vaio. Then she begins reading a printout of an article called, "The Case of AA, or What to Do with Opposing Theories of Disease." She makes notes in the margins, furrowing her brow. The article is about a dispute between Moscow and Saint Petersburg psychiatrists regarding expanding the parameters for the definition of schizophrenia.

(Gena from Shlyuz said, "What's sad isn't just that they're flying by in their palace, but that they don't even look out the windows. They can't be bothered to turn their heads.")

I try to look out the window, but it is actually painful—must be the speed.

The train reaches Moscow in four hours and fourteen minutes.

CHAPTER 4

JUSTICE VS. DECENCY

I THINK IT WAS Irina Bergalieva, my friend, the human rights activist, who called me. She told me a woman who lived in her dormitory, Manana Dzhabeliya, had been sentenced to deportation.

I'm saying "I think" because my memories of those days are very fuzzy. On October 7, 2006, Anna Politkovskaya was murdered—shot in the elevator of her building. Five gunshots. Anna Politkovskaya was the journalist whose articles made me want to become a journalist. There was nobody in the world I respected more. My office was near hers. Sometimes I'd leave her apples on her desk, but we never spoke—I thought I was still young and dumb, it could wait, I had time. I never let myself think she might die. After her murder, I spent many hours bargaining with death—if her killers were found right away, could she be resurrected? If I promised to tell her everything that I always wanted to say but was too afraid, about how much she had changed my life and so many others', about how grateful I was to her, would she come back to life? She did not. I was tormented by my pain, it burned me inside like fire and then, in a flash, turned to an icy hatred. The hatred was a lot easier to live and to work with. I'd open my eyes in the morning and my first thought would be: work. At night, as I fell asleep, I would think to myself: I'm going to rest up and then get to work more.

I had enough work to do. Georgia had expelled a handful of Russian army officers on accusations of spying. Russia decided to get revenge. Many Georgians still lived in Russia: from Soviet times, when we were one country; those who had come fleeing the war; those who had come here to work. They started getting rounded up and deported. It didn't matter if they had their documents. People weren't even taken to immigration court, their deportation papers were served directly by the police. Over 2,500 people got deported that way in the course of two months.

On TV, they said that the Georgians had always been Russia's enemies. They cut off all transport and mail connections with Georgia and stopped selling Georgian wine. The police would ask schools to submit lists of their Georgian students. Moscow markets were raided. Police rounded up people with Georgian last names. Manana Dzhabeliya got swept up in one of these raids.

She was fifty years old, a refugee who had come to Russia fleeing the war. She didn't have a home or family in Georgia. Her family was her two sons—her youngest, Nika, was the love and pride of her life, a student at Moscow State Law University. They arrested all of the Georgian merchants—over twenty people. Including Manana. Nobody even looked at her documents. They wouldn't let Nika, who'd shown up to the police station to bring his mother some food, see her. Manana was hungry, she spent the night in a cage. The next day, the Nagatinsky court ruled to deport her and six other people. The fates of these seven were decided in fifteen minutes. Manana refused to sign the ruling. It was signed for her.

She was taken to a detention center to await deportation. She was scheduled to be deported in nine days without a chance to appeal. But then my friend Irina found out about what had happened and called me and the Moscow Helsinki Group.* The Moscow Helsinki Group got the

* The Moscow Helsinki Group was the oldest human rights organization in Russia. In January 2023, the Moscow City Court permanently shut down the MHG for supposedly being in violation of the regulations on nonprofit organizations.

courts to issue Manana's copy of the verdict to her sons so they could appeal it. We had one and a half days to file a writ of appeal. We managed to do it.

The court did not set a date for a new hearing. Manana lived behind bars. She went on a hunger strike. It was all very hard on her, she had a bad heart and high blood pressure. An ambulance had to be called to the jail almost every day. The jailers didn't like that. Inspector Ekaterina Sokolova brought her a document revoking the writ of appeal, instructing her to just sign it and get deported immediately. Manana refused. Sokolova asked her, You're an adult woman. Why are you torturing yourself and your loved ones? It is indecent.

And now I would like to talk about decency, how people understand this concept in Russia. Decency is not the same thing as morality—it is actually the opposite. A decent person follows established rules. For example, they'll pay off a cop to avoid getting a speeding ticket—everyone does that. They obey their elders. They don't insist on their rights—especially if they are aging Georgian refugees. If the court tells you you're getting deported, you go get deported—don't piss off the people more powerful than you.

Manana was being indecent. She starved herself, got on the nerves of her jailers, attracted attention from human rights activists and journalists, she insisted on her rights instead of accepting her lot.

We were also behaving indecently. The human rights activists held press conferences. I wrote stories. Finally, she got a court date.

Irina and I and Manana's sons—big, grown men—all showed up to the hearing. They brought Manana in from the detention center. That was the first time I saw her. A small, heavyset woman with a soft face, warm brown eyes, curly hair that had gone totally gray. She clearly felt bad that everybody had come here because of her. She tried to sit up very straight and speak very clearly. The judge was hot in her robes. She dispatched the case quickly—the outcome was a foregone conclusion. She issued the verdict. The deportation was canceled.

But they wouldn't let Manana go home because the hearing was on a

Thursday and who works on Fridays? Friday is basically the weekend. She was taken back to the detention center with the promise that they would release her on Monday. Before taking her away, the transfer guards allowed us to take a picture together on the steps of the courthouse. Irina said, Let's get a picture so we can remember this moment forever. There we are in the photo, Manana, Irina, and me. Manana is smiling and you can tell that the smile costs her dearly.

She was returned to the cage. Her cellmates said she was laughing and even dancing a little, she promised to bring them all food when she got out. She died on Saturday. Simply did not wake up. The women banged on the doors, shouting until the jailers arrived. They didn't tell her family right away, waiting until hours later, after they'd filled out the documents. That morning, Manana's sons had been scouring Moscow in search of forbidden Georgian wine to celebrate their mother's release. When Nika called me, I thought that my phone had broken. The receiver was blubbering and wailing.

We met at the detention center. The first snow was falling into the darkness. Georgian consul Zurab Pataradze stood with Manana's sons. They weren't being allowed into the detention center. I started screaming at the consul—why did you only come now, when she is already dead? He put his arms around me, I tore myself out of his grasp. He said, There's no need to shout anymore. He said, Let me get you home, it's a bad winter.

Manana returned to Georgia dead. Her funeral was held in the Sameba Holy Trinity Cathedral, the largest church in the country. Parliamentarians and ministers, Georgians deported from Russia, and simple passersby all came to pay their respects to the refugee. Her sons stood next to her coffin. They never returned to Russia again.

Irina Bergalieva, who first told me about Manana and came to her defense, died four years later, in the hallway of the Podolsky courthouse. She'd come to stand up for people being threatened with eviction. She couldn't. She simply collapsed. People called her an ambulance, but she did not have a pulse. She had a bad heart as well, but she never talked about that. I thought of her as all-powerful. She wore the brightest lipstick and had the best laugh in the world. The police officers, the judges, and bureaucrats who had to deal with her thought she was secretly backed by the mafia because she wasn't afraid of anybody and fought for everybody she could. Their tiny minds couldn't comprehend how defenseless she actually was.

Irina was buried at the Perepechinskoe Cemetery. The ground is all clay, there's no grass. The people she saved came to her funeral.

I still remember her phone number, 8 916 926 27 06, and sometimes I find myself yearning to dial it. I called her up so many times over the years, when it was totally dark out the window, in bad snow, when I had no strength left and everything weighed on my chest. She'd say, Don't be afraid of anything, never fear anything, people are capable of everything. And so I wasn't afraid, I was never afraid. Irina, Manana, and Anna are gone. Now, when it gets frightening, I just keep running forward.

FROM SUNRISE TO SUNRISE

May 26, 2009

The police station where I went undercover as an apprentice criminologist is in a typical three-story building in a Moscow neighborhood that is so far from the center, it's practically not in the city.

The first floor has the main offices, that's where calls come in, the Rapid Response Group, and interrogation rooms. The second floor is the most restricted—the field officers, the archive, and the criminologists. The third floor has the investigative officers.

9 a.m.: shift change. The guard on duty checks everyone in and does weapons inspections. The department head observes the changeover. His role seems to be merely decorative. He vanishes into his office, never to reappear.

Sleepy Post and Patrol Service (PPS) beat cops drive away to their checkpoints. I'm not allowed to shadow them, "They have special operating procedures." The PPS are the ones who rip off migrant workers, extort bribes, and file phony reports. They only let trainees do PPS ride-alongs once they are sure of their loyalty.

The dispatch office is the heart of any police precinct. Here, it's a large room with a barred window taking up half of the wall, a makeshift kitchen (refrigerator, table, microwave), and a little room off to the side with two couches, where the desk sergeants take turns sleeping, plus a munitions closet. The phones are always ringing through a veil of cigarette smoke, there's morning rage in the air. The man yelling is Sasha*—today, he's a desk sergeant. First thing in the morning, before he has had his beer, everything pisses him off. Behind his back, people consider

* All names have been changed.

Sasha a loser. He used to be in the special forces of the GRU*, but somehow or other he ended up on the police force. Sasha is also a huge *Lord of the Rings* fan. He loves talking about how good always triumphs over evil. Which doesn't get in the way of his indifference to seeing the captives get beaten. Captives is what they call everyone they arrest.

Calls come in. Desk sergeants page whoever's supposed to answer them over the intercom: detectives, officers, sometimes the criminologists. People on their way out to the field want to know, "Was it a light crime?"

"Another dark one."

"Gonna be cold, then."

A light crime is when the vic saw the perp. A dark one is when they did not.

Policemen call themselves officers. An officer will do anything for another officer: he'll take a bullet, stick up for him in front of the administration, sign a phony report, get his son into college. Outside the precinct, the world is divided into the perps—suspected perpetrators—and the vics—victims. Both groups have adversarial relationships with the police. The feeling is mutual.

Between the calls, cops spend their time watching endless procedurals extolling the greatness of the Russian police. The best ones are the first season of *Avenue of Broken Streetlamps* and *Cold Case*, the more realistic version. There's something perverse in the cops' obsession with cop shows, which exist to convince people that the police are something they *really* need. Moreover, the cop shows' protagonists are always breaking the law, which is, according to TV logic, not only unavoidable but also right.

Egor the criminologist, who I'm supposed to be shadowing, and I are on our fourth episode of a drama called *Cops*. One of the cops is a lot like Egor: he'd signed up with the police to get out of doing compulsory military service, started believing in it, got into his job, became a pro, got disillusioned, but now he can't leave because "the boys" just won't let him go.

* The military intelligence service

It's very hard for them to let go of the kind of criminologist who covers up all their crimes and helps get the perps behind bars by readily tampering with evidence.

"It's not that I'm scared, okay? I'm not afraid of the boys. It's just that they really, really need me."

There's a page from the office.

"A vic is here. Come get pics of his ride."

"We're watching something. Tell him to wait."

"He's been waiting two hours already. He's freaking out."

"Let him freak out, then!" Egor explodes, getting up from the couch. A needed man needs to act out every once in a while.

We go down to take pictures of the vic's vehicle. It's completely covered in shit—totally, thoroughly, up to the very roof.

The victim, a young man in a fancy suit, is clearly in shock. "Can you believe this?" he moans. "I live by a school and this is how those little punks have their fun. They're usually doing it to Zhigulis or, like, Ladas. My car is *expensive*!"

"Does your insurance cover the contingency of a vehicle becoming covered in fecal matter?" Officer Zhenya asks. He likes to rub things in.

"It's not about money. I want them punished. Can't you find them? Call the school . . ."

"I'ma be honest with you," Zhenya says, sliding into informality. "We are not looking for them. We're not gonna call up the school. It's too hard to prove, and the most that they're gonna do is fine them and put it on their records. Just get your car washed, then park it in front of the school. Sit somewhere and watch it yourself. You'll see who it is. Then you can feed them that shit."

A CALL. First corpse of the day. It's not a criminal corpse, there's no need for a criminologist. However, the officers insist that I go anyway. The two in the car are accompanied by a strange man in a black suit.

"Is he an officer?"

"Yeah, unofficially."

The young man turns out to be from a funeral home. It's a long-standing practice: the desk sergeant unofficially informs the home of every dead body, and then their suits ride along. Each body gets the desk sergeant 3,500 rubles.

We greet the first responders in the doorway. The apartment is more or less furnished. A woman, forty, lies on the couch, covered up by a blanket.

Her son is twenty, surrounded by his bewildered friends. All of them visibly drunk. They were drinking beers in the kitchen while his mama was dying. He calmly recites the story.

"I heard her calling me. I thought she'd shit herself. She's been shitting herself a few days now. She says, 'I want to puke.' So I brought her a basin—there it is, right there. Then she let out a croak and died."

Exactly forty days ago, this kid buried his father. Both his mother and father drank.

"C'mere and help turn her over."

The officer unceremoniously examines the body. Her arms and legs hang off the sides of the couch. He carelessly tosses the blanket back over her.

One of the son's friends, a girl, runs out of the room.

We begin filing: no signs of violence.

We take down identifying features.

"It's dark in here. Intern, go see what her hair color is."

I go up to her, have a good look.

"Chestnut, dyed."

"Eyes?"

"Gray blue. Pupils almost the size of her iris."

"Are her armpits shaved?"

"That's not one of the blanks."

The officers exchange looks and burst into laughter.

"Not bad, intern, you didn't flinch. Good work."

Before we can even make it back, there's a new call.

The officer issues a tirade of curses into the phone.

"A kid's bike? A fucking bike? Have you fucking lost it?"

He listens in silence. Hangs up.

"Fucking horseshit. The vic is an officer's wife."

The anxious officer's wife is waiting for us at the door of her building.

"They stole my son's bike. It was his birthday present! He's four. It was right here in the lobby! The neighbors say it was the alkie from the next building over."

The alkie's a gray-haired old man who can barely walk. His apartment is heaped with filth. The kid's bike really is in there.

"What do you need a bike for, Granddad?"

"Huh?"

"The bike! Are you going to ride it? Sell it? Is it a gift for someone?"

"I don't know. I saw it and picked it up."

In the next room, an officer is going through the drawers and cabinets. He's looking for beer money. He can't find any. He is cursing.

It takes a long time to get the old man downstairs. He doesn't seem to understand where we are taking him and he starts yelling at us. One of the officers somewhat tenderly prods him in the belly with his fist. The old man quiets down.

We have a hard time shoving him into the car. When we get back to the station, we have to escort him into the fish tank.

Around 7 p.m., it's time to go to the store. Food and drinks: beer, vodka, cognac. The detective girls get wine. Our bottles clank through the checkpoint. But the cop manning it asked for two beers. After settling with him, we get right through.

The detective girls have already made salad. We pour out the wine into mugs. "Just hurry up," the girls warn us. "We're really slammed right now!"

The department has to submit its numbers. Detectives have to send forty cases to court every month, or else they'll lose their bonuses.

The girls say that only three out of the seven people in the investigations department actually work. Those three are spending their fourth night in a row at the precinct, only going home to shower and change their clothes. There's a nearly empty box of Red Bulls on the windowsill of their office.

"Shall we discuss the March case while we're all here?"

The March case is the whole station's headache right now. On March 8, International Women's Day, two men went to visit the same woman to wish her a happy holiday. They couldn't figure out how to split her attention. Their squabbling turned into a fight. Which ended up as a stabbing.

The wounded man claimed that he'd been attacked with the knife. The stabber said that he'd only gotten the knife out to scare him and stop the fight, but then the wounded man started trying to wrest the knife out of his hand and ended up stabbing himself.

They didn't call the police until the ninth. By then, the damsel had managed to wash her floors, and tables, and walls. They didn't find the knife. There were no witnesses—in the heat of the action, the frightened woman had run out of the room. It's a stab wound, which matches both stories. It would seem to be a clear-cut cold case.

But the wounded man has invested relatives, so the case took off. The officers found the right kind of knife, they falsified fingerprints. They loaded a witness. The crime scene report is in its fifth draft. At the same time, officers worked the arrested man. Although he still hasn't confessed.

The March case is what's called a zero: it is completely made up. The rest of the cases that they are submitting to court require corrections. In front of me, the criminologist signs a pile of blank crime scene reports.

"Now let's start drinking for real!"

Oksana, a bottle blond dripping in gold, once again tells everyone about how in six months, she'll be in the tax service, "My uncle—as you all know—has been promoted to deputy head for all of Moscow. He promised to help." Everyone listens attentively without interrupting her. Almost every police officer dreams of becoming a tax man.

An officer runs in with eyes bulging out of his head. "Shukher! Shklovsky!" Shklovsky is the head of the investigation department.

With a practiced motion, the detectives hide their glasses behind the legs of their chairs. An officer shoves a bottle under his jacket. Everyone hurriedly lights cigarettes and starts telling jokes.

Shklovsky, a short, sturdy man, saunters in.

"Having fun, are we?"

He stands in the middle of the room with a nasty smile on his face. Everybody except Oksana gets up to leave.

Through the door, you can hear him shouting.

"You're fucking up the quotas! Completely! I'm gonna fire you before you can get to your cushy job!"

A few minutes later, Oksana runs out in tears. A satisfied Shklovsky follows her out.

"What are you looking at, intern? You sorry for her?"

"Yeah."

"Well, don't be. She works day and night, you know! After twirling her ass all month long! Straight to the tax office!"

Shklovsky's still mad, and he sends me and Officer Zhenya to a drug pusher's interrogation. Escorting people during an interrogation is really unpleasant and Shklovsky knows it.

A small clique is hanging out by the interrogation room—two guys and some girls, the civilian witnesses. They're drinking beers and canned cocktails, listening to music on their cell phones.

"Our regular peanut gallery," Zhenya explains.

The regulars are all on the hook for minor infractions. Although there are also some psychos who volunteer, but not very many.

We relieve the escort guards, taking their places in front of the door. The interrogation is already going on inside.

The pusher is around thirty with sleepy eyes. His hands are cuffed and he's trying to rub his wrists. The cuffs clatter against one another. His fingers are long and thin, covered in fresh wounds. He's sitting with a detective—a little brunette with a can of Red Bull—and an older, tired-looking lawyer. The lawyer is working pro bono, they had to call him in.

"They pressured me. Psychologically," the perp says. "The officers wrote my testimony themselves. They said if I signed it, they'd let me out with just a travel restriction."

"Gross misconduct," the lawyer says.

"What are you defending him for?" the detective asks with a smirk. "It's all cut-and-dried: an innocent person would never admit to their guilt in exchange for a travel restriction."

"You don't make it easy to walk away." The lawyer mirrors the detective's smile.

"I wouldn't do that," she says. Then, turning to the arrested man, "Officers can say whatever they want to you. It's all up to the court anyway. And what makes you think those were really officers? You wouldn't be able to pick them out, would you? Did you get their last names?"

"Did you know that back in December, some officers down from Central got taken in for pushing false confessions?" the lawyer remarks contemplatively.

"Yeah. And then in January, Markelov* was murdered," the detective retorts. "So are we going to work this out or are we just fucking around here?"

"I can't talk," the perp says, suddenly exhaling.

"So you refuse?"

"No. Gimme water."

He drinks a half-liter bottle of Bon Aqua down in a single gulp. And asks for more.

"How long has it been since you had any water?" the lawyer asks.

* Stanislav Markelov, a lawyer from *Novaya Gazeta*, was murdered on January 19, 2009.

It turns out that the perp hasn't drunk, eaten, or gone to the bathroom since he was brought to the station at 2 p.m. that afternoon.

"Are you guys fucking kidding me?" the lawyer asks calmly. "What if his bladder explodes?"

We escort the perp to the bathroom. We refill his water bottle in the sink. I have a cookie in my pocket and I give it to him on the way back. He scarfs it down, then licks his palms. Zhenya is horrified.

"Hey, intern, you fucking nuts?"

We call the witnesses in for face-to-face questioning. The detective is angry—their testimonies are identical, word for word. She rewrites them.

The witnesses cover their eyes and take a long time answering the questions. Their accounts don't line up anymore.

The lawyer comes alive. "Did you actually see the drugs changing hands? Did you witness it with your own eyes?"

"No," a witness quietly says. "I didn't."

"He didn't see it!"

"What?" The detective asks again, looking hard at the regular witness.

The witness mumbles something unintelligible.

"He didn't see anything. He said he didn't see anything."

"He saw everything. We're just tired right now." She reads one of the identical testimonies aloud. "Do you confirm this?"

"Yes."

We escort the perp back to the fish tank.

People are tallying their totals for the day; those will get sent to the district. They're finishing up their reports.

"Sanya, give me some witnesses," the second desk sergeant, Dima, requests.

Names and addresses from an address book are copied down into the blanks on a crime scene report. These dead souls will serve as evidence for the prosecution in court.

"Does that junkie have any relatives?"

"A mom, I think."

"Has she been contacted yet? Call her."

She's called.

"Your son is here. He's under arrest. You can come, but hurry up, he's getting transferred soon."

The officer starts filling out the documents immediately, "Due to the absence of relatives in Moscow, it was impossible to provide the arrested party with a change of underwear or seasonal clothes."

"Let's call the mother back," I offer. "Tell her the things she needs to bring."

The officers laugh.

"This is a standard form, intern," says Dima. He has seniority. "It's the same one for everybody." Under his breath, he continues, "Don't think about it, don't even start. You'll lose your mind."

The mother runs in fifteen minutes later. We escort her to the visitation room. Five minutes later, Scheherazade shows up, the on-duty Central Directorate officer in charge of transferring captives. She's a tall, black-haired woman, unbelievably beautiful, wearing a quilted jacket. She puffs on a cigarette, complaining about the pileup of work. Now that it's time to file quarterly reports, everybody's been catching perps like it's their job. She takes the captive away.

We get ready for dinner. We set the table, cut up salami, pour cola into the cognac.

The holidays are just around the corner and the cops are telling colorful tales of their side hustles. On the lower rungs, you can't feed yourself on a cop's salary, even with bribes. Officer Vasya's a florist between his shifts. He explains that the most beautiful "big boy" bouquets are made out of garbage—flowers that no one would buy on their own. The main side hustle for most is doing security. Almost all of them want to work somewhere else. Their biggest, most unattainable dream is the tax service or customs.

Dima, who's been on the force for seven years, shares his most tender reminiscences.

"I remember there was this construction site with just Tajiks. They'd steal women's purses. Regularly. Two or three vics would show up here a night. We couldn't manage to nab all those slanty-eyed bastards. The boss was really on our tails about it. Then, one fine day, after a shift, we changed into plain clothes, called up our friends, got our clubs, and fucked their shit all the way up. They crawled away like cockroaches when we were done with them. After that, not a single crime anywhere near the construction site."

The other cops laugh in approval. Dima continues.

"But that wasn't the best one. Two years ago, we were lined up in a cordon on a bridge. Some district colonel was inspecting us. Giving us a hard time, telling us we looked bad, calling us jackasses. It was November, the snow was coming down, but the river wasn't frozen yet. And right at that moment, some girl decided to jump off the bridge. I didn't have time to think, I was already running and tearing my clothes off. That asshole was yelling something behind me. I dove in the water. I thought my heart was going to stop. I swam as hard as I could, but her head was already under. I went under, too, the cold burned my eyes, I could hardly see anything. But I found her. She wasn't breathing. I dragged her out by the hair. When I got out, I threw her down on the asphalt and just collapsed on the ground next to her. Both of us ended up in the hospital. They told me that she survived, but I don't know—she never came in to see me, maybe she was embarrassed. After that, I got chewed out real bad because I had thrown my holster down on the ground and disobeyed a superior's orders. They ended up taking my bonus away."

We are silent.

"That's my very best memory," Dima says.

The officers take out a bag of weed, already giggling. I'm sent to the criminology offices for some tinfoil. They make a bong out of an empty bottle.

"You scared?"

"It's fine, we're all friends here."

They have a deal with the district officers to warn them when the inspectors go out on their rounds.

The dispatchers are trying to call us. But we don't hear them. Finally, the soberest one of us crawls up to the phone and starts laughing into the receiver. The rest of us follow suit.

"Are you cocksuckers stoned again?" shouts the voice on the other end of the line. "Take the call!"

We do our best to write down the name of the street. We really, truly cannot.

No one answers the call.

Dima and I drag ourselves out into the hall, to the official bulletin board. The letter from the director of the Ministry of Internal Affairs to police officers feels fantastically, unfathomably hilarious. We laugh until it hurts.

A FEW HOURS of nonstop fun later, we go to sleep on the couches. The most sober officer stays up to man the phones. We get woken back up almost instantly.

There's a gorgeous blond in a business suit at the office window. She was just mugged in her building lobby, they took her purse. She's as cool as a viper.

"The purse doesn't matter, but my passport was in there. And I have to fly in two days. Can I get a new passport tomorrow?"

"Only if you call Pronin's cell."*

"Vladimir Vasiliyevich? His morning meeting is over at ten, right?"

The vic turns out to be a manager at one of Gazprom's† daughter companies.

* Vladimir Vasiliyevich Pronin was then the head of the Moscow City Police.

† Gazprom is a Russian energy company that extracts, processes, and sells oil and natural gas. It extracts 68 percent of the natural gas in Russia, which makes up 12 percent of worldwide production. Over half of the company's shares belong to the Russian government.

She gives us a ride to the crime scene in her Porsche Cayenne. The officers cringe the moment they see the building.

"Hey lady, you ever think about moving?"

"Why's that?"

"Cuz you got churkas pushing next door. Selling drugs. And the junkies need money. So they attack residents. You're not the first one. You ought to move."

"*Indeed*," she says in English, "I guess I'll have to. Thank you for the advice."

She doesn't ask why they don't just shut down the operation.

WE GET BACK at 7 a.m.

There's a man with a bloodied head and crazy eyes on the floor of the fish tank. Two weeks ago, he got two years' probation for robbery. Today he got wasted and broke the windows of nine vehicles. They nabbed him on the tenth one. When he tried to escape, they kicked the shit out of him.

"What'd you do that for?" Dima suddenly demands, sitting down by the cage. "Zveichik, why'd you do that?"

"I don't give a fuck."

"You have a fiancée. You're going to jail now, Zveichik. You're gonna die in there."

"I don't give a fuck."

Dima runs into the office and feverishly begins opening the doors of the cage with the clear intention of giving Zveichik a piece of his mind. The desk sergeant stops him.

"We still have to turn him in. They're not gonna take him, the state he's in, as it is. Are you related or something? What are you so mad about? It's cut-and-dried hooliganism. Good work, Zveichik, you're a real champ, keeping our numbers up!"

Zveichik grins drunkenly.

It's gotten light out.

CHAPTER 5

HELPLESSNESS

IT WAS PROBABLY the fiftieth apartment I looked at. No sun, practically night. The owner let me in and waited in the hallway. Nobody lived in it. The air smelled like sweet dust. Cracked wallpaper, floors, a ringing, stumbling parquet. A giant window. Outside, the long linden branches reached to embrace the red sky, a shining silence, the ruins of an abandoned building on the other side of the street.

No, there were bells. But I felt improbably calm. I still remember that feeling.

Mama sometimes tells me I'm crazy and not self-aware. But I knew exactly what I was doing. I made a choice and I couldn't have chosen better. It's just that there are some things that you don't tell your mother.

If I could have an honest conversation with mine, here is what I would say: When you decide to be an independent journalist in Russia, your life acquires new boundaries. You can't have enemies, pay bribes, or lie. You can't get into long-term disagreements with your colleagues—well, you can, but if they die, it'll never stop hurting. You're on the fringes of the media landscape, a laughingstock. During the innocent aughts, people saw us as lunatics, writing terrible things about our wonderful life for reasons no one could fathom. When the Kremlin began shutting down one independent media outlet after another, people looked at us like we were cult members obsessed with creating a major newspaper in a wasteland instead of saving our skin. But you don't think about safety, you think about what will happen to your loved ones if you end up in jail, in exile, in a grave.

Then, of course, there's the money. It's always very little or none at all. You can get used to that; half of the country lives that way, too.

That's why I'd never counted on having a home.

However, one time, I won two international prizes. And my job gave me some extra money. So the bank agreed to consider me for a mortgage at a god-awful rate.

I started looking for an apartment.

It had to be the cheapest one possible. But it also had to be the right one. My realtor quickly dropped me. I walked through the shittiest neighborhoods and let myself dream. If I got an apartment, I could have a baby. I would imagine my daughter being born. I got a notebook with a princess on it and pored over every option, the pros, the cons, distance from the subway, preschools and schools, where the light came in. I wanted to be woken up by the sun.

When that sense of calm came over me, I got out my phone and opened the compass app. The windows were facing southwest.

I bought the apartment.

Pretty soon, it turned out that it was impossible to live there—the wiring was bad. So the remodeling began. Denis did it. I never understood why he agreed to. He usually worked for prosecutors and detectives, TV anchors and oilmen. I paid almost nothing and even that he didn't always accept. He'd go and make some money on the side and then come back. Endlessly plastering walls and putting up molding. We smoked together. He was a Russian Orthodox nationalist. He probably believed that a lesbian journalist from *Novaya Gazeta* needed the help. He was right.

I went to work in Donbas, my first war. Between trips, I looked for tile, paint, light switches. Construction markets and front lines, plumbing and land mines, pipes, corpses. Denis never asked about the war, but when I went off, he'd go to church and ask the priest to pray for me. Denis would say, "Try not to get killed. The walls are so beautiful now, you'll be very happy here." Denis was Ukrainian. I'm a Russian whose job is describing how Ukrainians and Russians kill one another. We tried to make the world a better place where we were able, in a tiny apartment on the outskirts of Moscow.

Meanwhile, Denis started getting nervous. He'd tell me that something or someone was in the apartment. His run-ins with an otherworldly presence included blue liquid seeping out from under the bathtub, knocking, his favorite brush disappearing. He'd collect evidence and present it to me. I got nervous, too—what if Denis left me? I also felt a strange presence. It wasn't aggressive, but it was always there. I was sure I would get along fine with the ghost.

After about a year, we got to the ceiling storage. It turned out that the seller had been lazy and not cleaned it out. We found leather scraps, wooden molds, knives, and a rubber-tipped stick that looked like a magical staff. "A cobbler must have lived here," Denis concluded. In one of the suitcases, behind a bundle of rags, we found a pile of Soviet-era government bonds—a useless hoard. In another suitcase, there were receipts for fixing shoes. On the back of one, there was a draft of an application.

The man wrote: I am a cobbler from guild number X, this is my name. My wife is a homemaker, this is her name. We have children, a daughter and son. We gave our son up to an orphanage to be raised by the Soviet state, we couldn't afford to feed him. We are asking for a spot for our daughter in a day care or else we will have to give her up, too.

The daughter's name was Tamara.

They must have ended up getting that spot, because Tamara grew up here and came to own the apartment. She wasn't sociable, the neighbors say. She worked at the Moskvich factory. Lived alone. Never married. Had kidney problems, went blind. Never had kids. Tamara never saw her brother, who disappeared into an orphanage when she was three, ever again.

"Now our ghost has a story," Denis said, calming down. I also calmed down. Sometimes Denis would mutter to Tamara, asking her to give him back his favorite brush.

One day, the remodeling was over (the war was not). Denis talked to his Uzbek friend and he brought me a cauldron of fragrant pilaf. I invited the people I love over to celebrate. We ate the pilaf and other things and laughed a lot. I was supposed to feel happy and I did, but in bits and bursts; it was drowned out by anxiety. I couldn't understand where it was coming from. I thought that it had just soaked into me and I only needed the time to get it out and then the happiness would take its place.

Six months later, my government decided that the shaken economy needed stabilizing. They started doing their own round of renovations, taking down old buildings and giving the land to construction companies. They would move the residents into industrial zones. My home was on the list of buildings slated for demolition.

I tried to organize a resistance. My neighbors told me I was insane to want to go up against the state. All of their experience, all of their family history, told them that if you resisted, best-case scenario, you'd wind up behind bars and worst case, you're dead. "We'll go to Mars if they tell us to!" they shouted back at me at our meetings. "If the state has decided we're doing this, it means it's the best possible option. Who the fuck are you to disagree?" An elderly woman told me that she was just hoping to die before they took down our building. A young father refused to even look at the petition to save our building, saying, "I'm scared." My neighbor from the fifth floor said it was all in God's hands, and if the Lord wanted our building to survive, it would, but if He wanted otherwise, we mustn't go against His will.

I took my appeals to court. I lost every time.

The date for the demolition was set.

I locked myself within my beautiful walls. I cried. I slept a lot. I paced between the kitchen and bedroom, I lay on the floor. Outside, there was laughter, children going to the school my daughter would never go to. It was unbearable thinking about the present and future. I turned my thoughts to the past.

I thought about my family. How lucky we are. We didn't lose a single person for the whole twentieth century. Not during the revolution or the civil wars or the repressions. World War I chewed up my great-grandfather and then spit him out. World War II didn't swallow a single one of my relatives, though it held them in its mouth. Afghanistan, two Chechnyas, Georgia, Ukraine, Syria—all of it passed us by, no one was killed.

I thought about my grandmother. How tough and unsmiling she was. A peasant, she worked at a factory. After her husband died, she kept bees so she could feed my mother and uncle. She worked hard and saved her whole life, and then she put everything into an account in my name. "Your daughter will never need for anything," she told Mama. "If she wants to, she can even live in Moscow. If she doesn't want to, she never needs to get married." All of this money became completely worthless a month after her death. When I grew up, I withdrew it. It was 1,000 rubles: two pairs of socks, two pairs of underwear.

I thought about my mother, a girl from the barracks housing of Yaroslavl, the first person in our family to finish all of school and then the first to graduate from college. She also wanted to work at a factory but ended up formulating paints—for her whole life, until our country collapsed. Then she washed floors and taught middle school. Her dream had been a dacha, she'd saved up for it, but then all the money turned worthless in the nineties. It was enough for her to buy a refrigerator. The material end result of her life. She can't throw it away.

I thought about Tamara. Had she seen the words written on the back of that receipt? Did she know that her parents had chosen between her and her brother, and that they chose her? Did she know that her brother had lived?

Why did I ever think that my life would be any different?

I got up and walked out of the beautiful walls. I sold the apartment. I didn't get much, but it was enough for a new mortgage. Now I'm remodeling my new place. Denis is still working with me. We are close friends. He still goes to church whenever I go away on assignment.

Tamara remained in that apartment. She never appeared again, but I felt her departing breath as it fell asleep. She left behind her legacy. I inherited it.

I'm very lucky. I'm with my family. Life isn't too rough on us.

"Have a baby," says Mama. "There's never going to be a better time. Give birth."

NUMBERS

In 2021, Russian courts oversaw the trials of 783,000 people. Of these, exactly 2,190 were found innocent. Two thousand one hundred and ninety. The probability of somebody charged with a crime being exonerated was 0.28 percent.

CHAPTER 6

WHAT IT'S LIKE TO BE A WOMAN

IT WAS THE LAST DAY before my vacation. I came to work in a white dress. It wasn't completely white, the fabric was yellowish, as if it had come from an old trunk. The dress was lace, spaghetti-strap. I'd bought it at the mall—gone there myself and bought it. I wore it with white platform sandals with colored buckles.

I wanted to show the editorial office how beautiful I was, going on vacation.

There wasn't much work to do. I wandered the halls, it was summer, hot. I thought about buying cheap tickets to Egypt, going to the sea. All of it: my white dress, my white sandals, August, the sea ahead of me, my first vacation—a real vacation from my real job—made my head spin, my bones feel soft. This was the life, I hoped it would be like this forever. All of my work was done, my paperwork signed off on. I sat reading the articles on our website and choosing a travel agency.

A summer evening was slowly descending. It was starting toward twilight, the sky was going red, then the dark blues came in. I thought I had better go home.

My editor called me. A train had gone off the rails in Malaya Vishera, a terrorist attack. Twenty-five wounded, there might be dead. Somebody had to go.

Yes, of course I will.

I really wanted to write about terrorism. This would bring me closer to my dream of working in the North Caucasus, like Anna Politkovskaya. I was happy my editor had called me and not one of my colleagues. It meant that I really was worth something. Now I had to deliver.

Malaya Vishera is a small town between Moscow and Saint Petersburg. There were no trains going there, the tracks were damaged. But there were trains to Tver. I looked at the maps. It was a four-hour drive from Tver. They probably didn't shut down the highway; I would get lucky.

I printed out the initial reports of what had happened. I got out money from an ATM, everything that I had, 6,500 rubles. I ran to the train station.

On the train, I read the printouts and prayed that the train wouldn't be forced to stop before Tver. I couldn't picture what a terrorist attack looked like, how they were going to repair the tracks. What if they made us get out of the train? The other passengers had already heard about the attack, they were talking about it. The going opinion was that it had been the churkas, the Chechens, our enemies. I watched them with a sense of superiority: You people don't know anything, and you're never going to unless I tell you about it. I'm the one who will find everything out and then explain it to you. At moments, it felt like a soundtrack was playing in the background. The young reporter is traveling to the site of a terrorist attack. She's very beautiful, in a white dress—it is a movie, after all. She will surely succeed.

The train got to Tver. I ran out onto the square in front of the station, making my way to the taxis lined up at the curb. The first driver refused to take me, but the second one agreed. We negotiated a price of 4,500 rubles—it was night, a long trip, and we'd probably run into the police.

We were barely out of town when the driver took the checkered sign off the cab. He said the highway patrol always stopped taxis going between cities. Taking bribes. Wow, I said. We talked about bribes.

We got out onto the highway. Lights, cars, speed. The driver held the steering wheel confidently. He had reddish hair, chubby, between forty and fifty. Have you been driving for long? You could say I've been driving since childhood. I love cars. It's not how it used to be. Lots of churkas. They pick up fares but don't know where they're going. People get lost. Like you, young woman. Aren't you scared to be out on the highway at night? Of course not, why would I be? I'm with you, I can tell you're a professional. Aren't I? Of course, of course.

Where are you from? Yaroslavl. I'm from the Tver region. You've come a long way. Ever been to Tver? Only passed through it. Too bad, it's a beautiful city. Does your family live here? Yes, my wife, my daughter. Do you have a family? Not yet. How old are you, if it's not a secret? Although of course, we don't ask ladies questions like that. It's fine, you can ask me. I'm nineteen, I'll be twenty in September. I didn't know reporters could be that young. There are some even younger. I have been working since high school. So do you like it? Yes, of course. You travel, you meet good people. But the work you do. I wouldn't let my daughter do what you do. Going out at night like this. But you do it. Yeah, but I'm a guy. It's different for women.

We pulled over for gas. The driver asked me to pay him up front, to cover the gas. I handed him the money. He seemed dissatisfied, he kept frowning, like he had a headache. I wanted to ask him how he was feeling, but I was scared of offending him. The driver bought us some coffee and we drank it down. Giant trucks speeding past us, the city far behind.

We got back in the car and rode in silence for a while.

You're a real risk-taker. You got in a stranger's car and let him take you. But I can tell that you're fine, what's there to be afraid of? You never know. *You* tell *me* what you girls have to be afraid of, you would know better. And that dress. I was supposed to go on vacation tomorrow. Nobody knew about the terrorist attack. Uh-huh. What's your salary? Basically nothing, to be perfectly honest. But how much? I'm a correspondent, which is almost the lowest rung. Twelve thousand a month plus honoraria. Wow, that's actually nothing. That's what I'm telling you.

I didn't charge you enough. What do you mean? Well, if you think about it, going between cities, it's a minimum of six thousand. I just took a look at you—you seem like a nice girl, I ought to help you out. But now it occurs to me that I'm not making any money for this ride. What do you mean? What do I mean? Do you know how much gas costs? And maintenance? It's my cab, I have to fix it myself. You don't even know what it means to get a car repaired. No, I don't, I don't even have a license. That's what I'm saying. You have no idea. Meanwhile, you're trying to pay me four and a half thousand. For a trip like this, that's like nothing. With a terrorist attack at the end. But you agreed to the fare. So what! Who cares what we agreed to back there? I'm telling you now, I did the math, and it doesn't add up. I'm telling you in Russian. Don't act like you don't understand me. I don't like that.

It'll be six thousand, or I'm letting you out on the side of the road and you can go where you like. The truckers will think you're a hooker no matter what. They'll drag you into the bushes. So I'll get you there, but for the new price. Okay? I don't have a choice. And what choice do I have? This car's not a horse, it doesn't run on grass. I have a family, I work for them. Do you have any idea what it means to support a family? What could you possibly understand? You said yourself that you're only nineteen. A student.

I could see he was psyching himself up. I handed over the money. We were silent.

Why so quiet? I hurt your feelings? No. What do you mean, no? I can tell. Don't get upset. I'm telling you, do you know how much maintenance costs? I didn't realize how far away it was. What didn't you realize? You agreed to the fare. Well, I just didn't think about it is all. I gave you all the money I have. But you need to get to that Vishera. So I'm taking you.

Now tell me, do you have a boyfriend? I do. And he lets you out like this? Like what? He lets you go out riding around at night? Of course. Wow. That's because you're still young, you don't know what it's like out here. If you knew what I know, you would never. What do you know? Taxi drivers hear about everything. We've had girls disappear on this highway. Could be a serial killer, could be some regular guys out on a bender. Kids these days aren't too smart, they'll just get in a car and bam.

What, are you scared? I was just kidding about the serial killers. No serial killers out here. I just don't get it—a girl like you, in the middle of the night, in a white dress. It's crazy.

You and your boyfriend sleep together at least? What? Just wondering.

Silence.

Not to brag, but I'm pretty good. At that, I mean. Know what my wife says? I don't need another man as long as you're around. And she's a hungry one. All women are hungry once they have had a taste. But not all of them are so lucky. How about you? Do you like it? Like what? Sex. I don't want to talk about that. Uh-huh. You must be one of those. One of what? The unlucky ones. It's okay, you're still young. You'll have your fun yet.

He laughs, showing his gold teeth.

Laugh if you like, but I can tell right away. The unlucky ones. I'm even embarrassed for the guys. I believe that a man should satisfy a woman. That comes first. Do you know the kinds of things I know how to do? You wouldn't believe it. How did you learn? How? My wife taught me. You're the lucky one then. What's her name? What do you need to know for? Just asking. Just asking, huh? My family is none of your business. Of course not, I'm sorry.

What are you sorry for? Not like I care. I'm fine with you. I'm fine with you and you're fine with me, right? The road is long, or else we wouldn't get there.

He turns off the highway. Says, "We'll go through the villages here." I put my hand in my purse. Nothing that can protect me. A notebook, a dictaphone, printouts, a pen, an empty wallet, some coins. I squeeze my pen in my fist.

We drive through two sleeping villages in silence. The driver grumbles to himself, Should I ask the way? Night. We drive up a gravel road leading into a dark forest. Branches brush the car on either side.

The car stops. The driver starts putting his seat back. I jerk the door open and jump out.

He comes out on his side.

What's wrong? What are you doing? I'm tired. I need some sleep. You don't expect me to drive all night. I'm in a hurry. Hurry! It's not safe hurrying when the driver is tired. That's me telling you. I'll sleep and you'll sleep next to me. No. What do you mean no? I'll stay out here. You can sleep. There's mosquitoes out here. It's fine, I'll wait. Rest if you need to.

He gets back in the car. I step toward the bushes, wondering where I could run to. The forest rustles behind me. My body flushes with heat.

He comes out again. You change your mind? What? You ought to get some sleep, too. I can see your eyes glazing over. No, I don't want to sleep. Yes, you do. No I don't. You scared of me? You look like you think I'm about to drag you into the bushes. You're making a face. Nothing to be afraid of. I'm just a regular guy.

I'm not scared. What makes you think that?

I could tell right away you're the fearless kind. A normal girl would have never gotten into a car with me in the middle of the night. Why didn't you wait till the morning? I'm in a hurry, I said. There's been a terrorist attack, people may have been killed. You gonna resurrect them? I don't understand you journalists. Like flies on shit.

Well, fine, let's go then. You're not gonna sleep? How can I get any sleep with you around? Let's go. I'll get you to Vishera.

Half an hour later, it starts getting light. We're still in the woods, then we finally come out to a railway junction.

Vishera's on the other side. You walk from here, the driver says. Fuck, what a night. All for a shitty 6 grand. You got nothing to say? Fine. You out here in a white dress. I have a daughter, you know. I'd have a talk with your editor about sending a girl out like this. You got really lucky I'm not insane. You're lucky. Not everyone would be this nice. You better learn that. Journalist.

He gets in the car and turns around. I watch him drive away. I walk out onto the rails and sit down. I'm waiting for someone to come and tell me how to get to the blown-up train.

THE HIGHWAY

October 7, 2010

They wake up around 5 p.m., but Vika hasn't slept at all—she's just been lying on the kitchen floor talking to Andrei. Andrei's in prison, not far from the district center. Vika snuck off with Nina's phone while she was asleep so she could talk to him.

"One night, he came out to the post," says Vika, telling me their love story. "He took me out for two hours. Now we have been together for a whole year and a half!"

Out of their "year and a half," they've only actually lived together a month. Yes, drinking, yeah, fighting, but, looking back, Vika sees those four weeks as some of her happiest. Vika's been waiting for Andrei for a year and four months and spending all of her money going down to the penal colony to buy her sweetie li'l T-shirts, cigarettes, food, and to add money to his phone account. She's also been drinking hard this past year and a half and she's lost her front teeth. Even though Vika makes lots of money—40,000 rubles a month, four times the local average—she's putting off getting her teeth done "for later," after Andrei gets out.

"My little doll!" Vika shouts into the phone, having finally reached him. "How are you doing in there? I miss you!"

But instead of exchanging sweet nothings, Vika is now forced to answer for her behavior: Andrei's been on the phone with Sveta, Vika's boss, and he has been told that Vika didn't work last night.

"My face is all burned! I couldn't!" The 1.5-liter bottle of beer recruited to lubricate conversation is quickly draining before our eyes. "I came home and I fell asleep! I didn't fuck anyone, if that's what you care about!"

Vika has been a prostitute for two years. Andrei knows exactly where the money to buy his li'l T-shirts and other creature comforts comes from. The fact is, he doesn't think that it's very much money, and if Vika is skipping work, she must not actually love him. And if she doesn't love him, then why the fuck would he want a woman like that? He hangs up on her.

Vika calls back right away. "Andrei!"

The conversation goes on for two hours with breaks for sobbing. In the end, Vika sits down in front of the mirror and starts to carefully cover up the brown spots all over her chin—chemical burns from peroxide, from when she was wasted. From behind, Vika looks like a chiseled figurine, except there's her red, drunken face, her shipwrecked gaze, and the black abyss of her mouth. Vika specializes in blowjobs.

Nina and Sveta take turns in the shower. The bathroom walls are caked in years-old mold, the wallpaper's peeling off in the bedrooms, the whole apartment is dazzingly filthy. The girls pay rent here and, like the place where they work, it belongs to Martha. "She's like a sister to me," says Sveta. "That's what I call her." We dress. Sveta calls up a cab, and by six we are on our way to the post.

18:30

The post is four miles outside of town, at the Market, a strip of drywall and metal kiosks, the trailers, standing on either side of the federal highway. There are around fifty trailers: tire repair, coffee, girls. The girls only take up five of the trailers but they have stiff competition: salesgirls "who'll go with anyone in exchange for a drink," highway girls who work alone on the side of the road. Sveta's trailer is known as the best.

Sveta actually has two trailers, a "fucking one" and "the main one." The fucking one has two rooms, two beds, and that's it. In the main one, in addition to a bed, there's also a little café room behind a partition. A bar, two refrigerators, some dishes.

Sveta puts on false lashes and coats her lips in a thick layer of pearl. The girls are sweeping up in their trailers, changing the sheets, taking the tables and chairs out and arranging them on the sand. Then come the stereos and speakers, "You're tuned to Russian Radio—everything's gonna be great!" There are two melons out on the table. They are immediately bought by a family driving past down the highway. Sveta puts out two new ones.

"I can sell anything," Sveta says. "Over and over."

Sveta is forty-one, a real veteran. She's a short blond with a gripping gaze. She has been working the Market for fifteen years. Before that, she saw a lot in her day—was crazy in love with a drug dealer, which ended with her being sold into sexual slavery. It took a week and a half to pay off his debts. For a while, she was married to a Dagestani, "I ran away 'cause nobody's the boss of me." She also worked as a waitress at a café in the Karachay-Cherkessia mountains. Sveta likes reminiscing about this period best, "I even worked for the Karachay-Cherkessia government! One New Year's, I made 5 grand just in tips!" But she is happy now, too. She proudly lists these off on her fingers, "Two closets of clothes, a closet of shoes, I threw out my lotions three times just because I got sick of them." Sveta has an adult son and daughter. Her daughter basically never sees her. "She is an educated girl, a teacher, she doesn't drink, doesn't smoke," Sveta recites with pride.

Sveta also has a Dream. The Dream is named Singer Valeria. "Just a regular girl from Saratov, but look what she's made of herself!" Sveta went to her concert in the district capital with Martha, the owner of both of the trailers. That's another huge highlight. She got right up to the front and handed Valeria a bouquet of green roses and got her autograph. The autograph is now hanging up on the mirror next to the photograph of her daughter.

Almost all of the prostitutes in Sveta's trailer have kids. Vika the blowjob specialist has a six-year-old son; Nina, a twelve-year-old daughter. The children all live at their grandparents'. Taya has two kids. Her daughter is in the third grade and her son is just starting school. Taya arrives and goes in a trailer to sleep before the clients start coming. She's very beautiful: dark blond hair spread over her shoulders in waves and a sad smile. She's very quiet. Before Taya got into Sveta's, she was on the junk. That's why people call her CC. "She doesn't shoot up anymore, although you never know," Sveta says. "She's a good worker, not squeamish."

The one who's squeamish is Nina. First of all, it's "no blowjobs, not for any amount of money." Second of all, no churkas, "I despise them." Nina hates churkas for what she considers more or less ideological reasons, "They think of women as lower than them."

Nina isn't your typical highway girl: she's over thirty, short hair, kind of chubby, extremely smart, very sharp tongue. She even has an unfinished degree in economics. Nina's friend took her out to the highway about a decade ago. "I wanted to raise some cash for a plane ticket but then I just kept on working. If someone had told me that I'd be a prostitute even a year before that, I would have never believed them." Nina has stuck with the highway for the sake of her daughter; she was two when Nina first started, no father. Now her daughter is in the fifth grade, she's won lots of oratory contests. She is the apple of Nina's eye.

Nina is going to get married soon. Her fiancé, Vasechka, is about ten years younger than she is, he's down in Moscow right now on a job, doing construction. She's constantly sending him tender texts. Vasya is a former huffer, and Nina says that it was their love that cured his addiction. Although her feelings toward him are mostly maternal, "I think we'll be happy."

19:30

The first client drives up, license plates say Region 05, Dagestani.

"Mamen kuments!" Nina shouts. "As-salaam aleikum! In the name of the sheep, the cheese, and the holy pig ear! Call the riot police!"

"Blowjob three hundred, anal two hundred, five hundred—that's twenty minutes—a go, a thousand an hour, four grand for the night," Sveta rattles off. After a short round of negotiations, "Laila, this one's for you."

Laila jumps up from her chair, pulls down her tiny dress, and puts on a smile. Laila is half Dagestani herself, perhaps the only one of the girls who is sincerely glad to receive visitors from the Caucasus. "They're really easy to work with, they always fuck like it's their last time," she explains. "They go in, do a few thrusts, and it's over." Laila angles for speed. She can turn over up to twenty clients a night. She comes from a village. She brags that she once bought a new refrigerator for seventeen thousand and a plasma TV, "Everybody back home freaked out."

"Just me and Laila can make twenty thousand a night, just the two of us!" Sveta brags. "We recruited a really good crew back then."

Recruiting village girls to work on the highway is a routine affair. Martha has people who go around the villages, ones farther out, rounding up girls from large and poor families. Everybody loves country girls around here—they work hard, they're modest, "with a strong drive to do their jobs." Some come themselves. They are thoroughly vetted; it's important to weed out the drug addicts. Others are brought to the highway in the trunks of cars, to pay off debts. Better know what you're doing if you are trying to buy one like that. One time, Sveta's new purchase ran away on the very next day, "the ungrateful skank."

20:00

It's getting dark, the customers are arriving. Two guys buy a beer to share, it's 100 rubles a can, and attempt to haggle with Sveta. They sit down with the girls, don't say anything, don't answer the girls' questions. One of them matter-of-factly feels up Vika's legs. "Why don't you get us a chicken?" Sveta upsells them. "The girls are hungry. They could use some meat." One of the men replies, "Best meat around here comes from this very trailer!" Outburst of laughter. They order Vika and Taya, once each.

Sasha comes by, the mommy of the neighboring trailer. They need to talk about Zoyka the Dump, their fellow mommy. Zoyka the Dump rents out her stepdaughter, but that isn't the issue: the issue is that her trailer hasn't contributed to the thousand-ruble grounds-maintenance fee.

Sasha recruits her own girls. "I get in the car and drive around town. They'll be on the square in front of the House of Culture, at bus stops, you know the type. Bellies out, beers in hand. I come out of this white Mazda, come up to them like, 'Girls, you're sitting here picking up boys, drinking beer, wasting your money. We do the same thing but we're the ones who get paid. You'll be up to your ears in liquor. Come have a look.'"

Sasha brags that she had the daughter of the deputy head of the local city police working for her for a year. "Her parents wouldn't give her the cash for her trinkets, so she came out here herself. I wouldn't give her out to anyone from around here so that they wouldn't find out, I never sat her outside at the table. She stayed in the trailer. If the client was clean and not local, I'd give him to her. Now she's a freshman at the school of economics."

They talk about why there are so few trailers with girls at the Market. It's a very lucrative business, the overhead's low: a trailer costs between 50 and 150,000 rubles, plus 1,500 a month for rent and another 3 for utilities. All of it's run by the local police, but they mostly stay out of the business side. They just come around once a month for subbotniks.* The upside of that is you never have to pay them off. All of the mommies agree, "The only reason more people don't do it is that it's a real nerve-racking business."

20:30

A short, balding man makes his way out of a cab, grinning from ear to ear. An army man, he just got promoted to major and is out to mark the occasion.

"Hey, Svetka!" he shouts. "Get me a chicken, vodka, and beer! Or else we'll shoot up the joint!"

The girls laugh.

* Civic events in which participants do volunteer work for the social good—as a rule, these take place on weekends. Subbotniks were instituted in the USSR, during which they were essentially compulsory; they usually involved getting people to clean the streets. Today, any kind of unpaid labor can be sarcastically referred to as a subbotnik.

"Pay up," Sveta demands.

"What, don't you know me?" the major asks with a sting of surprise.

"Pay up front," Sveta says. "I know lots of guys just like you."

The major shows Nina photos on his phone, a new race car, Japanese, he picked it up on the cheap. He compulsively plays with his keys, trying to draw attention to his key chain, the military foreign intelligence agency's bat logo. He shares his big plans: four months till retirement, then he is going to open up his own detective agency. "My uncle's the major general from the district tax office and my aunt is on the Supreme Court. They'll get you right off the hook."

"My little Teletubby," Nina flatters him.

They polish off a bottle of vodka—300 rubles—and he asks for another. "Got in a fight with my girlfriend. I mean, not a fight. I just told her what's what and got out," he says with pride.

"Call her," says Nina.

"Nah. I'm a man. She'll call me."

A little while later, his phone really does ring. The major languorously pulls the phone toward his ear, then jumps up and starts cursing. Back at the base he's in charge of, a conscript has shot himself. Right at his post.

"Faggot!" the major shouts. "Some slut dumped him! So what! I never blew my brains out when I was dumped! Fucking snowflakes, those boys born in ninety and ninety-one—they're not fucking men. Crisis babies. Another one overheated out on the drill grounds. . . . That boot is in the ICU now. The doctors give him a fifty-fifty chance of survival. It's not my fault that the sun is hot!"

Now that he's gotten his yelling done, it dawns on the major that he really does have to go. He starts calling his driver, then stops himself: he is drunk, it's the middle of the night, he's at the Market—not good for his reputation. So he decides to dial up a man named Volodya instead.

"Enough is enough! I'm off for tonight!" he shouts. "And nobody better try and disturb me! I'm not going anywhere! Get the report on my desk by eight in the morning! I'll sign everything!"

"Phew!" he laughs. "Nerves. Taya, let's go for an hour."

The major hands Sveta a thousand. They leave.

23:00

A new car. A man with a boy who looks fourteen.

"I brought my nephew," the man explains. "To give him a taste of the chicks."

The boy clearly feels awkward. He drinks down his vodka and glazes over, leaving with Taya. His uncle begins reminiscing about his time in prison. Turns out he's gotten out recently. Was in for robbery.

"The people inside are totally normal. They're clean. Unlike you all."

"Have some more," Nina says quickly. "Want me to pour you some?"

"Have you drunk out of this glass? I can't drink out of a whore's glass."

"I, for one, went to school at a lyceum," Vika suddenly interjects. "A German academy."

"Don't make things up," says the ex-con.

"I'm not. First my mom was in for drugs, then I was on probation, but you know what, die Liebe ist ein Glück, die Liebe—Schicksalsschmuck. Die Liebe ist ein Traum, die Liebe—Sonnenraum."*

Sveta comes out. She silently pours the vodka out on the ground.

"You little cunt!" Vika yells. "Burn in hell!"

"If he wants vodka, then he better buy it," Sveta shouts in response. "This is the third time he's showing up to a table that's already set! Nothing's for free at the Market!" She flies up to the man, who is shocked. "Give me three hundred! Plus another two hundred for salads!"

00:10

The spectacled, elderly man doesn't step out of the cab—he falls out of it.

* Love is bliss, love—fate's necklace. Love is a dream, love—the sun room.

"Hey, there! Stasik!" shouts Sveta. "Come here, sit down at the table."

Sitting's not easy for Stasik but he never stops talking. "The tile work in the Yaroslavl churches? There's terra-cotta ones, green ones, glazed ones, enamel, with all the flora and fauna. Things used to have spiritual beauty! Where is that spirit today? Where is that power?"

Meanwhile, Sveta empties his wallet "for food and wine for the girls" and leaves him only 100 rubles for the cab back.

Stas teaches at a local college. At Sveta's, *college* has a specific connotation. Martha's son is studying at one; instructors will sometimes show up for a subbotnik. But Stas always comes here with money, so Nina starts dancing with him.

Half an hour later, Sveta is sending Stas home.

"He's in love with me. Has been for a long time!" Sveta brags. "He'll show up to order something, but he is always casting such glances at me!"

According to Sveta, about a third of the customers are in love with her. She lists them with relish: who's offered to have her move in with them, who has proposed, two of the guys even asked her to have their babies. One showed up and said, "You don't belong here. You're clean. Come work for me."

"What kind of job?" the girls wonder.

"You know what it was? Weaving funeral wreaths! That guy's obsessed with me too," she nods toward the major, who's literally buried his head in Nina's breasts. "I'm in his phone as his love."

01:30

Lesha stops by. He's one of the oldest regulars at the Market. He has been running a tire-repair trailer next to the girls for almost twenty years. He showers everybody with compliments. "You girls hold everything up! You're our hardest workers!"

He's mostly talking to Vika. He gets what he wants: she sits down on this lap.

"Get off there!" shouts Sveta. Lesha laughs.

"I know why you're laughing!" Sveta retorts. "I saw her going into your trailer yesterday morning."

"She was bringing me cash!"

"And then she got locked inside? Get out of here!"

Lesha takes Sveta aside to the tire-repair shop "for a conversation." When she comes back, Sveta says what she thinks.

"What I love about this job is that you can always put men in their place. He's in love with her. Says that he wants to marry her. He wants to buy her off me. But I will make sure that they never get married. I'll never forgive that Vika for what she did to me."

Last year, Sveta fell off the wagon and she got drunk. It was a long night. Led to a conflict with clients. Vika got scared and called Martha. Martha showed up, quickly got rid of the men, and fined Sveta 24,000 rubles. Sveta was forced out on the highway to pay back her debt.

"I paid it all back in two weeks. But I am no prostitute. I can never, ever forgive her for that."

03:30

"I'm on number twelve for the night. But I can do more. I can. I can do seventeen. I am just tired," Laila explains. It is unclear whom she is justifying herself to. "That last guy was all right. He kissed me and told me I'm cool. They don't usually talk much."

She's smoking.

"While I am fucking them, I am divvying up the 500 rubles," Laila says later. "That much is for Papa in prison, that much is for Mama—she's in the hospital, just had a stroke. This much is for the house, that much for clothes. I have a little brother and sister—she also just started working out here at the Market, as a cashier, and she's getting married right away. Doing the math passes the time. I'm the sole breadwinner for my family.

"The only good part is I am infertile," says Laila. "I'll never have kids. If I also had kids to take care of . . ."

"Laila!" shouts Sveta. "This one's for you!"

A washed-out man with frozen eyes. "Let's go."

"Uh-huh, one second," says Laila, downing a glass of wine in one gulp. Her hands are shaking.

They come back quickly. The guy walks her out to his car to get a photo with her. He grabs her and tries to sit her down on the hood. Laila wrestles out of his grasp and accidentally scratches his car with the heel of her shoe in the process.

"What the hell?" the man says quietly. "Do you understand what you just did?"

"I feel for you, brother!" the major shouts.

Everyone at the table is arguing about how much the repair's going to be. Somewhere between 5 and 7 grand. The men are riling each other up. Sveta runs out of her trailer.

"What is your problem? You are the one who dragged her on there! You did that!"

"Your sluts . . ."

"Sluts? What did you come here for?" Sveta shouts. "What do you want from these sluts?"

"Want me to call the district office? To sort things out?"

"Go ahead! I'll call them myself! Try me! I can do worse!"

The girls calmly sit on their clients' laps. The man really does go to his car and makes a phone call. He comes back out.

"Here's the deal. I'm offering a peaceful resolution. It's that or in seven days, your flophouse is gone. Up to you."

"Get the hell out of my face!" Sveta shouts and starts making a sign of the cross over his car. "You won't even make it home! Good luck, buddy!"

The man leaves. Sveta starts laughing.

"That was nothing! I remember how one time, this thug showed up. Says, 'Put your hand on the table.' I did. He takes out his knife and—bam! I barely had time to pull back. Says, 'You've got good reflexes.' We ended up drinking with him, upsold him for a couple of thousand . . . Or this other guy, shows up with a grenade. High out of his mind. He keeps taking the safety out, then sticking it back in. Toying with me. He does it again and I put my hand down right on top of it and I grab it real hard. I tell him, 'Let's blow up together!' He sobered right up. You can't drink on the job at the Market. You gotta stay sober. Or else they will find my girls down by the spring like they did with those other girls last year."

"I hate you even more!" says the major. "One drink? My treat."

"Pour 'em out!"

All the glasses are filled. Sveta covertly dumps hers into the dust.

04:00

When the ex-con went out to take a piss, he stumbled upon some "khaches." The drivers were hauling some watermelons and stopped to sleep right on the side of the highway.

"Five trucks of watermelons and two of those animals in each one. And only one of those bitches gave me a melon! Right here on our own Russian soil!"

Everybody agrees that those "khaches" ought to "have their asses kicked in." The major and the ex-con get up from the table, but they don't get far—the ex-con immediately hits the dirt. The major pulls him back up and sits him back down. He still wants to fight, though.

"Which one of these fuckers should I fuck up, Ninochka? Killing's all right if it's for the sublime . . ."

"Wow, a real Rimbaud!" Nina cuts him down. "Tell us about your cool car again."

Anka, a highway girl, stops in to eat. She's just twenty-three but looks a lot older—deep wrinkles, hair filthy and matted, her body desiccated. She's been an addict for a long time.

"I'm a band saw operator! I work in the first division, shift A!" Anka announces. She keeps telling us this.

Eats hungrily and leaves quickly.

"She must not have filled her quota yet," Sveta explains.

Anka's "quota" is 700 rubles—one dose.

04:30

Sveta sends Vika and a client down to the city for two hours. Laila leaves after Vika, she's getting dropped off in a village, onto a passing train.

Soon Taya calls a cab, too. Her son had a cough yesterday, she needs to get him in compresses in the morning. "She's always fucking things up," Sveta says. "Her husband, he's also in prison, he had his eye gouged out in a fight after she cheated on him with a guard. He tried coming after him. . . . Don't be fooled by how sweet and quiet she is. She is cursed."

Everybody who works on the highway is very superstitious. There are icons up in both trailers. Curses, hexes, jinxes, protection spells . . . These women believe that the world is ruled by invisible forces beyond human control. It's probably the only way to survive around here.

The cab brakes so hard, it sends the dust flying in every direction. Two guys, all dressed up: straight from the club and headed straight back afterward. One of them is forcing himself to have a drink, the other one's wasted. They're on day five of a bender. The drunk one needed to get some air—his wife just died.

"Sick for six years. Then four days ago . . . I couldn't sleep for some reason."

"Some vodka? Some wine for the girls?" Sveta offers.

"I'm fine."

"Then what did you come here for?" Sveta shouts. "Trying to score a freebie?"

Nina's gaze silences her. She quickly walks off.

"My dad died in 2006," Nina says. "We partied a ton for my birthday, and then a week later they call me and say to come home."

Tears run down her made-up cheeks. It happens so suddenly that everyone turns away. Just the guy whose wife died strokes her hand. "I wish all you girls good health. That is the most important thing—health. Health."

Nina finishes her vodka and goes to the main trailer to sleep.

"Goddamn alcoholic," says Sveta. "They never wanted her to set foot in the house again after her father died. And they were right. Back when Martha and I were working, we'd upsell the clients, then go out behind the trailer, two fingers down the throat to keep a cool head. That one . . . Lots of people come work for us to keep their drinking in check. But you can't. Martha once tried getting Nina into aversion therapy.* She managed to stay sober one week and that's it. Nina's not interested. She says, 'I don't have a problem.'

"Nothing will ever work out for any of them. Because they don't have any brains. If they did, this wouldn't be their life. They tried to hire them to work the registers, but their counts always came up short. . . . That's why they're the prostitutes, all that they're good for is making some cash off of them.

"One of the tire-repair guys around here once wanted to marry Nina. She lived with him, they had a plan. Then one day she walked out on the highway and up and rode off with some guy. Came back three days later, and it was over for her. . . . That guy is now marrying another one of the girls here, also a prostitute. You have to deserve it if you want somebody to marry you. And with this new one, you mark my words, she'll be back here in a month, tops. The highway won't let you go just like that."

05:00

Six guys pile out of a car (how did they all fit in there?): muscular, buzz cuts, real ghosts of the nineties. "Township boys," Sveta says under her breath. "Completely fucked up. They'll get sloshed, then they'll head straight here."

* Aversion therapy, known as "coding," is a treatment for alcohol dependency developed in the USSR. Providers attempt to convince patients that if they drink alcohol, they will die. Patients are also given drugs that have bad side effects when mixed with alcohol; sometimes, a capsule of drugs will be implanted in their muscles. There is no scientific evidence for the efficacy of coding, but it continues to be a widespread addiction treatment in post-Soviet countries.

"You got a girl for us?"

"Nope! They're all gone."

"Best you remain polite with us, Mother . . ."

"I'm not your mother! Beat it! Go to the twelfth or the thirty-seventh!"

"We went! They don't have any, either."

One of the guys is on speed. He's running in circles around the table and screaming. "Drives me fucking crazy! I hate everyone here!"

"Keep acting like that and you'll never get any girls here ever again," Sveta tells them.

The speedy one is sat down at the table, the vodka's poured out. But then he immediately gets in a fight with the fourteen-year-old boy, who'd been quietly dozing off in a chair. He punches him in the face. The table's turned over. Blood, juice, and vodka drain into the sand.

"I'm calling the cops!" Sveta shouts, waving her cell phone over her head. "You'll have the rest of your party in the drunk tank!"

The boy and his ex-con uncle leave quickly.

"We'll sit here awhile," say the township boys. "Bring us some beer."

The situation grows tenser. A taxi drops Vika back off. She's totally drunk now and only wearing a bra.

"Oh hey! Boys!" She collapses onto somebody's lap.

"Oh, I remember this one," says one of the township boys. "This is the one who hit me on the hand, guys! She isn't very obedient."

"Means she's incompetent!" says a guy in a rust-orange shirt. "A prostitute's job is to lay like a log and keep her mouth shut. I'm renting a product, its purpose is giving me pleasure. If it doesn't work like it's supposed to . . ."

"Yup, that's a whore, brother," another township boy chimes in. "Whores have a pretty weak grip on life as it is. Plus, twenty sticks a night . . ."

"Maybe, but don't you agree that you ought to love what you do? Say, I'm a stick layer. So I lay, like, twenty sticks every shift. If somebody asks me to lay twenty-one, I'll do it. I won't turn my nose up. All of us are just robots. How is she any different? Her job is to take as many sticks as can fit. Plus, sex is something you could enjoy if you wanted! What if she is a nympho? Maybe she comes."

His comrades matter-of-factly feel up her chest and grin, exchanging glances. Vika is blotto, she stares ahead with total indifference.

"Hey! What the fuck are you living for?" the guy in the orange shirt says, leaning over the table.

"Fuck knows why I live," Vika suddenly says very clearly. "But who the fuck are you, asking me that?"

"Go to bed, now!" Sveta pulls Vika up from the table, pushes her into the trailer, and locks the door. "I'll sit with you boys."

The township boys plod through their beers. The wail of the penal colony siren out in the distance washes through the air. The sky quickly brightens. Horses and cows slowly tramp down the other side of the highway. Yurka the cattle driver flashes his whip from atop a red mare. "I got two months left, then I'm free!" he shouts over to us. "Two more months, Svetka! Wait for me!"

The boys finally get up.

"Forgive us, Mother, if anything's wrong. We'll come back tomorrow, all normal."

That's when they realize that they've locked their keys in the car. While they are trying to figure out how to open the door, the speedy one picks up a rock and breaks the passenger-side window. Then he starts taking the shards out, cuts open his hands, blood everywhere.

"Sveta, get us some water!"

Before he gets in the car, the speedy one takes a long time washing the blood and dust off his boots. Fastidiously, until they shine.

05:50

Sveta wakes up Nina and Vika. They bring the table inside. Sveta puts the unfinished bottles back in the fridge, "I'll sell them again." They turn their radio all the way up. A pop version of the Russian national anthem fills the sky over the Market. The girls dance to it and their dancing contains all their exhaustion and anger, all their disgust at this world.

"Take pride, Fatherland!" they shout in chorus.

And that is the theme music for the appearance of an unmarked Lada 110 carrying two men. One of them waits in the car, the other comes out and flashes his badge—city police.

"I like that one." He nods toward Vika. Then he grabs her by the waist and starts dragging her toward his car, shouting out to the driver, "Open the door!"

Vika struggles. Squealing, the girls throw themselves on him to wrest her out of his grip. He doesn't manage to shove her into the vehicle, so he comes after Sveta.

"You are the mommy here, you are responsible for your daughters' behavior."

"Why didn't you ask me first? That's not how it's done."

They go into the trailer. Quiet negotiations. Nina runs after them.

"You're out of your mind, you bastards! You think she's a thing that you can just throw in your car? Like she's just an object?"

"Nina! Shut up!" Sveta yells.

"We'll be back tomorrow," the cop says after some silence. "Three of us, with my friends. A table and girls, you got it?"

He winks toward Vika, calmly gets back in the car, and drives off.

"You've fucking lost it!" Sveta goes in on Nina. "They could have just put all of us in the back of their car. Fucking drunk!"

"Calm down. Get over it." Nina leans up against the wall. She is shaking.

"You fucking drunk. You're not a prostitute, you're a whore. Gimme a cig."

"This fucking drunk has no cigs," Nina calmly replies. "As for being a whore . . . you're no different from us. Highway girl."

"Me? I've accomplished a lot in my life, thank God."

"At least I'm still human. You're Grandma Shit."

"You're gonna regret that," says Sveta after a moment of silence.

06:20

Before calling a cab, Sveta gets out a big notebook and goes deep into bookkeeping. They made a total of 13,670 rubles. Out of the 8,000 the girls made, they will get 4,000. Sveta will get 4,670 (her commission off the sold goods). The rest is for Martha.

The girls stay in the car, only Sveta goes up. A fat woman with a vigilant animal gaze counts out the money and lays it in stacks. She mumbles, "Money's for money, fools are for fools." In the next room, you can hear her eighteen-month-old daughter sigh in her sleep.

Martha hands Sveta 500 rubles each for each of the girls, "for their expenses." The rest of the girls' money Martha hangs onto for them.

Sveta spends a long time complaining about Nina.

"We'll work it out," Martha says.

They think about going down to the Volga but they decide to go home instead. Nina turns on the TV right away. The morning cartoons have already started—"I am obsessed with them." Vika goes to the kitchen and calls up Andrei. Instead of a dial tone, a scratchy voice sings out of the phone, "The years go on without an end, but still they won't release our friend."

"He put on that song just for me!" Vika whispers to me.

"Andrei!" she shouts into the phone. "Andrei! How are you, my little doll? How did you sleep?"

The next night, as a punishment for her drunkenness, although it is actually for Grandma Shit, Nina is given out to the township boys for the night.

CHAPTER 7

MY LOVE (INVISIBLE AND TRUE)

ANYA AND I met at a lesbian club, back when they still existed in Moscow. It was the second time that I'd been. I had just recently come out to myself, fallen in love, confessed, gotten rejected, wept, and googled how to cure myself of being a lesbian. Turned out that there was no way. I had enough tears to cry for a week and two days. Then I decided to pull myself together and figure out my new routine, like somebody in a wheelchair or with diabetes or HIV. I needed to learn how to be a lesbian. That was my goal when I went to the club.

We watched *Lost and Delirious* and then there was a discussion. After the discussion, we played a game—everyone got a number, then you had to write down the numbers of the women you liked. If you got a match, you could get each other's phone numbers. I got nothing.

Somehow it happened that Anya and I walked to the subway together. We talked about politics. Anya was clearly older than me but asked extremely naive questions. I thought she was making fun of me and I kept getting more and more annoyed with her. We got onto the subway car in silence. After a few stops, Anya had to get off. She got on the platform and shouted, Give me your number! I shouted it back at her. She sent me a text. I replied.

We moved in together fast. It was my first serious relationship. It was funny. I'd get up two hours before her to iron her shirt and make her poached eggs in hollandaise sauce. After a month, it became clear that she liked going around with her shirts rumpled and preferred macaroni and hot dogs. Anya always bought the cheapest groceries; she washed, dried, and stockpiled plastic bags. She was older than me and remembered not only the 90s (crime, poverty, terror of the future) but also the 80s (shortages of every commodity, food ration cards, the sense that the country was about to collapse).

We were poor, we rented a corner in a studio apartment. Then I got a raise and we started renting a one-room apartment ourselves. On the weekends, we slept and watched movies. Sometimes we went to the park. Sometimes, if it was summer and we had the energy, we'd take the train to small towns outside of Moscow. In one of these towns, I saw a painting of a lilac branch and Anya bought it for me. We hung the lilac up over our bed.

Anya was tan, sun-kissed, with hazel eyes full of laughter, her front teeth made a little house. Her favorite blue sweater was gray with age. She had four college degrees—math and physics, translation, economics, and law. She worked as an oil and gas analyst.

One blue winter morning, I woke up and felt like my stomach ached. I couldn't figure out where the pain was. I lay on my back, running my hands over my body, and suddenly realized how much I loved Anya, with my whole body, for real. From that day on, I started thinking about the future. I started thinking about how we would have children.

On February 14, Alfa Bank* announced a promotion where they would help anyone who was in love become homeowners. Their slogan was "Love Matters Most." It didn't matter whether a couple was married, they would still give them a joint mortgage at a good interest rate. I found out about this at work, from an ad. I immediately called up the bank: Is it true? Yes, it's true. They asked me how long we'd been dating,

* Russia's largest private bank.

I said a year and a half. Wow, the girl said, and you're already ready to buy real estate? Yes, we love each other a lot, I told her. Let me put you in touch with the manager, we can do a preliminary estimate, the girl said. I need your names. I told her our names. And then she said, No, then it's not going to work. A couple is a man and a woman, not you. That's the bank's policy. While I was thinking about what to say, she hung up on me.

I couldn't believe it. I called other banks. I didn't even think to go out in the hall to make these phone calls. I called from our shared office. I felt like I was in free fall. I said we both worked, we were both college educated, we lived together, and they would all say it doesn't matter, it doesn't matter, goodbye. One bank said: 18.9 percent. I asked, How much? And the man said, Nobody else is going to even consider it. You know that perfectly well.

After that, I read about marriage and the rights it confers. Then I read about marriage in other countries and how those countries had decided that everyone could get married. I read about LGBT activism and googled LGBT activists in Russia. They seemed unattractive, rude, and insane. I spent another year griping to my best friend that Russia had bad LGBT activists who weren't any good at defending my rights. My friend said nothing. I started getting embarrassed, becoming more and more ashamed, but I couldn't explain where all that shame came from.

A year later, on February 14, Anya and I were sitting at a café. I wanted to tell her I loved her. Instead of that, I said, Anya, we need to go to gay pride. She answered, Yes, I've been thinking that, too. We have to.

Here's how gay pride events went at that time: Activists—no more than ten of them—would come out in the center of Moscow and raise their rainbow flags. Nationalists, Cossacks, and Russian Orthodox people would show up to the locations announced by the LGBT activists and attack them. The cops would wait for the activists to get beaten up and then they'd arrest them—the people who'd been attacked, not the ones who attacked them. Journalists stood by, taking photos and laughing. I'd already been to a gay pride event as a journalist. For a journalist, going meant a good laugh.

Anya and I went to gay pride. We wrote "Hate Is Boring" on our rainbow flag. We unfurled the flag and stood there with it for about ten seconds. Then I was hit in the temple. Anya got arrested. I was hospitalized and started losing my hearing. Journalists called me for comment. Before, they had thought it was funny when gay people got beaten up, but when it was one of their colleagues, someone just like them, it wasn't so funny.

We went to gay pride every year after that. We'd get beaten up and arrested. One time, people ripped off my dress—I was left standing naked in the middle of Moscow. I made friends with LGBT activists. Turned out they weren't crazy, just very exhausted.

Then the State Duma proposed a law against "gay propaganda." It said that we were socially unequal. That I was socially unequal. I decided I didn't want to just stand around with a poster and flag anymore. I announced I would go to the State Duma with Anya and kiss her in front of it. I invited anyone else who wanted to kiss there to join us.

There were four days of kisses. We kept getting attacked and arrested.

Orthodox activists brought urine and rotten eggs, they threw shit at us. They brought their children so they would beat us, too. You can't fight back against children—they're small, you could hurt them. The State Duma passed the law.

When Russia hosted the Olympics, I decided to go out on Red Square and sing the Russian national anthem while holding a rainbow flag. Me and everyone who came with me got arrested and beaten at the police precinct. A cop spit in my face. I wiped it off with my hand and then wiped my hand on my pants. Wow, there's cop saliva all over my pants, I laughed.

A lot more happened.

All that time, Anya was by my side. And I was by her side. We were running out of strength, but we didn't realize that. Then, one day, we ran out. We stopped loving each other.

I felt it because the place in my stomach that had been filled with love now felt empty. We lived together for a little while longer. Then Anya left. That was the end of my love and the end of our future children. I didn't have it in me to fight for the common good anymore. I stopped being an activist. I stopped being the one getting attacked and arrested. The one who was going to get killed.

What had I wasted my love on, I wondered.

What do you waste your love on? It burns and burns until it burns out. Sometimes it lights up a piece of your life, like the lilac branch, and life comes out of the darkness, reveals its full colors. But then the darkness returns.

WITH LOVE AND SORROW

February 2, 2019

Ilsky lies under soft new snow. Every line is traced in white—each branch, the rusted carcass of a bus, the green fence, the young cherry trees planted in rubber tires, the Living Flowers kiosk.

Water streams down the streets—pooling in lakes, flowing through gutters, into drainage ditches. Every street has its own ditch. Dogs scramble over them, children leap, and women cross by little makeshift bridges. But the dams and ditches can't hold everything. More water keeps flowing.

Seventy-year-old Vladimir Dubentsov and sixty-four-year-old Nikolai Galdin were found on the evening of January 10. There had been no tracks in the snow beside their house for two days. It was very quiet.

"I came home from work. There's this unhealthy silence. I look over the fence, the padlock's missing from the door. They always used to put the lock on when they went out. We found the sister's number. She says, 'I don't know where they are.' If they'd been normal people, talked to their neighbors like everybody else, we would have raised the alarm earlier. But everyone just thought, 'They're keeping to themselves, thank God.' Her husband came, and he says, 'I'm not going in their yard.' Right. So some of us went in. It reeked of smoke. They'd tried to burn it down, I guess. Good thing it didn't take, or else it would have spread to our place, too. We called the cops. One was lying right by the door. Kolya. We didn't go any further or touch anything. It was all obvious already."

The Street

Proletarskaya Street, where the murders took place, is not exactly short, but it's bisected by a highway—the road from Krasnodar to Novorossiysk. Ten of the houses are set apart from the rest. The rumble of the traffic mingles with the sound of running water—there's a lot of it here; you could imagine you were near the sea.

The Dubentsovs' house was the poorest. Brick, painted ocher, a wooden attic, stains on the facade, windows covered in plastic film. A spotted puppy peeps out from the doghouse. A mud bank props up the green fence, thick with layers of paint—the old men's attempt to stave off the water. A few years back, all the other neighbors raised up their plots, and now the all the water runs down here.

One of the neighbors, Edik Gorbenko, is clearing the ditch that runs by his plot. He's using a long-handled hoe to poke in the water.

"Everyone was real upset about them getting killed! So sad, we could have danced for joy!"

He's chuckling as he talks. He lists his grievances.

"First of all, they threw nails into the road. They poured water on the fence. Quarreling all the time, all the neighbors were shit, all the women were whores. Kolya, the boyfriend, when he'd see my wife in the street, he'd say to her, 'Home again, are you? You bitch, you whore.' My kids have known about gays and what they do since they were small. What does that tell us? That those two didn't even bother to hide it! No wonder they got killed. If any of us wanted to do it, we could have just poisoned their vodka! That's what I told the cops, too!"

Tatiana Nikanorovna Kharchenko ("Just say Nikolayevna," she tells me. "I've run a preschool all my life, it's what the children can pronounce") is another neighbor. "How can a person just kill somebody? I mean, a brawl, okay. But to murder someone? I can't understand it."

"He wasn't exactly friendly with anyone, Volodya. Nadya Petrova, she used to live here, they were friends, but she died over a year ago. He came to me often enough, though. They'd have a bust-up with the neighbors and then he comes to me to talk it over. I mean, what a thing. Such an unenviable life, then dying like that."

Her great-granddaughter Evelina is hanging around, eavesdropping. She's one of the neighborhood kids who had waged war against the two old men. Unfazed by her grandmother's presence, she tells me how they booby-trapped the couple's front yard.

"Pipes, you know the kind? For fireworks? We made little bombs out of them. Kirill, he also used to throw trash over their fence, push nuts and things into the gaps."

She sets out the chronology of the conflict, "This summer, and last summer, and the one before." "Why did you do it?" "'Cause there's nothing else to do."

"I'd wring all of your necks if I caught you at it," her great-grandmother grumbles.

"Whatever, Gran! You never even said anything!"

Her eleven-year-old brother is in the next room, arms wrapped around a hairless Chinese crested. "It's got skin just like a human's."

Who Are They

I reconstruct Vladimir and Nikolai's biography piece by piece, and even then it is patchy.

Vladimir's mother, Evdokia Nikitichna, fought in the Soviet-Japanese War. "She was called up in '45. They were living in the Far East then. She served in the navy as a radio operator. She fought too, her ship went into battles. So she was a veteran of the Great Patriotic War, just not with the Germans but out in the East. The Japanese attacked us, too," Vladimir's cousin Elena is telling me.

Vladimir's father, an army man, died before he was born. Vladimir moved to the Kuban region with his mother and stepfather, also a World War II veteran. He graduated from teacher-training college and worked in elementary schools in Ilsky and the neighboring Severskaya. At forty-two, he qualified for a disability pension.

Everyone here—absolutely everyone—is positive his diagnosis was something psychiatric. "They must have both been mentally ill." People mention specific conditions. All of this will turn out to be untrue. Vladimir was prescribed medication, but "nothing out of the ordinary," the providers all say.

He also bought bones—to make soup with and for the dogs. Had very little to live on and he complained about it.

He met Nikolai through the local paper.

"I subscribed to the paper myself, so I used to see the ad all the time. 'Seeking a man to share a home with, no drinkers, no criminal record, willing to officially register suitable person to the address,'" says his neighbor Valentina Vasilyevna. "He needed help around the house and yard, but he had no use for a woman. He didn't need them. So that's how that Kolya ended up there."

Even less is known about Nikolai. He was from around Kanelovskaya stanitsa.* He'd mentioned Medvedovskaya stanitsa, as well. "Maybe he lived there at some point, or had relatives there." He drove a truck, did security, and then retired.

They moved in together ten years ago. And they were never apart after that.

They didn't conceal their relationship. "Kissy-huggy, touchy-feely." They split up the chores: Vladmir shopped and ran errands, Nikolai kept up the house and yard.

Every single one of the neighbors mentions how Nikolai swept the street in front of their house every morning. "Their house was unbelievably clean." They were guarded, they kept very much to themselves.

But for the last five years, they were at war with their neighbors. They moved in tandem. "If you had a beef with Kolya, he'd set Volodya on you. You'd hear him screaming all the way down the street." The old men had each other's backs.

At the same time, they were fighting the municipal board—"the

* A stanitsa was originally a Cossack settlement and is now just a kind of village.

administration, housing and communal services, the village council, the police." Armed with the law, Vladimir lodged complaints and demanded the services and benefits due to them. Installing a dumpster, connecting gas and electric meters, digging a ditch. The head of the administration himself would come down. "He knew his rights, he made them do their jobs."

The village is hardest on the old men when it comes to the way they tried to get public housing. "Picky, picky!" "We offered them a room, back when Vladimir's mother was alive!" says the zone housing officer Alevtina Pavlovna Kokoreva. "Sure, the bathroom was communal, but we've got teachers here who don't even have it that good. Those two refused!"

Stray remarks paint a clear picture of the fact that people had had it in for Vladimir for a long time. "The children who first started writing things on his fence are already grown up now." They'd write, "Straight fence, gay owner!" Vladimir and Nikolai were attacked several times.

The neighbors talk about Vladimir's conflict with the local Cossacks.* As the son of a World War II veteran, he wanted to walk in the May 9 Victory Day parade, but they wouldn't let him. "They said they didn't consider him a man." (The Cossacks strenuously deny everything, "People are just bad-mouthing us.")

Everyone who mentions the bullying asks for their name to be redacted. But what they feel ashamed of and reluctant to talk about is not that the old men were bullied, or that they were murdered, but that old men "like that" lived in their village at all, right on their street.

* Cossacks are the descendants of peasants who fled central Russia to the southern and eastern borders of the Russian Empire, and the non-Slavs who joined them. Cossacks worked the land, traded, were hired by tsars and princes. They helped the Russians conquer the peoples of the Caucasus, Siberia, and the Far East. They fought wars. On several occasions, Cossacks mutinied against the tsars and fought the Russian army. By the nineteenth century, the authorities had established a relationship offering Cossacks certain privileges in exchange for their military service. The Cossacks became the main Russian military class, distinguished by their loyalty to the authorities and lack of political convictions. The Cossacks were used to put down civil unrest. After the 1917 revolutions, Cossacks took the side of the Whites against the Bolsheviks; they lost, and many of them fled Russia. In the final years of the USSR, the Cossacks declared themselves a persecuted people. In 1999, a law on Cossacks was passed, allowing Cossacks to receive land and serve the government. Some 190,000 Cossacks banded together into a military society. They are officially involved in "maintaining public order," which includes dispersing protests. Five million Russians consider themselves Cossacks.

The bullying seems to have somehow confirmed the men's "oddness" and therefore does not need to be mentioned. "Why come all the way out here just to write about something like that?"

Vladimir's cousin Elena is a medic. She would not meet with me in person, "I don't want to talk about it, it's still too hard." According to her, she only knew Nikolai as her cousin's tenant and "never socialized with him at all, I wasn't interested in him." I ask how she likes living here. "I know everybody, they all know that that was my cousin. Everybody was used to his peculiar ways. People expressed their regrets, their pity."

She denies any bullying took place, "He would have told me, wouldn't he?"

The Stanitsa

Victor Finko, Severskaya Investigative Committee's senior detective, tells me they currently view homophobia as one of the leading potential motives. He's optimistic, "We'll solve it, of course."

Down at the precinct, they've put together a round-the-clock investigation team. The deputy head of the village police volunteers that they've already flushed out and interrogated all of the gays here.

"I had no idea that we had so many of them. And that age, too." He grins.

This is how the policeman describes the murder, "Somebody picked up a club and bashed their heads in, but obviously got other places, too. He probably acted alone." Then he tried to burn down the house. "Maybe a crime of passion?" he jokes.

Both men had recently collected their pensions, but the killer didn't take any money. Not a thing was missing from the house.

Last week, they had word from the police in Krasnodar that on January 12, the body of a man, wrapped in a blanket, was found on the riverbank. It turned out that this man had also been gay.

"Someone's been going after the fags," says the policeman, then apologizes for using the word *fag*.

The local youths are investigating, too, just out of curiosity. "We checked out the ones we thought might have done it, guys who'd done time, especially. But it doesn't look like it was any of them. They were all passed out drunk that day." There's not a lot to do for fun around here: You could have a rumble between neighborhood crews ("Actually, there's some guys coming over to beat us up today") or hang out at Three of Sevens, the local bar, or at the club. You could drift—go racing around the village while smoking hookah. The guys say there are no neo-Nazis here, or any youth groups. They didn't know about the old gays, or they "would have given them a couple of knocks" themselves.

Ataman* Victor Nikolayevich Pikalov confirms this, "We have no goths or emos." The rules are different out here. Some Chechens came a while back to beat up on our boys—with cause, so I took myself out to Krasnodar, had a talk with the diaspora. You're coming to settle scores, I said, but why bring guns? It's not worth having a shootout over two idiots. We've already dealt with them ourselves.

He's sad that I missed the Cossack Ball.

Outside it's pitch black. The ataman lines three Cossacks up in front of the village administration building. A Cossack patrol makes rounds of the village on Wednesdays, Thursdays, Fridays, and Saturdays. They're trawling for juvenile delinquents—in the Kuban region, all minors must be off the streets by 10 p.m. He reads out the orders: street patrol, site checks. We load into two vehicles. The ataman tells me not to buckle up, "You don't need to with me." But then we don't follow the planned route.

The ataman goes on and on about how lucky he's been with the administration head—"We're on the same page about everything"—and points out to me that although the streets may be flooded, the water is perfectly clean.

We stop by to check on a "dysfunctional family." We wait by the gate for ages while the ataman shouts for the man of the house to open up. A small woman, her legs bare, steps out into the snow.

* A Cossack leader.

She's outraged that her family's been deemed "dysfunctional." Her husband beat her up, she "wasn't thinking" and called the police. "When was that?" "Back in the summer."

"Why'd you call the cops? You should have just phoned me," the ataman tells her.

A kid, eleven or so, trails her out of the house. "Get back inside!" mother and ataman yell in unison.

For some reason, we drive up to the former factory dormitory. The ataman knocks on one of the doors, peers in, and shuts the door again. He shouts, "Get dressed, you've got visitors!"

A young man in a black sweater comes out, looking terrified.

"Smoking indoors?" the ataman harangues him. "And the second floor, we're running orgies there now?"

The young man walks the Cossacks to the exit.

"There were rumors about him, too," the ataman explains. "But now I've seen it with my own eyes. A naked guy lying on his bed. As soon as I open the door, he dives behind the wardrobe."

"So what?"

"So nothing. I won't shake his hand again, that's what. It's his own business, though. You know, democracy and all that."

After showing me real-life gays and their "reasonable" treatment of them, the Cossacks take me to watch army-style fighting: kids twisting one another's arms, tossing each other onto mats, doing kicks. Then we go to the woods: the swimming hole is a square of cold turquoise water.

"Up the hill, further on—that's where the Hare Krishnas are camped. Farther back, there are those other ones, tree huggers, cultists. They wouldn't let anyone in the woods. I said to them, 'I'll put a circle of men around your camp, you're not setting foot in the stanitsa.'"

The Suspect

The next morning, the yard in front of the murdered men's house is heaped with their things: parcels of clothes, books, suitcases, old boots, jars, the pitiful remnants of life. The puppy, sensing something, wails.

Next door, a woman peers carefully over her gate and begins wailing too. Yesterday, the cops hauled away her fifty-three-year-old son, Aleksandr. Valentina Vasilyevna Panteleyenko is eighty-two and she's terrified.

"We're scared of everyone now! I'm so upset, I haven't slept a wink. We never went anywhere near there. Never said a word to them! We know nothing about it! And now they've been on him since the eleventh, pulling him out of work! He's got hepatitis C, he's got arthrosis. He's a porter at the tile factory in Afipskaya. They showed up here in the evening, a whole gang of them. Then they searched the house for a weapon, brought people with them to witness the search. Last night he came home hungry, he hadn't had anything to eat. They showed up again and took him away. I called Severskaya stanitsa, they tell me, 'Yep, he's here. We're holding him for hooliganism.' He was probably raising a ruckus, complaining. The hearing's today. For what? I ask you! He's got a job! He wouldn't hurt a fly! 'You're withholding,' they say, and they threaten you! 'We'll stick you in a cell with the pansies, and then you'll squeal!' What am I going to do? Why won't they leave him alone?"

For the moment, the search for the murderer is confined to the two men on Proletarskaya Street who have already done time.

Aleksandr Panteleyenko was sentenced back in 2000 for drug possession and released two years later. He'd lost an eye just before the release and can barely see with the other.

They are desperately poor. Valentina Vasilyevna slices some bread to go with our tea and weeps. A deep breath, and she starts up again, "It's only the pills that are keeping him going, he's got rheumatoid arthritis. And now they're holding back his pension, too. Go and get certified for disability, they say. But then they won't certify him! He's managing, as long as he takes the meds. He never spends nights away from home. Doesn't see anyone, he doesn't even have a girlfriend, he lives with me. He's even scared of the dark! When the cop came and told us about what happened, Sasha put the outside lights on and kept them on all night long. He told me, 'Shut yourself in!'"

She phones the police station, "Don't you dare beat him up in there! He washes my clothes and takes out my bedpan! I'm elderly!"

Aleksandr Panteleyenko is released three days later. He says they didn't beat him, but "it got very close."

"They're like, 'Confess!' What am I supposed to confess?" He's worried he will get fired, worried that there'll be "rumors going around," and asks to be kept clearly separate from the murdered men.

"So what if I live alone? No wife or kids—doesn't mean I don't want them. I am not like that!"

The Graveyard

In recent years, the old men only went "into the world" for funerals. "Well, Vova would go. Kolya wouldn't. If anyone died, Vova went. Always making sure that he had the right time, the right date, so he wouldn't miss it. He could get a meal then, a decent meal. He would always pack some to take home with him. This and that, a few piroshki. He had his friend to feed, too! I mean, men . . . What could they cook, between them?

"But on the thirteenth, I was walking to the market and I saw a towel tied to their gate. That's our custom: when the dead have left the house, the last person out of the gate ties a towel on. Then anyone can untie it and take it home. Rich people put up a good, thick terry cloth towel. Those who haven't got much, something more modest. Whatever you can afford. They had something striped, terry cloth. White and green stripe, I think."

Only Vladimir was buried. Nikolai's body is still at the regional morgue. Vladimir's cousin says that she wanted "to take away the other one too. He was a person, too, after all," but she lost his passport. Now the police are searching for his relatives.

The old men will not be buried together.

Tatiana Nikanorovna believes this is right.

"I buried my husband in Chernomorka because that's where his first wife is, and his son. So I figured . . . It's right and lawful to bury him over there. We were together for nineteen years but never formally married. So we are nobody to each other. That's how people see us.

"He died in the spring, two years back. It was so strange! He was in the hospital in Afipskaya. I came to visit one morning, and the doctor, she was there too, and he says, Listen. Just please discharge me, I'm dying to go home! I'll drink goat's milk and get some sleep. I can't eat or sleep properly here. She says, Well, I'm not keeping you! and discharges him. I called his younger brother in Krasnodar to drive us home. They wheel him out, put him in the back seat. I climbed in there with him. His brother turns to look at him, says, Hey, something's not right. He doesn't look too alive. I tell him, He's probably asleep. He turns back again, Look, maybe we should call an ambulance? We drive up to the hospital in Ilsky a doctor comes out. The doctor listens to his chest and he says, He's dead.

"He'd rested his head on my shoulder and died like that, on my shoulder.

"Yegor Matveyevich, that was his name. I miss him! He was a good husband. Attentive. I felt like there was a man in the house. Who could go and do things. I felt like I wasn't alone. It's scary to be alone. It's important to love."

There are three graveyards in Ilskoye: the old one, the new one, and the newest one. Vladimir is in the new one. And that's a good thing, because the newest one is under water, while this one is just thick clay. His mother's grave is next to his. It has a portrait of her, Evdokia Nikitichna. Her gaze is stony, her lips pressed tight. I think of her surviving the war. Snow has covered Vladimir's portrait, leaving only his eyes visible. I clear the snow with my hand. He's about forty here. That same look: he's trying to smile but can't manage to, his chin is drawn in.

The wreath says, "With Love and Sorrow."

Beyond the graveyard, horses graze, the water runs on.

P.S. As we went to press, we learned that a suspected murderer had been arrested and charged. It was twenty-three-year-old Aleksandr Fet-Oglyh, another Ilsky resident. He had a previous conviction for burglary and did a term of hard labor community service for the municipal board ("chopping down trees at the cemetery"), where he stayed on as a general laborer. He was involved in the local Cossack activities. Ataman Pikalov said that it was actually Aleksandr's father who was a member, not Aleksandr himself, "that one is not on any of our rosters." There was a glowing report about Aleksandr in the local paper, after he and the other Cossacks went out to Krymsk to do aid work after a flood. He'd been considering becoming a contract soldier, and according to some sources, his contract was due to start February 1. He was arrested the day before.

Fet-Oglyh confessed. His story was that he'd been drinking with the old men, they'd tried to come on to him, and so he fought them off. "Looks like he overdid it, though," said the police.

CHAPTER 8

NON-RUSSIANS

An Englishman, a Frenchman, and a Russian get abducted by aliens. They lock them up and give each one of them two metal orbs. The aliens say, "We'll be back in an hour. You're going to have to impress us. And if you fail, we'll dissect you." An hour later, the aliens come back to check on the Englishman. He's in there rolling one orb into the other. "Look," he says, "I made billiards." The aliens watch for a while—they're not impressed. They dissect him. Then they go in to see the Frenchman. He's juggling the orbs. Not impressed. They dissect him. Finally, they go into the Russian's cell. He's fast asleep. The aliens wake him up.

"Where are our orbs?"

"I lost one and broke the other one."

Ha ha ha. Tell me another.

I'm Russian. I was born in Russia. My mother is Russian and so is my biological father. My name is common among Russians. Sometimes people will call me Alena and I will answer to that. My last name is Ukrainian, it was my mother's from her first marriage. Our family name is Malyshev. I have blue eyes and white skin, Slavic features. I braid my long hair. My native language is Russian, which I speak without any accent.

I've never felt like a foreigner in my country. I belong here.

People always called our neighbor Maria Markovna "careful." I thought this meant cowardly. When the gas service came to the building, she wouldn't let them in her apartment. She was afraid of "the state"—all bureaucrats, anyone vaguely official, military, police. She never went to the building meetings, she always kept to herself. She loved me, though, and let me come to her place. It was filled with books, from the floor to the ceiling, and had gleaming wood floors. Maria Markovna taught Latin at the university.

Mama told me the story of how Maria Markovna came to our house once. Mama was still a little girl, it was the Soviet Union, and they were denouncing bloodthirsty doctors in all of the newspapers, all of them Jews, every last one of them had close ties to international Zionism. Maria Markovna brought in the paper and asked, Do you still think of me as your friend? Even though I'm a Jew? Mama's mother said yes.

When I started to go out to gay rights protests, Maria Markovna came to our house once again. She was very old now. She said, Stop your daughter. She doesn't understand what it means to be an enemy of the state.

And I really did not. I didn't understand why Maria Markovna, who had been educated in Moscow, had come back to teach in Yaroslavl. They tried to keep Jews out of the colleges in the capital. They called it the "war on cosmopolitanism." Before the Soviet Union, there was the Russian Empire. It had the Pale of Settlement where the Jews were allowed to live. It was made up of parts of Ukraine, Belarus, Poland, Lithuania, Moldova, Latvia, and Russia. But if the Jews were wealthy enough, or if they'd served in the army, or had a useful profession, they could live anywhere that they wanted, just like the Russians.

It's good to be Russian. You can live wherever you want.

Mama is singing me a lullaby:

Hush my baby, rockabye,
Hush my baby, don't you cry,
Or a little wolf will come, and he'll bite you on your side,
And he'll bite you on your side, pull you to the forest wide,
Pull you to the forest hush, underneath a willow bush.

I lay there with my hands under my cheek, thinking about the wolf taking me into the dreamy wet forest.

Mama came from the village of Larino. That's where her parents were from, and their parents. They'd all been peasants.

It's a small village in the Yaroslavl region. Mama says twenty houses, a single street running along the river.

We had a three-window house. Made out of logs. A room with a stove—people slept on it. In the corner, a smoke-darkened icon of the Virgin Mary and an oil lamp. White curtains, a white tablecloth on the table, a sack of white flour. They built a cattle yard behind the house. The Malyshevs kept chickens, geese, ducks, sheep, and a goat. No cow. Mama still says, If only I had a cow. I ask her, Are you planning on keeping it in the city? Mama sighs. She says, A cow smells and has eyes.

Grandpa had beehives, he produced honey. When he died, after returning from the Second World War (his heart stopped), Babka took care of the hives. She had already moved to the city, but she would travel back to the village over the last of the ice (once the ice broke on the river, there were no roads that led there), and she would stay until May. The honey she sold at the market would feed our family. Mama says that they kept a pet swallow. And a pet hedgehog. The swallow flew away and the hedgehog was killed by the neighbor's pitchfork for eating the chicken feed. How much of that feed could he have eaten? says Mama. He wouldn't have starved those chickens of his. Mama pities the hedgehog.

The Pakhma River flows past the village, mellow and sweet round a bend. The river was once full of water, dammed, with a mill. People used to take boats to the neighboring village of Bogoslov, where the church was. There were crawfish. People would catch them at night. Mama was scared of the crawfish, scraping and crawling on the boat's bottom—what if they pinched her toes? Little fish called vyurok lived in the sandy bottom of the river. If you stepped on one, it would writhe out from under your foot—it was funny, it tickled.

They mowed the hay, then they raked it, piling it up, making bales. Everybody had livestock, they needed a lot of hay. "No land left unmown." They even mowed in the woods—those woods were filled with light and soft, low grass. The kids would run out into the woods gathering honey berries—they called them voryanishki in the village. They made kisel and unleavened cakes with them. Raspberries, too. Slippery jack mushrooms, which are so much fun to pick but so annoying to clean. The caps are all slimy, they slip out of your hands, it's gross.

Mama once saw a moose in the woods. "We looked at each other and went our separate ways."

Here's how you get to Larino from Yaroslavl: first, take the bus, then walk through the fields for two hours. The fields are abundant and colorful—filled with oats, peas, wheat, barley, cabbage, hemp. You are never alone. Northern lapwings hop on the dusty path, skylarks trill in the air. The lapwings have crests on their heads and rainbow wings.

Mama would take me when I was little.

I remember the fields overgrown with rust-colored weeds. There were no birds.

The village was dying. You'd rarely see anyone.

The weeds wove up toward the sky, growing taller than me. I struggled to tear my way through them.

Our house didn't have a floor anymore. Mama's first husband had wanted to save it from rotting by lifting it up on a foundation, but then they broke up.

The house was rotting.

Instead of a floor, it was filled with tall grass. It was strange walking through it. There wasn't a roof everywhere, the walls would break off into the sky. When it rained, we hid from it in the ruins of the stove. I'd sing, Let it rain, rain on down, down on me and everyone, and a bucket down on Baba Yaga, too. I was putting a spell on the rain to make it stop.

We weren't going there just for fun. It was the 90s, we didn't have enough food, so Mama was working a small patch of soil, trying to grow vegetables. The grass always crowded out the tender young shoots; our harvests were small.

We'd pull the grass out around the shoots, cutting our fingers. We'd pour ash on the cabbages to stave off the caterpillars. We'd go to the river for water. The Pakhma had lost its dam and grown totally shallow. I walked out into the water, and it would only come up to my little-girl waist. I thought: the river feels that the people have left it, that it no longer belongs to anyone.

After completing our peasant tasks, we'd sit down at the big wooden table in the middle of the yard. Mama would feed me canned borscht. You had to keep an eye on the can—an old crow with a reputation for stealing lived in the village. We caught her one day, rifling through the jar with her beak, looking for meat. There was no meat. The crow croaked and complained.

Behind the dark house: the abandoned field, then the forest. The gray alders kept inching forward, stretching up toward the gray sky. With every summer, the forest came closer.

I see it advancing on us.

Eventually, we stopped going to Larino—Mama didn't have the energy.

But back in the city, Mama kept trying to figure out how to get a deed to our land to make it officially ours. Our country had changed its name and now land was private property. We had to pay for a specialist to come. But the specialist couldn't help—according to the existing documents, there was a house on the land. But a house without a stove doesn't count as a house. "Build a stove, any kind." Mama didn't have the money for the specialist or a stove.

Several years later, we learned that the village of Larino had burned to the ground. Every last house.

And the forest had finally grown all the way back up to the river.

Mama's afraid to go back there.

I'm not afraid, it just feels like the earth is bottoming out from under my feet.

When I turned thirty, my mother gave me a big, empty book. You're supposed to glue photos in it and label them.

We'll label them all and that's how we'll keep them, she said.

The unmarked photos are black-and-white, blurry. Mama tells me what to write. That's your grandfather Fyodor, that's your babka Evdokia. Your great-grandfather was named Pavel, but there is no photo of him.

Three years ago, they posted a cache of documents from World War I on the internet. You could search them based on location. I entered "Larino" and found my great-grandfather's name. He'd been a private. All that is left of him is a single document: a blue discharge form from the army. On June 12, 1916, he was wounded in the vicinity of Vilna. Now it's called Vilnius, the capital of Lithuania.

His name is written in black ink: Malyshev, Pavel Osipovich. Then, next to his patronymic, penciled in purple, it says "Iosifovich."

Which means my great-great-grandfather's name was actually Iosif.

I called my mother.

Mama, are we Jews?

Of course not! she said. We are Russians, all Russians, all the way back, the most Russian people imaginable.

THE LAST HELICOPTERS

March 19, 2021

By the River

Nina Dentumeyevna Chunanchar sits on the riverbank. The river is called the Avam, it's wide and gray. Behind her, the star-shaped cement war memorial with the names of the fallen; before her, the drop down to the water. Below, the boats. Farther off, some children are bringing in fishing nets. The tundra is changing from rust to black. The snows haven't settled yet.

Nina Dentumeyevna says, "Our gods. Sudiu Nguo. The sickness that's everywhere, that's Sudiu Nguo. Kotura is the suicide god, when they shoot themselves. That's how most of them do it, shooting themselves with a gun, that's Kotura for you. Then there's Deiba, the orphan god. The god of orphans, he's probably an orphan, too. Do we pray to them? No. We don't."

She is seventy-three. She's had two husbands—both dead. Six children. All of them dead.

Four of the children died when they were small. Here, they stitch goose wings to the shirts of children who die and bury them in the trees. The dead children turn into birds.

She used to be able to see her youngest girl's burial from her window, but then they put up a house that blocked out the view. One day, the house burned down, and now Nina Dentumeyevna can look at her daughter as much as she wants to.

Her son Lenya lived the longest. "His name was Ngotesia. As if his father and I had split up, and I took him for myself. That's called Ngotesia." He was thirty-one when he hung himself. He did it sitting on the floor beside his mother's iron bedstead.

There's still a rope tied to the head of Nina Dentumeyevna's bed, "but it's not that one."

He had money sticking out of his pocket, the government check he'd gotten that day.

Why did he hang himself? "I don't know," says Nina Dentumeyevna. "He was probably drinking."

She had three sisters and three brothers, but they are all dead now.

She lives entirely alone. She stokes the house stove every three days but feeds the shaggy street dogs every morning. She applied to the nursing home in Dudinka but was turned away. "Come back when you're older."

"Wouldn't you be bored in town?"

"Ha. What good is the tundra to us nowadays? We don't need it anymore."

She is the last of her line.

She is Nganasan.

The Nganasan People

There are seven hundred Nganasan people left.

They are the northernmost people on our continent.

They have never been numerous. Yet only thirty years ago, their number was nearly double—thirteen hundred souls.

They are the descendants of primeval tribes that hunted the wild northern deer. Their culture is genuinely ancient, and so the greater part of the Nganasan pantheon is not made up of male gods but mothers—of water, underground ice, fire, earth.

At the beginning of the seventeenth century, the Russians imposed a yasaq—a Turkic word for tribute—to be paid in pelts.

This is how the yasaq worked: the Russians took the most important and respected members of the community hostage and demanded payment for their lives.

The Nganasan were in no hurry to submit. There were rebellions. But a minority people's resistance is limited. The largest revolt, in 1666, ended in the killing of thirty Russian "government and manufacturing men," plus four Tungus men. The killers were hanged.

Under communism the Nganasan way of life was ended by executive order. The new authorities instituted an official policy of settlement for all tribes and peoples whose "nomadic civilization" was deemed "intrinsically incompatible" with the principles of a communist society. Villages to house the Nganasan began to go up in the 1930s, farther south than their nomadic routes and right on the ancestral lands of another people—the Dolgan. To this day, these villages are a mix of Nganasans and Dolgans. The regional and national powers have always been represented by ethnic Russians in the roles of mayor, police chief, village medic, and schoolteachers.

The Nganasan still inhabit these villages: Ust'-Avam and Volochanka.

They fish and hunt reindeer.

But this year, there are no fish, and it's been three years since the deer left for other lands.

Ust'-Avam

The village is hidden away from the world by unbroken tundra and rivers. The nearest town is almost two hundred miles away through impassable wilds.

There are four streets: Stream Street, Sunny Street, Riverside, and Central. Houses with crumbling plaster, patched up with strips of tin. The tin is cut from old oil barrels, so the walls sport oil company logos.

Each house is subdivided into four "apartments" consisting of a one-hundred-and-forty-square-foot room plus a tiny kitchenette. That's for a whole family.

There is no sewer system. Everything goes in a bucket, and the bucket gets emptied into the street, away from the front porch steps.

There is no running water. It has to be carried from the river or bought from the water truck (50 rubles a barrel).

A gray schoolhouse clad in aluminum siding towers over the river.

The building's enormous. People call it the Cosmodrome. It has indoor toilets and running water.

Another defining feature: the bags of coal. Huge white sacks piled up beside the porch. The government supplies ten tons of coal per family for the winter; the winters here last seven months. The coal must be sifted—poured through a wire-coil bed frame—to shake out the dust and crumbs that would otherwise choke a coal fire. It's crucial to get this done before the snows really settle. Every street is spattered in black coal crumb.

Dogs mill about, some of them blue-eyed.

The houses seem to be inching toward the helipad, an empty space lit by floodlights. Behind it is the village dump—the goldmine—and the morgue. To get to the other side of the village, you cross the stream. People are always drowning in it, but right now, the water is low, gray, and safe.

Beyond that, tundra. Hilly, rust red, and barbed. Where it comes up to the village, the tundra is thickly dotted with pillars and crosses.

That is the graveyard. We won't be going there, it is forbidden.

Why There Are No Fish

The Nganasan do their fishing in small guild teams, working the Pyasina River and its tributaries, the Avam and Dudypta.

An industrial spill of diesel fuel has emptied the Pyasina of fish. On May 29, 2020, 21,000 tons of diesel burst out of a rusted reservoir belonging to metals manufacturer Nornickel. That summer, *Novaya Gazeta* and Greenpeace ecologists registered the disappearance of the Pyasina's fish.

Something else seems to have happened in the Avam and Dudypta.

The fishermen say that the fish in these rivers come from the lakes scattered throughout the tundra. In autumn and spring the lakes overflow and stream to the rivers, where fish go to frolic and spawn.

The Nganasan say that it's global warming. Spring came a full month early this year, rapidly and all at once. The seasonal flooding receded almost immediately. Lakes had no time to unfreeze. The fish didn't come.

When they speak of the summer's fishing, it usually involves swearing. They did manage "something." The something is just a third of their usual catch.

They bartered the fish for gasoline and food.

Gasoline also means fishing and hunting and keeping the lights on in the baloks.* By autumn, pretty much everyone has run out.

The Mayor

The square white room has two windows. People sit around a table, the only woman present is wearing a medical mask. There is a crimson flag, a portrait of young Stalin, a machine gun cartridge and helmet, several icons, some mammoth bone (falling apart and of little value), deer antlers, and sable furs.

A portrait of Putin hangs on the wall next to the icons. Putin is looking off into the distance. "Take care of our North!" is written across his chest.

The village chief, to whom everyone including himself refers as "the mayor," opens the meeting, "One of the dogs has attacked three people. Something has to be done."

People respond:

"Dogs bite when they're protecting their territory. That's how they think."

"Well, if a dog bites one person, that's one thing. But not three!"

"Dogs should always be on a leash and muzzled, like they do in the city."

An envoy to the dog's owner is deputized. The wind outside howls and yelps.

The mayor is Sergei Mikhailovich Naberezhnev. He is ethnically Russian, gray-haired, dressed head to toe in camo. He's lived on the Taymyr Peninsula for thirty-seven years. He used to be the village police

* Wooden tundra huts.

officer, "back when we still had chums* up around the perimeter of the village." He says that he was called up to be mayor. "Putin never shies away from the task at hand. So I didn't either."

No one respects the mayor. People say that he's useless, all talk. They think that he's stashed away municipal building supplies—the hottest currency after gasoline—in his cellar. They resent the newly built banya behind the mayor's house.

While talking to me, the mayor is using his elbows to cover a document with the heading "A list of Ust'-Avam residents leading an antisocial lifestyle."

There are 359 people living here but only 54 jobs.

The mayor considers his greatest achievement to be the reduction of deaths to six or seven a year, from the previous rate of twelve to fourteen.

"But I did the math. If every year, ten people die and only two are born, like we have now, by 2054, our village will be completely gone."

Olya

The chopper fans its blades—whoosh, whoosh, a flat circle—and lands on its round belly.

The whole village comes out to see its metal paws touch the ground.

People ring around the helipad. Black quad bikes, wheels half buried in coal.

The crowd moves in under the spinning blades. The helicopter disgorges its passengers. The villagers stuff parcels and packages deep into its womb, the pilot curses ornately.

He's going to lift off now and fly to Volochanka, the next village over, and then he'll come back and pick up the people going to town.

A Russian girl in a gray shirt jumps down to the ground. Her long red hair streams in the wind. She looks around, purses her lips.

Her belongings, two bags, are loaded onto a quad bike.

* Conical huts made of wooden poles covered in deer pelts. Chums are easy to erect, disassemble, and move, so many nomadic peoples use them.

She is the new math, physics, and IT teacher. Olga Andreevna Bespalova. Olya. It's her first time in Ust'-Avam.

She's twenty-two. She's just graduated from Novosibirsk State University. Everyone in her family is a teacher, and now she is, too.

She will live in the school itself: a windowless little room, a bathroom and shower.

She unpacks her books (*How to Live a Good Life*, *Norwegian Wood*, *20 Something Manifesto*) and writes out a schedule in her rounded cursive (7 a.m., yoga and mindful breathing).

The colorful little envelopes are from her friends, each labeled "to be opened at the ends of the earth."

Tomorrow, the very first lesson is going to be math. Tomorrow, Olya will discover that her ninth graders know the multiplication table, but not comprehensively.

There are two ninth graders, Eva and Stepan.

"My dear lady, might you write down a class list for us?"

Eva writes down three names.

"So we have two thirds of the class with us? Intriguing."

Olya is dressed for the occasion in brown trousers and a flowery blouse. A huge crimson rose is knotted into her red hair.

"Do you remember about square roots? Today's lesson is on expression values and square roots. Stepan, did you write that down? Eva, can you remember what an expression value is?"

Olya writes 2x + 4 = 0 on the blackboard in a large, looping hand.

"What is the expression value here?"

Silence.

She writes: 24 + 3 = 27.

"What is twenty-seven in this expression?"

Silence.

"The answer is right on the surface. I'm trying to make contact."

Stepan is staring at his desk, Eva, straight ahead. Olya walks up and down in front of the blackboard.

"What is the answer?"

"The answer is something vital," says Stepan.

"Going with the theme of today's lesson?" (Silence, silence, silence.) "Right. We're going to remind ourselves about square roots. And let's write it down. Pens at the ready!"

Olya adjusts the rose in her hair.

"Styopa, will you go on with your schooling?"

"I'm done after this year."

"And then?"

"I dunno. I've had enough of the school kind of thing."

"But learning is a lifelong process! You have to keep gaining new skills so you can be an in-demand specialist!"

Eva rests her face in her hand, eyes brimming with universe-spanning ennui.

"Stepan, I can see your eyes blazing with intelligence," Olya insists.

Evdokia, the village's sole eleventh grader, comes to the next class. This is Olya's shining hour. Evdokia—known as Dusya—is the best student in Ust'-Avam. She has bleached hair and long green fingernails. The two young women are soon bent over the textbooks, their conversation livelier by the minute.

"You remember the trick with negative degrees?"

"Yes. I like this one and this one here. And I like the equations themselves."

"I'm sure you remember that a graph is the expression of dependencies," Olya says. For the first time today, she is smiling.

"And everything in this world can be expressed as a function," says Dusya. "Absolutely everything."

Casting Nets

A knife scar cuts across Artyom's face. He tells me that he's got nineteen stab wounds, but "God keeps sparing me for some reason."

He's tried leaving the village. He served in the army, on the Finnish-Karelian border, worked as an airplane mechanic. There was no chance to stay on as a contract soldier. "They didn't want me." For seven years, he lived in Norilsk, working at a plant with enormous fuel tanks. He came back "to twiddle deer tails."

He says that people ought to stop whining, "You need to just live and be happy, without all this nonsense."

His fishing partner is Igor Falkov. People say, "God gave him a talent, but not a brain." His dark face looks caved in, his eyes are dull. He used to paint designs on baloks along the river, and even made paintings, but stopped entirely after his mother died.

The sun touches down on the tundra, and the tundra flares up and then blackens. Artyom and Igor set off to cast their nets in the dark.

Artyom inherited his seine net from his father. It's long and gray, patched up in places. It's one of the only two seine nets in the village.

There are no big fish in the rivers. The rivers are empty. "Nothing but burbot, dog food."

But in the night, shoals of a little fish called tugun, or Arctic herring, come close to the shore.

Tugun are neither sold nor stored. They're food for that day—fried, cured, or raw. The flesh is fatty and slightly sweet.

Softly, the sky is extinguished, joining the pitch-black land. Igor sets a course along the riverbank. He unfurls the net over the dark water.

The net envelops a piece of the river. The men clamber back onto the bank and, flicking their headlamps on, grab either side of the net. Slowly, slowly they come together.

It's as though somebody's tossed a handful of coins into the tightly stitched netting. They heave the little fishies onto the bank. You can hear their fins crunch as they break.

There's a ruffe fish trying to wiggle free of the net. Useless and extraordinary, it's translucent, covered in glassy spines, and throwing rainbows. They pry it out of the net and toss it to the cold sand for the seagulls to scarf. It's tiny, smaller than my finger. I carry it back to the river. Artyom harrumphs. He plucks up another little spiny guy and sets him down in the water, saying, "Well, maybe something good will come back to me, too."

Toward midnight, the sky finally goes black, but you can still make out the riverbanks. There is a white glow from the village.

Artyom tells me about the local serial killer, Kostya Tuglakov. He shot two guys with his shotgun, was sent to the mental hospital, came back and murdered a woman, went into rehab, and came home again. "We told him not to come around anymore. I wonder where he is now."

"Rip him up for spare parts," Igor Falkov says. He's not much of a talker.

The boat sits heavy in the water. Igor breaks an oar pushing off in the shallows and starts using a Styrofoam seat cushion to paddle.

The fishing is done. The men set a course for home.

Artyom slows over unseen rocks, finding his way through the many shades of darkness. He points up to the sky. "There. The North Star. All the other ones wiggle."

When you're in a motorboat, the stars tremble and move.

There are boats on the water here every night. The villagers cast for burbot. Their Chinese-made headlamps swivel at us as we pass; each fisherman sits in his own pool of light.

Dogs await their owners' return on the riverbank, pawing at the wet, dark sand.

A big brown one named Baby greets us as we crest the slope. He is angling for fish and he gets fish.

The Children

The watchman checks his phone and starts ringing a copper bell. It's recess, the kids run to the old village hall. That's where you go to pay your utilities; the building also houses the satellite internet router. Ust'-Avam does have Wi-Fi. It's almost impossible to connect to it, but the schoolchildren seem to manage.

What are they watching online? TikTok. Batman versus Pennywise. Life jitters, backlit, across tiny screens.

There's a boy huddled up in the corner, behind the door, large headphones covering much of his head. He only watches horror films, one after another. His name is Sasha.

The school has a playground, that's where you'll find the little ones.

You could go to the dump—the goldmine—and see what you can dig up. Or climb Bald Mountain, a hill rising gently behind the village, but that means going around the graveyard. Girls go berry picking, boys jack the grown-ups' boats and go fishing for burbot. You can sit at the river's edge and chug energy drinks and toss the empties over the drop. Smoke whatever you've nicked while your parents were out in a drunken stupor. Circle the village, one street, the other street, turn. The little ones try to tag along with the big kids. Nighttime is thick with children's voices.

At night, flaming trash barrels light up the darkness. Here's a square marked out in the coal dust, a corner each for a king, a prince, a jack, and a turd. Arguments about whether the ball was in or out, tempers running white-hot. A tall girl threatens to "kick the hell" out of someone. A boy is squealing that it's all unfair, cursing them all.

"Say you're sorry!"

"She won't forgive me anyway."

"Do it for your own sake!"

"Dumb idiot!" says the boy and wanders off into the darkness.

Another one says, "We've got a big village, right? If you count the graveyard, I mean."

The Shaman's Daughter

Evdokia Demnimeyevna tells me, "There used to be a people called Nganasan. They had endurance."

She's blind. Her eyes are dark, with white dots in place of pupils. She can see light, just a little.

For the Nganasan, life begins with the eyes. Their name for the earth is Mother of All That Has Eyes. Eyes are only borrowed; after you die, they go back to the mother. Dead eyes in a living face look beyond the boundary, to where no living person should look.

Evdokia Demnimeyevna is eighty-two. Duzymyaku is her Nganasan name. She is a shaman's daughter.

Her house is the outermost of the village. Beyond it, the stream, the hills, the graveyard.

She is the oldest Nganasan in Ust'-Avam. Her father, the shaman Demnime, was the next-to-last shaman of the Nganasan people. He did time in prison. He refused to join the collective farm. He lived at a hunting outpost in the tundra, not in the village. He mostly used his powers for his family, although occasionally, when boats went past his place "without an offering," he broke their motors with his mind.

At the peak of his powers, he resurrected a drowned boy. They say that the child came back to life, but his eyes never moved again.

His brother, Tubiaku Kosterkin, was also a shaman, and he was also imprisoned. When he returned from the Gulag, he announced that he had swapped himself for Stalin.

"He came back from prison in February and was trance-walking up by Volochanka. In one of his trances, he told me: 'Today, on this day, you wouldn't have seen me. When I was in prison, Deiba Nguo told me that if I want to come home, instead of myself, instead of my head, I had to give him a big man, and then I would see my children again. If I hadn't given him that man, I wouldn't have been freed. I gave him that man and came home. No doctors will save him.'

"We got to March and then came the news: Stalin was dead. No doctors could save him, nobody could."

The shaman's ancestral line must not be allowed to die out. After his death, Demnime's gift was supposed to be passed down to his grandson Igor (Nguchumyaku—"won't let you go"). They had prepared Igor for this. Demnime pulled him out of school after third grade, took on raising the boy himself. Taught him. But Igor did not become a shaman.

"Grandpa died, but he hasn't come to me. I can't see any spirits. There are no real shamans. They don't exist," Igor said.

Igor lived in the village, fishing and baking bread, which he would give away to anybody who needed it. He hauled water, worked as a laborer. July 17, 2012, was Evdokia Demnimeyevna's birthday and Igor went to catch fish. They found him facedown in a lake, dead.

The shaman's line—Ngamtusuo—ends with Evdokia Demnimeyevna's great-granddaughters. They live in town. "They don't know themselves."

When a shaman performs rituals, he needs a helper—someone to take up a place between him and the people. Usually that's his wife or daughter. That is how women learn how to speak with spirits. Evdokia Demnimeyevna begins a ritual song, but her voice keeps breaking. She clears her throat. "I've been to Paris, you know, by the river Seine. With a choir I sang in."

Her son Oleg is sifting coal. He pours some over the bed frame, watching it move through the wire.

He asks me for 600 rubles, for groceries "for babushka." Six hundred rubles is the price of a bottle of vodka in the village shop.

Nganasan Lesson

Once a week, on Saturdays, the Nganasan language is taught at the school. Even this single lesson was almost derailed when a boy crossed it out of the schedule with a pen: half the class fell for it and never showed up.

English is taught twice a week, though, so when the teacher, Aleksandra Saibovna Momde, asks the children to recite the Nganasan alphabet, a girl begins with *a*, *b*, *c*, *d* . . .

The third graders are struggling to recall the words for numbers, and the teacher herself is doing no better, "Five, six, seven—what's that, how do you say that?" They recite, "This is my mother, this is my grandmother," in Nganasan, but *mother* and *granny* seep in somehow anyway.

"So what? English will be useful to them at least. When the old folks die out, that's the end of it," says Aleksandra Saibovna. "These kids have forgotten everything they learned last year over the summer. And no one speaks it at home."

The children recite, in unison, "I, *mene*; you, *tene*; we, *myng*."

Inside Nganasan there is another, hidden language. *Keingeirsya* is double-talk: every word has a second meaning. It is the language of songs—a young man sings of a woman who spurned him (the words of the song tell of a river that forks—in a good direction and in a bad one); two friends discuss which brother each one should marry (which Arctic fox to yoke to a sled); hunters match wits. Any mistake, whether in grammar or sense, invalidates the entire phrase and makes the speaker lose face. The Russians did manage to write down some of these songs.

It's hard to believe that just forty years ago, in 1979, 90 percent of Nganasans considered Nganasan their native language.

Linguist Valentin Gusev explains that the Nganasan language was effectively killed by the boarding school system. It was forbidden there, with punishments ranging from being hit with the teacher's ruler to getting kicked out of class for saying a single word in it. The curse didn't work right away, it took a generation. Children born in the sixties could still speak their native language with their parents, but their own children were completely Russophone. Ethnographer Andrei Popov described the Nganasans' linguistic purism—an extreme, almost religious reverence for their native tongue—and named it as one of the contributing factors in elder Nganasans' unwillingness to teach their grandchildren who grew up in the Soviet school system. Hearing Nganasan mangled was more painful to them than the sound of a foreign language coming from the mouths of their children's children.

Nina Dentumeyevna sometimes speaks Nganasan to her neighbor Elizaveta Barbovna. It is the only Nganasan still spoken in Ust'-Avam.

"We don't say 'goodbye' in Nganasan, we say 'until tomorrow,'" Aleksandra Saibovna says at the end of her lesson. But she does not say the word.

The Store

"Mashenka, please, just sell it to me."

"No."

"I'll dance. I'll dance for you! Watch this!"

The woman sways and stamps her feet. She spins. She hops. Masha turns away.

The woman dances some more, weeps, and leaves.

The store belongs to Salamatov, an entrepreneur known for his chain of supermarkets, called Fire.Bird, all across the Taymyr Peninsula. He's put his stepson German Shapovalov in charge of the Ust'-Avam kiosk. German is not finding it easy.

Food is delivered by barge in the summer and trucks in the winter, over winter roads tamped into the snow. Coal and petrol come before food. This year, the last barge, the fourth one, never made it. Its captain refused to push on through the shallows and he was fired.

There's no more flour or salt. Masha phones German every morning but he is out of ideas. The water level is low and it won't be long before the first snows.

Masha Barkhatova, the cashier and "proprietress," is a large, handsome woman with short, bleached hair and thick eyeliner. "Half Dolgan, half who-knows-what," Masha says. Her ancestor, the shaman Roman Barkhatov, led the final revolt against the Russians. Masha's not from here, she ran away from Volochanka the moment she turned sixteen. She was raised by her grandmother and great-grandmother; the stories about her childhood are horrific. She used to drink, but then she got married and "we quit together." She and her husband spent years living in a baloks up north. "We came up from nothing." She has no pity left.

You need to know everything about everyone to be the shopkeeper in Ust'-Avam. The size of people's pensions and whether they've taken out loans; who drinks, who hunts, who has enough gas for his motorboat; who's fighting and won't go out fishing together anymore.

Masha has a notebook where she logs the villagers' credit at the store.

The overwhelming majority are constantly in debt. Pensions and state benefits arrive with the helicopter at the beginning of the month. That's when everyone files into the store to settle the previous month's debt and start a new one. For the next few days, the streets are "full of zombies"—that's what they call drunks.

Prices are exactly double those in Moscow.

The bestselling item is vodka, of course. A second shipment comes on the second barge, with the coal, and it never runs out. The store's back room is stacked to the rafters with crates of weird brands of vodka.

A bottle costs 600 rubles. After hours, under the counter, 1,000. But Masha doesn't sell at night, no. The previous cashier, another woman, was murdered right here in the store. She lived in the back room, where they now keep the vodka. She'd come to Ust'-Avam from Ukraine with her two children. She was battling cancer, wore a kerchief on her head. The village doesn't remember her name. But they remember that when she was being raped and killed, she didn't scream, for fear of waking the children. Everyone found this touching, and they all came out to send her off when the helicopter took her body away. She had opened the door because it was someone she knew—Kostya Tuglakov, Ust'-Avam's very own serial killer. You can make a lot of money at night. Masha loads people buying vodka on credit with "extras"—things she can't sell. Cans of borscht, baby shampoo, canned sweet corn. She just shoves it at them without a word. People take what they don't need. She writes it down in her notebook.

The village hunters and fishermen sell to the store, too, and so the supply barges and trucks returning from Ust'-Avam are laden with meat, pelts, and fish. The men are paid in groceries. But in order to survive for several months at a time at their hunting or fishing grounds, their teams must buy food, tea, coffee, and grains—and all that on credit. They settle their debts with everything that they catch.

There is a price list tacked up on the window: pike is 50 rubles a kilo, a large whitefish called muskun goes for 140; cleaned reindeer antlers, 500. "As you can see, we're all slaves," say the villagers.

Masha is the most powerful person in Ust'-Avam. The Russian mayor doesn't even come close.

How the Nganasan Were Tamed

In his book *Arctic Mirrors*, Yuri Slezkine details how the Russian government's attitude toward northern tribes changed over time. Their status evolved from that of savages forced to pay ransoms to being classed as a new kind of junior subject, whose tithes (the same pelts) were determined by special arrangement. Parity with the Russians was inconceivable given the consensus on the tribes' "insufficient neuro-mental ability." At the dawn of the modern age, on the brink of the revolution, for a short while, the "noble savages" did capture the intelligentsia's hearts and minds. The populist Narodniks* looked to Siberia for their "young and mighty land"—undeveloped and therefore pure, uncultured and therefore honest, a feasible exemplar for the future Russian collectivism that was sure to come. "The mores of the Siberian races are a strange blend of revolting vice and patriarchal virtues," wrote the polemicist Alexander Shishkov. The natives were a sort of mirror; people wanted to see themselves through this other. Ethnographer Nikolai Yadrintsev produced an entire monograph on Russians as benevolent colonizers, "no worse than the Spanish or British."

The Bolsheviks saw the minority peoples as a challenge. The Committee of the North was formed and tasked with a truly historic mission: to lift the tribes up from their primitive lifeways straight into the radiant

* The Narodniks were a faction of ideological groups active from the 1860s through the 1910s. They believed that the intelligentsia should deepen its ties to the common folk—the *narod*—in search of its roots, its place in the state and the world beyond. Narodniks believed that peasant society was the natural realm in which to build socialism. Narodniks would become doctors, medics, scribes, teachers, smiths, move to villages, and propagandize among the peasants against the tsarist authority.

light of communism, bypassing slavery, feudalism, and capitalism altogether.

It took the new powers until 1920 to reach the Taymyr in full force. They traveled among the tundra camps convening tribal councils and executive committees. In his 1929 book *Indigenous Soviets,* N. E. Leonov describes the first negotiations between the Nganasan and the Bolsheviks. The Nganasan wanted to know whether they were "required to obey the new instructor as unfailingly as they had the previous bailiff." The "instructor" said no, they were not, but at their very first objection to the new ways he declared, "You, old men, have the old law in mind, praying to God and going against Soviet rule. If you keep talking like this, soldiers with rifles will come here from Krasnoyarsk and lock you up in a metal box." A Nganasan recalled, "We were frightened then and kept silent, and so the meeting ended in silence."

Class theory proved tricky to apply to the Nganasan.

The Bolsheviks searched for kulaks to root out, but there weren't any. Their whole wealth was in reindeer, their own herds and the wild ones. A wolf pack, a flare-up of disease, or a blizzard could "disappear" any herd at any moment. Thus, lucky herders always helped out the unfortunate, taking on more mouths to feed, giving the unlucky ones work.

Nevertheless, kulaks were duly discovered and dealt with.

The Bolsheviks forbade the great culls of reindeer that took place seasonally along the riverbanks, deeming them poaching. Small-scale deer herding was first collectivized, then passed into state ownership. In 1973, the combined deer fell prey to an outbreak of hoofrot. The entire herd, numbering in the thousands, had to be culled.

The village remembers this year as "the blackest of all."

Was the disease preventable? Nikolai Vladimirovich Pluzhnikov of the Russian Academy of Sciences thinks so. For centuries, the Nganasan had successfully managed the deer count, and the mixing of the wild and domesticated populations. The Taymyr Peninsula was the only place in the world where vast domesticated and wild herds coexisted.

With hunting effectively outlawed, the Nganasan stopped tracking the wild reindeer routes, which weakened the breeding stock and effectively ended deer herding on the Taymyr.

In the place of the reindeer cull, the Bolsheviks started the Gospromkhoz, a state industry manufacturing center. Hunters had to hand over their pelts, meat, and fish—paying a kind of Soviet tribute; women sewed shoes and souvenirs from the hides.

The Gospromkhoz outlived the Soviet Union by a decade, closing down in 2000. At last, capitalism had come to the Nganasan lands.

And with it, a host of strange deaths.

Kotura Nguo

Evgeny Chuprin left Ust'-Avam on April 9. The polar night was over. He was going to see his wife and daughter in Dudinka. He went alone. His sledge, secured to his snowmobile, was laden with deer meat.

"He was an experienced hunter, barely ever had to fish. He knew the tundra so well, he could drive with his eyes closed."

"He always gave out the first kill of the season to elders. That is the custom—it goes to the old and infirm, women living on their own. The following hunt is for you."

Driving along the river, Chuprin made it to the deer camp called Kresty, where the frozen Dudypta River met the frozen Pyasina. He had a cup of tea there and set off toward town. Then the blizzard descended.

They say you couldn't see the houses for the blizzard. They say that the snow was wet and froze into a crust of ice straightaway.

Chuprin carried on.

His snowmobile broke down.

He attempted to walk back to Kresty. He got close but veered right, turning instead toward the houses. He froze to death.

"An absurd death," says the mayor. "We wanted to get a search party together the next day, but the blizzard was still going. It was a three-day blizzard. Once it finally ended, we asked for a helicopter, but now the blizzard was in Dudinka. We finally got it to come here to look for him. Around Kresty. How come we didn't see the snowmobile? I couldn't tell you. We only had to fly two or three kilometers out."

On April 19, Chuprin was buried in the tundra behind the village. The deer carcass he had intended for his wife and daughter was served at his wake.

Evgeny Chuprin's death was a good one. People like to tell the story.

Not so with the others.

What does death look like in Ust'-Avam? Of the six people who die here each year, only one will die from natural causes. Two or three will have frozen to death or die of drinking some other way. The rest will be suicides.

Two suicides annually in a population of three hundred people.

The circumstances defy understanding.

The head of a family. Has breakfast, has lunch, hangs himself.

A husband goes off to town without telling his wife, she hangs herself.

A father and son are drinking together, then they go to separate rooms. At some point, the father notices that the son is sitting too upright. He comes closer and sees that the son is not sitting, he's hanging.

A hunter is traveling down the river, his boat motor breaks. He tries to get it going again—no luck. He shoots himself, bleeds to death.

The suicides around here do not provoke reflection or feeling. There's suicide in every family. It is quotidian.

Galina Durakova tells the story of losing her husband of fourteen years, "That summer, yes, June. He hanged himself. I don't know why. He seemed normal that morning. Everything was all fine, but then later, in the afternoon . . . I went out to a friend's. When I got there . . . people came and called me home. 'Galya,' they said, 'go home quick, something has happened.' And the doctor ran over with me, and the policeman. When I got back, they'd already taken him down. He was forty-five. Completely sober. He did drink, sometimes, but he hadn't that day.

Didn't say a word to me. We have three children—two girls, and the oldest girl from my other husband. That one also died. He drowned."

The only person who attempts to put her sense of loss into words is Tatiana Tkachenko. Tanya is an orphan. Her older sister Lyudmila Popova was like a mother to her. Four years ago, Lyudmila took her own life. Tanya buried her sister "the Nganasan way," face covered, after stepping over three fires on their home's threshold. Then she converted to Christianity. "I needed your God."

She doesn't talk about suicide, it's considered improper, but she writes poetry that "not many would understand."

"I want to scream to silence them all! And so I can hear your reply . . . Why, why did you have to leave? You left your son behind. You always said you loved him. He keeps growing, he wants to know, 'Where did my mama go off to?' It hurts to stay silent and lie. I tell him, 'She'll come back soon.' And he waits, but he must know."

Lyudmila's son is named Sasha. Tatiana is raising him along with her own two sons.

Sasha has just turned eleven, they ordered a cake from town. Sasha's the one who obsessively watches horror films. I've seen him before; he was hiding in the corner of the old village hall, wearing big headphones.

Tatiana explains, "He's got all this fear, these phobias. It started after his mom. He sits in front of the computer sometimes, and he doesn't want to watch, but he's determined to conquer his fear, so he'll sit through the movie anyway. At first he used to write me notes, cut paper hearts out. And drawings, his mom in heaven. He would write to me: 'Tanya, I love you,' and hide it in my makeup bag. I start to hug and kiss him, he gets shy. Sasha thinks that my boys are jealous, that we don't love him as much. We love all our kids. He's stopped writing me notes now. He had this other thing, like he was in another world. He would start shooting, dropping down to the ground like this, and even in school he would just suddenly stand up and pretend to be shooting, then leave. Like in a game."

"Go on, then!" shouts Masha Barkhatova to a retreating customer's back. "Somehow, you can find money for vodka, but not for your food and smokes!"

"Are there many suicides here?"

"More. More suicides in Volochanka and Ust'-Avam than natural deaths. People break down, the young especially, there are more suicides among the young. There's no work, there is nothing. You look to the future, it's empty.

"Take Vasya. He died in spring, hanged himself. He'd come back from prison, lived quietly for a bit, and then raised some hell. No one reported him, but he went and hanged himself. Maybe he wanted to be sent down again. Prison is somewhere to be at least, and they feed you. Here, you have to pay for electricity, you have to work for food. There's no food, no work, no money to keep the lights on. Your dad's drunk all the time, your relatives don't help out, they don't take you in. That's it. We tried to help, we did what we could. He didn't want our help. So that was it.

"Andrei Sotnikov. Really strange, that one. He hanged himself even though he had everything. He was a good hunter. It had something to do with the cop, he wanted to take their guns away. How are you supposed to feed your family then? What do you eat? That was the only way that he could make money.

"The strongest survive. The ones who break down, they go. Look at how many of our people moved to town then just started drinking. Died. Some of them have gone missing without a trace. Half our people don't know how to live in town. Here you've got neighbors: you can get a bit of salt or sugar off somebody. Who are you going to ask in town? Half are in jail, the other half missing."

Masha's sister Olya went to live in town and hanged herself there, though not before celebrating her housewarming and birthday.

"We've reduced the death rate from twelve to fourteen people a year to six or seven. Even then, I think that's too many," the mayor says. "Two deaths, that would be the normal, you can't avoid that. The worst thing is that it's the young people. For every ten dead, it's only one death from old age."

Maryana

Maryana's suicide is considered a special case. She was twenty-seven. They say she was beautiful, but there are no photos left. She died on January 19, 2017. Everyone blames the mayor.

Rosa Timurovna, Maryana's mother, roams the village. Teary little eyes in a tiny face, a small red hat with earflaps. People share their liquor with her. She doesn't invite us in—there's no glass in her windows, just plastic film, no guessing what is inside.

Rosa Timurovna says, "She came back from the kindergarten, from picking her boy up. I thought to myself, Why does she look so sad? I never saw her again." She says, "I don't talk to him!" She says, "The mayor has to go."

She makes a few circles around the village, then sets off down the well-trodden path to beg for vodka on credit. Masha refuses and Rosa Timurovna leaves the store without protest. Once she is gone, Masha says, "I used to feel so sorry for her. Her daughter died—I even paid for the funeral myself, I was so sorry for that fool. But she doesn't give a damn about me, she's completely ungrateful. She's only got a small pension, the government pension. She had a nice daughter, Maryana. Nice girl, but she drank, I felt sorry for her. A cheerful girl, never lost heart, always dancing, but then they decided to take her son away. She hanged herself. Sober. They stopped taking kids away from the villagers after that.

"They came for her a couple of times, trying to take her son away. It terrified her. She was running around so scared. I don't know why they were on her case, there's others that ought to have their kids taken away, for sure. She never asked for anything. Her husband was alive, and he was a good one, even though she grew up in all this. She even had a cell phone! Other people who drink lose everything. Even though she drank, she got everything for her son online. She was pretty, and she didn't hold her mother's drinking against her.

"There was supposed to be a village meeting. It was decided that we needed to have a meeting about her. Who could have known that she'd do such a thing? She got a rope and hanged herself in the old house where they used to live. Her son ran into the meeting, saying his mom had gone over there with a rope. Her husband rushed there but it was already too late."

The mayor says, "There'd been no court case with Maryana. Then social services decided to send her case to court. I put in a word with a few people, the way you do. Said that I'd speak up on her behalf and say, 'Yes, they used to drink, but they weren't currently, everything's fine.' Ask social services to extend the probationary period for another six months, so we could keep working on Maryana, rather than taking the case to court. We were all up for it, everyone, we organized a village meeting. I show up to the meeting and then they tell me she's hanged herself.

"We had this project running, Our Village, Our Home, for making Ust'-Avam a better place. Maryana worked on it. She was a very good worker, the secretary, always on the computer. She was like an assistant to me. She put all the papers in order, made a list of all of the residents. She was a competent person. There was the one time, though, when she beat up her mother. She beat her up bad. After Maryana sobered up, the police chief and I called her down to the station. She told us, I'm going to hang myself. I said, Maryana, you've got a kid. Your baby boy, Alyoshka.

"I was walking down the street in Dudinka a couple of years ago, and I hear Uncle Mayor! I look back and see Alyosha, with a teacher from the orphanage. I said to her, Don't worry, I don't mean any harm. We chatted. I told her, Here is a thousand rubles, buy his whole dormitory a cake. She took it. He is a great little kid. Sergei, Maryana's husband, he's really handy. He can do just about anything. As soon as he sees vodka, though, as soon as he's through the shop door, he can't take his eyes off it. He keeps saying to me, Sergei Mikhailovich, I'll stop drinking and get Alyosha back. I catch him at it again—Sergei, didn't you give me your word? That's it, I won't do it again. It's been three years since Maryana died. Alyosha's still in that orphanage.

"Of course, everybody just goes, Blame the mayor! It's the mayor's fault she hanged herself. The mayor's to blame for their drinking, too. Just imagine what would happen if I tried to ban vodka."

Vodka

The vodka arrived with the Russians. Collecting the natives' tribute of fur pelts, the Cossacks would treat them to bread and vodka. Vodka and the "tsar's gifts" of tin, oil, and tobacco were used as a lure for nomads whose tributes needed to be collected—it would have been impossible to chase down the tribes otherwise.

Later, when the first merchants arrived in Siberia, they continued the custom. Slezkine writes, "Vodka was the customary refreshment, no trade could proceed without it—owing both to the hunters' passionate demands for it and the merchants' cool calculation. In theory, the selling of alcohol was against the law, but in practice, it was pervasive." In 1877, ethnographer Ivan Poliakov described how trade occurred along the lower Ob River, "First you give the Ostyaks a cup of good vodka for nothing; the first bottle for a ruble; the next two bottles, half-watered, at one-and-a-half rubles apiece; the next three bottles full of nothing but water, at two rubles apiece. The Ostyaks will go away dead drunk."

The manufactured goods were vastly overpriced and often defective, while fish, furs, and meat were taken in trade. In exchange for supplying the tribesmen with goods and collecting tribute, the merchants had exclusive license to purchase all they produced and lease the greater part of their lands. A merchant named Kobachev trading around the Yenisei River actually applied to the government to write such leasing arrangements into law, which would have ceded him exclusive rights to the entirety of the Turukhansky District. His petition was declined. The lands and rivers, as well as the tribes themselves, all belonged to the Russian Empire already.

Yura the Painter

The diesel station is the heart of the village. Electricity is life. There are three cisterns, each barnacled with usage meters, bent pipes, and green municipal oil paint.

There is a tiny box of a room just before the main generator hall. Yellowing walls, a table with mugs, a kettle, an ashtray made out of a stray piece of pipe, tea.

A young man in blue coveralls hunches over a sheet of paper. The tundra rises up from it. He drags a juicy blue line across the sheet. He touches the sky here and there, and the marks become air currents. He does it without thinking. Picks up a little more red. The sixteen squares of his pigments transform into a river, a rushing forest, the air above them. The ruddy tundra pulsates as, for a moment, gray clouds block out the light, throwing shadows down on the earth.

Yura Kosterkin is a diesel station attendant. His wife, Bedty (it was supposed to be "Betty," but the passport lady didn't know how to spell it), is at the kindergarten, teaching the children the names of fruit. They only have fruit in the winter, that's still a long time away.

"I paint what I see all the time. This one is summer. Summer is ending, I miss it already."

He maps out the dimensions. Makes a few marks on the water, and the river grows dangerous.

He usually tries not to paint while on the job. He paints from five to nine in the morning, while his wife and children are asleep on their cots. They have one-hundred-forty square feet between the five of them, so Yura goes in the closet they call the kitchen, puts on his headphones, and puts on Ellipses, a rap group from Moscow.

He never studied art. Well, he was accepted to the art school in Dudinka but got asked to leave after six months. "I was fucking around, not doing jack shit. . . . Bedty was pregnant, so I went back to her."

He never signs his work. "I remember it anyway." He gives it away, leaves paintings with friends. And now a Moscow festival has requested some of his wild, raw watercolors and he doesn't have enough of them. He had to bring his paints to work.

Three birds, one veering slightly in the wind. "Something living."

It takes half an hour to complete one painting. Yura's shift is twelve hours. A day shift, a night shift, then two days off. "We get people gas, keep an eye on the readouts. You need to dampen the diesel down sometimes, or bank it altogether. There is the pressure, the voltage, the frequency. The fuel levels—you have to keep feeding in more fuel. If something needs taking apart and fixing, you get covered in oil." There are five of them: two young and three old. It's a plum job, and stable, the best one in the village.

"I got headaches at first. From the noise. I'd get home and holler instead of speaking normally."

This is his fifth year working here. Before that he drank. In the village, they ask him, "Why don't you drink?"

"I don't know how."

"Well, then learn."

"I was drinking once with the guys in Dudinka. Five days' leave, and I drank the whole time. I ended up getting arrested three times in five days. On the fourth day, you're not even drinking to drink anymore, it's just so you can check out for a while. It's no fun anymore. Bedty took me home. She put all my clothes in the laundry so I couldn't leave. But I needed a drink really bad. I put my wet jeans on, I'm going for the door, but it's locked. Bedty says to me, If you leave, I'll divorce you. I tell her, Give me the key. She gives it to me, I try the door, but the door doesn't open. I can't get it open. I'm superstitious, it has to mean something. I went to Norilsk and got the aversion therapy.

"People around here don't think much of teetotalers. They say I'm too good for everybody now.

"She probably saved my life."

Ugarnaya

The villagers sign one another up to various manufacturing posts and tundra stations so that they're eligible for "nomad money"—a government subsidy for those who "practice traditional lifeways"—in other words, reparations for colonization. Currently, that's 6,000 rubles a month.

But how many people are there, really, who make their whole living from the tundra?

Ugarnaya Station is thirty miles from Ust'-Avam. Three hours by river, over the cold water.

The tundra rushes past, wind riffling my clothes.

Round-faced Kostya is taking a worker over to Ugarnaya. Kostya's hired his neighbor for the fall fishing season. He doesn't actually need a helper but "this way, he won't drink himself to death."

In the boat, their faces are transformed. They look relaxed, focused, precise—like men who are exactly where they want to be, doing something they know well.

The Nganasans have a verb—*argish*—it means to follow a herd of deer with your caravan of sledges. It describes a way of life. Everyone used to do this. They lived in constant motion; we stopped that motion dead.

Here's a hare running low among the bushes. A bird in free fall. Silently, Kostya motions to a splashing fish, a seagull hanging over the net, a man's footprints from yesterday.

Kostya's younger brother Lyokha waits for him by the water's edge. Lyokha is Ugarnaya's foremost fisherman. He's thirty-two but tells everyone that he's twenty-nine, embarrassed to be a grown man without a wife or children. The villagers make fun of him for watching a TV show hosted by a blind fortune-teller and following her pronouncements. He says, "They're all blowhards. It's easy to lift up a glass of vodka. They should try lugging coal."

He is the only young person I meet who holds the Nganasan language in his mouth. He doesn't speak it—there's no one to speak it with—but he knows the words, about two hundred of them, and he says them to himself, "*koly,* fish; *kobtuaku,* young woman; *lapseke,* child; *tyi,* flame." "Kodiumu teingu?" he asks me. "Do you have a boyfriend?" Then he gets shy.

Waters from the Pyasina don't reach the Ugarnaya River, and this is a miracle. It means that the May diesel spill has not affected Ugarnaya. The Pyasina is done for, Kostya says. He tells me about taking a motorboat to town and seeing dead fish everywhere along the way, carpeting the shallows. "My phone was out of battery, or else you would have had your proof."

There's only one house here, it's wide and black, and standing over a deep ravine. It has a shallow Russian-style roof and strips of tin along its sides. Beside it is a small chum for smoking fish. Two puppies scuffle underfoot. High white grass grows in front of the house, cradling a blue metal boat. A flock of birds is borne aloft on the wind toward the horizon, the birds look like a necklace of beads tossed up into the sky. Behind the house, the Ugarnaya flows toward the Dudypta to where they join. This is the third day that the water's rising; it's murky and churning. The nets get choked with silt and then the fish, spotting the nets, retreat.

Lyokha prepares to check the nets. He wears bright orange coveralls, luminescent, the greatest possible visibility.

His cousin drowned right here and Lyokha could not save him—he couldn't find him in the murky water.

The river burns beneath him.

He pulls up the nets one by one, his clever hands rifling through them. Things flash beneath the water: gold- and silver-bellied whitefish, sly-faced pikes. The fish thresh in U shapes, blood pours into the boat, mixing with gold. The slow north sun leaches Lyokha's skin, the boat, and the water, of color.

Fish blood is brighter than human blood.

The icehouse, a shining kingdom, a tunnel in the earth, is split into sections. Lyokha sorts the catch, placing the still-trembling fish atop previously frozen piles. They only managed to catch two tons this summer. One ton went to Salamatov's store. That bought them diesel. And that was it, no more money.

The other half of the fish they stashed away.

Come winter, the black marketeers will come to Ugarnaya. Their prices are much better. The icehouse fish await the winter, too.

Back home, Lyokha chops up a fat whitefish and dresses it with salt and onion. Water burbles in a scorched kettle on the house stove. The men start up the diesel generator and arrange themselves in front of the TV.

The TV tells them that a resident of Ulyanovsk was taken to court for putting a photo of Hitler up on the Immortal Regiment* website. Electric scooters have been mandated not to exceed twelve miles an hour. A farming and manufacturing forum in Samara has ended successfully, the governor gave a shepherd a prize.

The men lie still.

"What's Putin even for?" says Kostya. "It's just a shitty mafia. Putin, then Medvedev, then back again."

The night is much bigger than the house. Than us. Over the ravine, infinite stars. The northern lights—the green sun of the dead—rise up through them. An eye half the sky wide, an impossible city glittering like a long smear on the horizon. The snows are close now.

Lyokha dreams of his drowned cousin.

* The Immortal Regiment is a Russian patriotic movement. On Victory Day, May 9, its members march down city streets bearing photos of their relatives who either participated in wars or labored on the home front. Its website allows users to add information about their relatives to the National Chronicle. The movement was founded by independent journalists in Tomsk in 2012 in order to preserve the memories of the generation that lived through World War II. Soon, it essentially became a government organization. In 2015, the Immortal Regiment parade was held in Red Square with the participation of Vladimir Putin, who carried a portrait of his veteran father. In recent years, people have also started carrying portraits of veterans of the Afghanistan, Chechen, Georgian, Syrian, and Ukrainian wars.

"If he looks at you, you will get sick," Lyokha will tell me in the morning. "You shouldn't greet him. But I didn't."

"Don't dry the dishes with your apron," says the blind soothsayer on TV. "You'll wipe your happiness away."

The Old Camp

Vitya, a.k.a. Amba—which is short for his nickname, Ambassador—also lives in the house on the Ugarnaya. He has his own entrance. He fishes in his rowboat and cooks for everyone. He is shaved bald, has a brushy mustache and round cheerful eyes. He wants to know if there are vampires in the big city, like in the movies. The Kosterkin brothers think that he's off his rocker.

It takes a long time to persuade him to take us to the old, abandoned camp. He says his leg is hurting. He says, "There's nothing to see there."

We talk him into it. Amba puts frozen deer liver through the meat grinder. Then he gets into his boat and starts taking apart the motor. "The moon is waxing, so we'll have some wind," he says, sing-song, then bursts out laughing.

We must cross the Ugarnaya to get to the abandoned camp.

We have to walk across the cracked sand. Climb up the enormous hill.

The hill is overrun with black crowberries and lingonberries like little red drops. Amba eats them by the handful and mutters at the grass.

He's walking fast, we can barely keep up.

The hills are like shaggy beasts. The hills are barren.

The wind is blowing into the world like it's a conch shell.

Below, the Ugarnaya choppily flows into the wide Dudypta.

Deer antlers poke up from the grass like white branches. If you look closely, the tundra is filled with all sorts of things. A teakettle. A child's sled ("That's a grave, don't go near it," says Amba). Wooden deer saddles.

"My chum was right here. This is where we used to play. Second, third, fourth grade. Here's where we lived. I used to run out from here to there, barefoot, just in my underwear. It'd rain and I'd run in the rain.

"There were chums all over this hill. Two old men used to live on this spot with their wives, the grannies. Babushka Valya. What did you come for, my boy? Mama's asking for sugar. The other kids used to tease me: Scrounger, scrounger! But Babushka told them to hush."

Amba sits down in the grass.

"Would be good to build a house here. Just live right here. High up where you can see everything. We could see the deer if they came back again. The water couldn't reach us."

Back in the village, Amba's wife had gone outside drunk, fell, and froze to death. His children were taken away after that. He says his oldest daughter must be all grown up now. She lives in Krasnoyarsk and Amba asks how much a train ticket to Krasnoyarsk costs.

There's broom grass growing in patches of gray sand beneath the hill, its broom tails furry white. Amba pokes at the sand under his feet.

"An ermine passed through here. And that's sable there. And that's me."

How the Nganasan Bury Their Dead

Nina Dentumeyevna tells me how Nganasans become dead.

A person is put underground. They walk down a dark path. Then they get to the place where the dead live. There is a river that runs red with blood. The land of the dead is on the other side. The dead don't accept people right away; they have to live apart for three years on the riverbank. Until then, the dead see the person as unclean. They have to wait for three years to cross over by boat. Before they get into the boat, they must wash themselves with the red river water.

What is it like in the kingdom of the dead? "Almost the same as life here." Except they all live in chums. A hearth in every chum. The dead go about their business. They marry. But they don't grow any older, they stay as they were.

"It's better to grow old in this world. That's what I'd like," says Nina Dentumeyevna.

You can't go visit the dead except just before they travel across the river, three years after the burial. You should not speak of the dead. That border must be kept closed.

The border is carefully maintained. Returning from a funeral, you have to cross three flames before you step over the threshold of your house. One woman always stays back during funerals, preparing flames and plucking dog fur to throw in the fires. Where are the fires made? In summer, on metal sheets, otherwise, in old pots and pans, or in dog bowls. The living come back from the funeral and cross over the flames. They wash their hands and sit down to eat.

The dead must be equipped for their journey. They need three parkas—one to wear, one to rest their head on, and one under their feet.

Women are sent off with two untanned kamusses—hides from the legs of a deer—a flensing knife, a needle, and a thimble. The needle is broken, the thimble crushed. The woman will sew herself shoes in the land of the dead.

Men go with an axe and a rifle butt. Nowadays they're buried with a bow and two arrows; all guns are licensed and registered.

Both men and women get knives "to fight off all the rats that rush in."

Nowadays people are buried Russian style, in the ground. Before, the dead were left out in the tundra. In summer, people would make little chums and carry the dead inside on their shoulders. In winter they'd be laid on top of their sleighs, unharnessed from the reindeer.

Children were buried in trees. Branches wound with wire or twine, the small coffins tied on to them. No need for coffins for the littlest ones. Mothers sewed small goose wings on their clothes. A brand—a kirbir—same as the one for their parents' reindeer—would be drawn on the clothes and coffins with a piece of coal. That way the child could be recognized by their departed relatives, or their father, if he was already dead.

Dead children did not go underground. They turned into diamaku birds, tiny like sparrows. Sometimes they'd fly up to the sky, to the seat of the seven sisters, where they would lull the children to sleep and untie the youngest sister's sack. That's where summer fell from.

The Mayor's War on Drinking

"I tried it one Victory Day. Just forbade the sale of alcohol, on my own authority. This was back in 2014. The official celebrations began at noon and the store opened at ten. Around eleven or so, I get a delegation coming to my door.

"Apparently, I'm the Russian occupiers here. We're all so bad, we oppress them. They filed a complaint about me with the prosecutor general, about how I was depriving them. The district attorney informed me that vodka is no different from bread, salo, cucumbers, or tomatoes. We have no right to ban it."

"Do you ever feel defeated?"

"You want to know the truth? I had no idea how things really are around here. When I was a policeman, it was different. I had a clear-cut task, a mission. Now, there's just so much to do. And the things I want to do don't match my resources. I don't know how to make them stop drinking. We've tried everything. I collar them by the store, I talk to each individual. Look, Valera, here comes your son, I say, and quietly motion the kid to come over. Want to go to the store? We get inside, I tell the woman to let the kid have some candy, 500 rubles' worth. I give her a wink, she knows what I'm up to. She weighs out the candy and goes to the dad, Valera, pay up! He's grumbling and grunting, who knows what he says behind my back, but he pays. Now he can't get his vodka. Masha sells them alcohol under the table, at night. I had a talk with her. She said, Sergei Mikhailovich, I've got a large family to feed. It's pointless to talk to these hucksters about it. All of them do it. Olya Durakova. Natasha Barsukova. Yulia Steputenko. They bring alcohol in and then sell it to people. The worst part is everyone's for it.

"We wanted to bust them, but we needed to find someone willing to buy the black-market alcohol with our money. No one would do it. Sergei Mikhailovich, no one would ever sell to me again. We even tried to change the law so that just the sight of a person carrying alcohol out of the store after hours would be enough to initiate proceedings. The city was for it, but the regional government turned us down. This should have been raised at the regional assembly ages ago. But they couldn't be bothered to change the law, not for us.

"I tried arranging a tea party social for the young people. No alcohol? We're not coming. We do a special day for the elders: What, you couldn't get any vodka? On Victory Day, we give out kasha, buckwheat kasha, me and the head of the village club, canned meat, more buckwheat, and sugar. We pay for it all ourselves. One in every three or four grannies gives us a dirty look. You might have put some vodka in there. Never mind your tea.

"There's no talking to them. What else could we do? Use a stick? You can't ban it. If we tried to do that, smugglers would bring it in by boat.

"At least they've stopped trucking it in over the winter road. The police chief and I, we had a serious conversation with those guys. I told them, We will find out anyway. We won't nab you for vodka, we'll get you for vehicle disrepair or we'll catch you drunk driving and revoke your license. You get me? They got it. One guy said, 'I only brought in two bottles of champagne, for New Year's.' Champagne I can put up with. But not twenty crates of vodka! I went complaining to one of the bigwigs, and then his wife tells me, I am the one selling those guys the vodka, stay out of my way."

The Mirror Chum Master's Daughter

Nina Dentumeyevna sings:

The master of the mirror chum,
Cast his full gaze
Across his chum (across the flame),
And, booming, said:
"Daughter of the mirror chum's master,
Daughter of mine,
It seems to me

From outside, from the entrance
Come the ringing footsteps
Of the one who had flown in

She comes to say this:
That since the master of Bely Yar,
The one called Bridge-like Bow,
Has gone away from us.
A little boy
Who was not there before
Has come into the world,
Walking the deer paths,
Carrying a rope."

Hearing this, his daughter
Put on her traveling clothes,
Pushed off from a double bow,
From two bows
Stacked atop each other,
Sprang up
Through the chum's smoke hole,
And flew away
Into the air, out to the west.

As the wings of the biggest eagles
Were the flowing sides of her parka.
As two stars,
Bright polar stars,
Were her blazing eyes.
With the dawn
She came to Bely Yar,
Drawing close to the chums.
Softly, softly she bent
Over the smoke hole,
To see inside:

Bridge-like Bow
Had found himself a wife,

He found her long ago,
He got himself a son
A baby girl's cradle, too
Right by the mother's side

Now the one who flew down,
Comes in with ringing steps,
"Son of the master of Bely Yar,
Prepare for battle.
I've come
To face you.
Let us fight to the death.
Let us fight to the life!"

Bridge-like Bow
Came to meet her outside
Not far from the chums.
They raised only their bows.
The first arrows
Touched one another,
Sparked a thundering wind
That was not there before,
Raised thunder and lightning,
That was not there before.
Again they loosed their arrows,
And struck one another
Straight in the heart.
Wounded, they came together
Slowly toward one another,
Wounded, to hold hands,
To fall to their knees,
And, kneeling,
Fall to their sides.
Like cloudberries they fell,
Fell together.

Time to Leave Ust'-Avam

You get your helicopter tickets at the former medical clinic. There's no physician here anymore; the village is dying and shriveling up; what was once a full clinic is now just a nurse's station. I ask Yulia Steputenko, the one in charge of medical supplies, "Is it true that you sell alcohol?"

"Yes," she tells me simply. "A thousand rubles a bottle. My husband is ill, and my daughter's at university. We owe the bank a million rubles. I work three jobs, but it's not enough. We wouldn't survive otherwise."

A young, blue-eyed, Russian electrical engineer—his work takes him across the entire Taymyr—tells me, "I secretly went to the graveyard. It's strange there. Twisted-up crosses, posts. They put little tin birds on top. So many of those birds."

The mayor finds me waiting by the side of the helicopter and gives me a hug. "Don't write anything bad about us. It's hard enough here as it is," he whispers in my ear.

I'm handed a baby boy and a sheaf of documents. Both need to be delivered to his mother in Dudinka.

He sleeps, a heavy, unnatural sleep.

I'm cradling him in my arms. Beneath me, the gray tundra flies past. It's waiting for snow, deep and long-lasting, to come and cover it. There has never been anything but the tundra and never will be.

Snow

It came in October and swathed the tundra in snowdrifts. The river froze. December brought -60 °F frosts and the village went still, huddling by the coal stoves.

December also brought news that Nornickel was going to compensate the Taymyr's indigenous people for their murdered rivers. They would pay 250,000 rubles apiece to anyone registered with a fishing collective or receiving the nomad subsidy.

People took helicopters to Dudinka and made their way to Norilsk from there. They brought their children and elders along. They opened new bank accounts. For many, their old accounts had been blocked when they defaulted on loans. They went to the offices of NTEK, the Nornickel subsidiary, to sign the compensation contract.

Clause three of the contract states, "Disbursement of compensation shall be deemed to fulfill the company's entire obligation in regard to the diesel spill at Norilsk Power Station No. 3 and indemnifies the company against any further claims for compensation, whatsoever may arise."

Clause four of the contract states, "The parties acknowledge that they have negotiated on an equal footing."

People signed it without reading. Barely anyone understood what clauses three and four actually meant: that for 250,000 rubles per head, they were giving up their right to pursue justice and accepting the fact of their murdered rivers for all time. Seven hundred people signed: all of Ust'-Avam, and Volochanka, and many from town. Another list is being drawn up for May.

Pretty much everybody bought themselves a Yamaha 5 snowmobile and drove back to the village.

Money coming into the village means mass drinking.

Maksim Porbin was the first to die. He choked on his own vomit and his heart stopped.

Tolik Popov died next. There were bruises on his body, which triggered an investigation, but the forensic expert said the beating was an old one. It was alcohol that had stopped his heart.

Andrey Bolshakov stabbed Pavlik Stolypin. But not to death.

Next, Ust'-Avam expects its two annual suicides—"they're mostly a spring or summer thing"—and one natural death from illness or old age.

It's hard work, digging graves in the permafrost. If you believe Nina Dentumeyevna, what comes after is a three-year wait and a blood-red river, and then the other world, where reindeer graze around a multitude of chums, where fish can breathe, where there are no Russians, where the Nganasan will stay forever.

CHAPTER 9

MY FIRST WAR (MAMA AND CRIMEA)

FOR MAMA, the USSR was and will always be the greatest country in the world. She lived there for forty-four years, her entire youth. She doesn't care when I travel, she never asks me for souvenirs or even to see my photos. She says, I'm not interested.

She says, It's because you can't even imagine what it is like to go wherever you want and feel at home wherever you are. She's been to Georgia, Ukraine, Latvia, Estonia, Lithuania, Belarus—all of that was the same country.

She says, I still can't believe that that's how it was.

But most of all, Mama remembers Crimea.

I remember her stories about it from childhood: the enchanted peninsula. The sea, the warmest, the sky, the bluest, so many cliffs, some of them white. The palaces—real palaces—every one of them different. The ruins of an ancient Greek city, columns amid a wasteland. Going to Crimea was a dream for every Soviet person. People would make jokes about it, call it the central beach of the Soviet Union. But was it really about the beach? The whole place was magical, almost unreal.

Mama would ask, What did Ukraine do to deserve such luck? It used to belong to everyone.

I'd tell her, It's okay, we'll go there anyway.

(I've never been to Crimea. Now it looks like I never will.)

I gave Mama a laptop and taught her how to search for things. Look, here's some music, here's movies. Here are my articles, it makes me happy when you read me. And here you can type in "Crimea" and see it all over again—the palaces, the sea, the overgrown cliff that looks like a sleeping bear.

Mama learned how to use her laptop.

Then my sister decided she needed to show her she loved her as much as I do, and so she bought her a television—a small one, but with a flat screen.

It's easier to watch TV—you just turn it on and that's that.

And with the TV, you are never alone. Neither my sister nor I have lived with my mother for a long time now; we both moved to Moscow to work.

Mama would turn the TV on when she came home from work, and the apartment would fill with voices, sounds, laughter. She'd only turn it off when I called. I'd call every day, but just briefly. Ten minutes, twenty minutes. And then she would be alone again, and it would be quiet, so quiet.

In the autumn of 2013, I kept getting colds and depression. They sent someone else to cover the Ukrainian revolution. That revolution began because Viktor Yanukovych, the pro-Russian president, refused to sign the EU-Ukraine Association Agreement, aiming instead to bolster Ukraine-Russia relations. People chanted, "Ukraine is Europe." From afar, I watched the tent city form on Maidan, followed the fighting on the streets of Kyiv. My colleagues found themselves in the line of police fire. There are always two forces opposed in a revolution: the state and the people. The people won. President Yanukovych fled to Russia. I was excited about the Ukrainians' victory. I thought, We need to learn from them. Maybe one day we will get a change, too.

Mama would call me and say, Thank God you're not there, God protected you.

"From what?"

"Do you know how many Nazis they have over there? They would have hung you because you are Russian."

"That's nonsense, Mama."

"They hate everything Russian now, they prefer Europe, they consider us enemies. That whole revolution of theirs is just against Russia. What, don't you know anything?"

"What do you know?"

"I watch TV."

"And I read my colleagues' reporting. They're Russians and nobody hangs them."

"Because your newspaper is anti-Russian. That must be why."

"Do you really think that I'm anti-Russian?"

"They'll start shouting that everybody has to jump up and down, and call anybody who doesn't a moskal!* So people jump up and down!"

"So what? It's cold there. They're just keeping warm."

"So what?! Doesn't that hurt your feelings?"

"I don't care what the people are shouting in Kyiv."

"See? You don't care. To you, it's a foreign country. But I still remember when Kyiv was ours."

We would hang up on each other. Mama would probably go to make tea in her empty apartment and pet her white cat. Get back in front of the screen. I'd smoke and think to myself, Fucking hell, why did she have to get her a TV of all things?

My sister and I came to see Mama for New Year's. We made a rabbit with dates and it turned out pretty well. The onion marmalade didn't and nobody touched it. The three of us sat in front of the television. After the midnight chimes, they played the Russian national anthem and we all stood up and sang it, our whole little family.

The winter went on. In February, there was news that people in unmarked uniforms had started infiltrating Crimea. One day, they took

* Moskal is a Ukrainian pejorative originally referring to Russian soldiers or officials and now to all Russians.

over the Supreme Council and the headquarters of the administration. They didn't say who they were, their faces were covered in black balaclavas. Journalists started calling them "the polite people." And they really were very polite, agreeing to pose for pictures with locals, cracking jokes.

The Ukrainian authorities said they were Russian soldiers. Putin said no, they were just local self-defense groups. So what if their uniforms looked like the Russian ones? You could get ones that looked like that at any store.

Mama and I talked on the phone. Mama was really worried.

"What if they are Ukrainian insurgents?"

"Who?"

"Ukrainian insurgents. Like the ones who shot at people on Maidan. On the square, during the revolution."

"Mama, the people shooting into the crowd on Maidan were the police."

"How do you know?"

"From the photos and videos of them."

"No, the insurgents were shooting at the police and into the crowd and the police were firing back at them. And now their fighters might be in Crimea. Crimea! There are so many Russians there, everybody speaks Russian. Those Nazis hate Russians, they're going to kill them."

"Is that the TV talking again?"

"So what if it's from the TV! Those are your colleagues, too."

"Those aren't my colleagues."

"Then you're not a journalist, either, if they're not your colleagues."

Mama would hang up the phone. I would go smoke.

The seized Supreme Council announced they were holding a referendum about Crimea's status. Then it turned out that the referendum would actually be about Crimea becoming a part of Russia. Ukraine said the referendum would be in violation of its constitution. The seized Supreme Council said that the revolution had also been in violation of the constitution, because it wasn't a revolution, it was a coup. They said that nationalist forces had forcibly taken power in Ukraine and now extremist groups were trying to infiltrate Crimea. And so the task of the Supreme Council was to protect the Crimeans.

I would call Mama. Mama was worried.

"What if the insurgents start organizing terrorist attacks? Of course they need to hold a referendum. If Crimea becomes a part of Russia, nobody will dare to lay a finger on the Crimeans. Do you know how protective Russia is of its citizens?"

"Sometimes I feel like we're living in two different countries."

"I know the feeling."

We fell silent.

The referendum was held in the cities occupied by the polite people. We were told that 96 percent of the Crimeans voted for annexation. Two days later, President Putin and the new chairman of the Supreme Council signed an agreement on the incorporation of Crimea into the body of the Russian Federation. They organized a celebration with fireworks.

Mama called me herself.

"Can you imagine, people are going out into the street to celebrate! They are dancing! Crimea is back! It's returned to its native harbor—that's what people are saying. Can you believe I have lived to see this day, Lena?"

Listening to you disgusts me.

"What?"

"Listening to you disgusts me! We—we!—just seized a chunk of somebody else's land."

"What did we seize? Crimea has always been ours. Historically and spiritually—ours, Russian. The people there support Russia, they don't want to live in Ukraine."

"So let them move to Russia."

"Why are you talking like that? Aren't you ashamed of yourself?"

"Aren't *you* ashamed of yourself? Don't you understand anything? They had a revolution, they still don't have a president. We took advantage of that!"

"We did not! Crimea was always—"

"We did! It's like stealing your neighbor's goat while his house is on fire."

"Crimea isn't a goat! The people took charge of their land themselves. I thought you supported democracy."

"What democracy? There are armed men in the streets, and most likely, they're ours."

"Putin would say if they were ours."

"What, you've never heard Putin lie?"

"Don't you respect the president? You have to have basic respect!"

"What do I have to respect him for?"

"And you don't respect me, either. Talking that way to your mother. Why are you yelling at me?"

"Because I'm ashamed! And you're not!"

"You're stupid. Just listen to me. Listen. So what if you don't need Crimea. Your children will get it anyway. Your children will go there. It's such an amazing inheritance. The cliffs there are white, literally white."

"I can't talk to you anymore."

"I can't talk to you anymore, either."

We hung up the phone. I tried to cry, but something was burning me from inside, like when I was little and hurt myself or had my feelings hurt. The tears wouldn't come. I called her back. She wouldn't pick up. Fine, I won't call anymore. She can just rot in front of her television.

At work, my bewildered colleagues recounted their conversations with their relatives. I'd listen to them and I'd hear my mother—my poor, beloved mother, who'd suddenly revealed a monster inside her, greedy and shameless. How could this happen? What would I do without her? And she without me?

The photographer Anya Artemyeva came up and told me, Cut it out, now. Use your head. What do you care about more, Crimea or your mother?

"My mother."

"Then that's that."

I called her again. We talked about the dew on the window, about how the cat had spent the whole night climbing the cupboards and only fell asleep toward the morning, about how at school, the kids have the flu again, it's the second wave.

And only at the end of our conversation, I said, "So do you understand that there's going to be a war?"

"There won't be a war. Russia is strong, no one would dare."

"And just because it is strong, does that mean that it can do whatever it wants?"

"Of course. Isn't that how the whole world works? The U.S. attacked Iraq."

"I don't care about the US!"

"You don't care about Russia!"

"I love you."

"I love you."

A month later, Putin said that all those "polite people" had actually been Russian soldiers.

A month after that, Donetsk and Luhansk announced their independence from Ukraine. And the war began.

YOUR HUSBAND VOLUNTARILY WENT UNDER FIRE

June 17, 2014

The driver of the freezer truck crossed the Russian border in the early hours of May 30, 2014, through the Uspenka checkpoint. A black Land Cruiser met the driver at the border and had the truck follow it. They unloaded around 4:30 a.m. The driver doesn't know where. Some morgue, could be on an army base, on the edge of Rostov-on-Don.

The border guards on duty in Uspenka that night said that three men in camouflage showed up, turned off the security cameras, told them to turn off their cell phones. Then, while the truck was crossing the border, they also took their cell phones away. The guards didn't review any documents for the cargo, didn't search the truck, they didn't even log it. The cargo was thirty-one bodies—Russian fighters killed in the battle for the Donetsk airport on May 26.

Alerted by Donetsk Republic authorities, the truck was accompanied to the border by journalists. We learned two names of the dead: Sergey Zhdanovich and Yuri Abrosimov. Then two more names came up on social media: Alexey Yurin and Aleksandr Efremov, who'd previously done their compulsory military service in the 45th Regiment of the special forces unit of the Russian air force. That's it.

I called every single morgue in Rostov-on-Don, although it was clear that "a morgue on an army base" could only be District Hospital 1602, in the remote Rostov neighborhood called Voenved. It's a sprawling military complex with bases, transfer stations, and an airfield. The hospital has a center for receiving and dispatching the dead called the CRDD and a huge cold-storage facility with a capacity for four hundred corpses, a relic of the Chechen wars.

Allegedly, there were no bodies at Voenved. CRDD deputy head

Alexey (who refused to provide his last name) said, "We only have soldiers and only from Chechnya. Families and paratroopers have been asking, we've even let some of them in so that they can see for themselves. We don't have anyone here." Elena Volkova, the head of the administration department of the military forensics center, told me, "People have called from the city and regional forensics offices, they're looking, too, they're being hounded by relatives. We don't have the bodies. We get all our bodies through courts; I would know if we had them."

The press service of the Northern Caucasus Military District tried to convince me that military morgues only have soldiers, while the people I was searching for were civilians. They told me to look somewhere else.

Russia does not acknowledge its participation in the war in Donbas. "There are no Russian combat instructors or special forces or troops over there—none of our people are there," Putin said.

TWO WOMEN AND three men are standing near the hospital entrance at Voenved, in the sliver of shade cast by a construction trailer that's been converted into a chapel. They're going through iPhone photos, choosing one for the tombstone. One of the men is clearly a stranger among them, gray-haired and tall with a soldier's bearing. He steps away to make a call on a giant phone.

I ask them if they are here to pick up a body. They nod that, yes, they've come to collect a dead man, yes, from the Donetsk airport. "And who are you?"

When they find out I'm a journalist, they immediately ask me to get "at least ten meters back, but actually, please, just leave."

"If you have any shame, don't take any photos," pleads a tortured young woman in a long turquoise dress. There's something strange about her facial expression. I'll realize later that it's not the irritation of someone being distracted from grief, it's acute fear.

They walk away themselves, out of the shade, into the blasting noon sun. It's over 89 °F, there's nowhere to sit, just the dusty cement roadblocks. There is an air-conditioned office with chairs sixty-five feet away, but they don't seem to want to go anywhere near the hospital. They don't leave. They stay but keep their distance.

Forty minutes later, a group of five tanned men in stretched-out and dirty T-shirts appear. They approach the man with gray hair to talk over details. I overhear them, "We need an order from someone inside." One of the men comes up and asks me, "How did you find out the bodies were here?" He turns to the soldiers smoking near us. "Don't talk to her, she's a journalist." The soldiers quickly pile into a vehicle, lock all the doors, and start sweating. They don't dare crack a window or start up the engine. I go to the sunniest zone, give them more space. The soldiers get out for air, but the relatives are still too scared to go back in the shade.

An hour later, one of the tanned men shouts at us from a passing jeep, "Go eat lunch, we are still deciding!" The family leaves.

I later learned that they managed to get the body they'd come for. No authorities contacted them, they figured it all out themselves. They called Donbas directly, held conversations between Donbas and Rostov. The body was handed over under the table, unofficially.

The following day, also in secret, the body of Sergey Zhdanovich was picked up from Elektrogorsk. The head of the executive committee of the United Russia Party* and representative of the local chapter of the Combat Brotherhood,† Roman Tikunov, personally traveled to Rostov to make it happen.

Per my request, veterans' organizations met with the leadership of the Northern Caucasus Military District. The leadership earnestly informed them that there were no bodies in Rostov, it was all a red

* United Russia is the largest political party in Russia, known as "the party in power." Since its foundation in 2011, it has wholeheartedly supported the course charted by Putin. As of the 2021 assembly, 324 out of the 450 deputies in the State Duma are members of United Russia.

† The Combat Brotherhood is an organization for veterans of so-called local wars and military conflicts. At the time of its foundation in 1997, it brought together participants from thirty-five wars and conflicts taking place in nineteen countries. Today, the organization counts ninety thousand members and has offices in almost every Russian region.

herring, there was nothing to look for. Alexander Titov from the district administration press service was at a loss after having spoken to many officials. "They're not telling me anything, either. For now, all I can say for certain is that we're not transferring any bodies or contacting any relatives."

A YOUNG WOMAN in a Shoecenter T-shirt is standing in front of the mall. She gives me a silent half hug, leads me up the escalator, then to the Shoecenter storeroom. The other employee is getting ready to eat a sandwich in there, but he quickly leaves.

Her name is Lyana Elchaninova. On her colleagues' advice, she put out a notice on VKontakte* about her missing common-law husband, Evgeny Ivanovich Korolenko, born 1967. That day, I'd been given his name among a list of the dead. Donetsk confirmed that Korolenko's body had been transported to Rostov in the freezer truck.

Lyana has no more tears.

"I'm just glad he's not in a pile out there. So many bodies were left behind. I was told that they're all decomposed already. That the Ukrainian army wants to just burn them."

Lyana's been looking for Zhenya for seven days. She gives a brief summary of her personal hell.

"He left without telling me anything. One night, I got home from work—I work until ten—and all that he left was a note. He took the car somewhere. He wrote, 'Andrik has the car.'

"On May 30, I figured out that Andrik must have served with him in Afghanistan. Like, he was a buddy from there. Andrik's the one who first saw Zhenya's name in the list of casualties. I called him. 'Yeah, he is dead, but I still haven't seen the body. I'll call you back and let you know when and where you can go pick it up.'

"I waited until eleven at night, then I called him again. "'I don't know

* Russian social network with 100 million users.

where they are, leave me alone with your stupid questions.' He called me back later, 'He's not in Rostov. He's on one list but not on the other one.' Then he told me that there is no way to ID anyone, it's exactly like Chechnya, and started telling me horror stories.

"But by then, my brain had started working again. I can ID him from his hands and feet. The teeth—you can't do anything to destroy them. Plus, he had implants, I can bring in his dentist to look. His DNA. 'No, don't do that, expert analysis is expensive.'

"Then the post about the truck appeared on the blogs. How they were taken over the border.

"The next day, I went to work, but the girls could see the state I was in. They started looking for him too, through their acquaintances. Some knew people in the police, some in the FSB—everywhere, nothing. Like they hadn't even heard that that many bodies had been transported out here. One of our boss's daughters works at Rostov City Hospital 2. She confirmed that the truck had come through, but they didn't have space in their morgue, so the bodies were sent to Voenved.

"I called them. But I am an idiot and I said that it was a body from Donetsk. As soon as they heard Donetsk, Ukraine, they were all, 'No, no, no . . .'"

Lyana is calm. Her tears flare up and dissipate in an instant.

"Even if I can't have it to bury, I would at least like to see the body. Or at least a picture of it."

I called Roman Tikunov from the United Russia Party again. I knew that he was, at that very moment, accompanying Sergey Zhdanovich's body to Elektrogorsk. I explained I was sitting next to the wife of a man who had died alongside him. Tikunov told me that I was mistaken and that our newspaper publishes nothing but lies and unverified information.

"I'm with a widow who's on her eighth day of searching the morgues. Would you like to speak to her?"

"Don't you dare call me ever again," he said, and turned off his phone.

We called the Combat Brotherhood, Afghanistan veterans, soldiers. They all promised to help but advised us not to expect very much.

Here is the letter from Zhenya's notebook.

Sweetums!

I couldn't bear to tell you yesterday, I didn't want to upset you, because I know how much you care about me.

You can see for yourself how everything's going.

It's getting too hard for me to keep living this way—not working, not living, stuck in a dead end. So I've gone to Donbas, they're waiting for me, I have opportunities there. I'll tell you about it if I survive.

I love you.

I'll be on roaming, my dear.

They'd been together for two and a half years. Not officially married. During the May holidays, they'd talked about how they should figure out where they should file the documents.

"It was this absolute happiness. We never fought, not even once."

From May 1985 to May 1987, Evgeny served in Afghanistan as a gunner in a motorized rifle unit. He didn't tell Lyana much about Afghanistan. "He tried to forget as much as he could." He was burned inside his armor and hospitalized. "His mother received death notices twice. After each one, she had a heart attack." His parents are no longer living. His only relatives are Lyana, a six-year-old daughter from his first marriage, and cousins.

He was a locksmith by trade. On his military record, it says that he had a previous conviction for something. He read a lot, mostly fantasy. He played *World of Tanks, War Thunder, Stalker, World of Warplanes.* Tanks, airplanes, shooting. In recent years, he'd worked at his friends' computer and office equipment repair company, delivering and picking up orders. Then his friends stopped paying him. He needed the money for child support and to live on. Lyana says that his finances may have been a deciding factor in why he went. "On the forums, it says that they pay them. But do they really?" "Why would he go?" she asks me.

"I didn't see him pack anything. His phone never rang. The only time he ever said anything was last fall, during the Maidan protests, when the first shots were fired—those snipers they couldn't find afterward, remember that? We were watching the news and he said, 'If a war breaks out, we're right on the border. They're going to call people up and I'll be the first to go.'

"If he'd told me that he was going, yes, I would have gotten upset, but then my brain would have started working again. We would have sat down and talked about it, discussed what I should do in the event of whatever. But no, he did it all secretly."

EVGENY NEVER LOGGED OUT of his VKontakte profile. Lyana said he'd been discussing his imminent departure in a chat on the site.

The chat is only several hours long, from May 19. Evgeny's profile name was Shiva (that's also his gaming name; Lyana explained that Shiva is the god of war). He was talking to a user named Fat Epiphan, a volunteer from the Russian Volunteers/Donbas group. Zhenya had written, "I got a call about the competition." Fat Epiphan asked him to fill out a form: call signal, date of birth, previous combat experience, specialization, size, city, equipment, phone number.

He asked when he would be able to arrive at the post for deployment in Rostov. They never mentioned the address. "If you have a uniform, bring it," Epiphan instructed. "We prefer mountain uniforms. Boots, olive cobras. If you already have boots, don't get extras. Don't bring your RUSPAT uniform, either."

"I wrote back to Epiphan, and on the twenty-third, Zhenya finally called me. I started yelling at him, 'Where are you, why did you abandon me?' 'Don't worry, I'm here, we're right on the border. We've been working out, running, everything's going to be fine.' I said, 'Stay out of trouble. And please, just come home. Why did you have to go?' 'Don't worry about me, I'll call you. And if I don't, it means that we're not allowed to.'

That was the last I heard from him. After that, his phone was turned off again. They came under fire on the twenty-sixth."

Now Lyana is sending Epiphan Zhenya's distinguishing characteristics. "He had surgery on the lens of his eye; there's a crown on one of his upper incisors; a tattoo on the middle finger of his left hand, he'd tried to get it removed; a birthmark in his right armpit the size of a pea . . ."

"Roger that," Epiphan replies.

Lyana uploads photographs in which the tattoos are visible.

THE RUSSIAN VOLUNTEERS/DONBAS VKontakte group has ten thousand followers and a good security system. The administrators are anonymous. The demands on the volunteers are quite strict: only people with combat experience, twenty-six and up, only certain specializations, no criminal record. Right now, they need armored infantry vehicle crew members, portable antitank guided missile launcher operators, antiaircraft missile system operators, automatic grenade launcher AGS-17 operators, grenade launcher and flamethrower operators. Volunteers seem to come under the auspices of the First South-West Interbrigade. They're recruiting civilians, too: mechanics, drivers, command center staff, logistics specialists, doctors and paramedics.

In addition to online conscription, Rostov-on-Don's enlistment offices are signing up volunteers in person. Veterans say that a few days before the May holidays, they received phone calls from the enlistment offices inviting them to come in and talk. Only those who had combat experience, officers, and warrant officers got those phone calls.

The callers told them that they needed men to help prevent diversionary tactics like the ones that had been used in Odesa. Everything totally on a volunteer basis. They issued contact numbers for the men to call if they chose to sign up. In other words, the enlistment offices were recruiting cadres.

"Tons of people signed up. The boys were optimistic about the outcome. Half of the people in the Rostov district have relatives over there. They have people they want to defend."

The Rostov region really is the perfect place for recruitment. It's home to 68,000 veterans of recent conflicts, from Afghanistan to Georgia. Almost every last one of the local Cossacks took part in the Transnistria conflict in the Dnieper region.

It feels as though everyone here is immune to the inevitable evils of war. Rostovites are well aware that there are official wars and unofficial wars, which can be called many things: counterterrorism operations, deployment of limited contingents, peacekeeping missions, or nothing at all.

Veterans don't approve of searching for bodies. "Until the authorities come up with the story of how they ended up there, nobody's going to say anything. If it turns out our men are over there, the ones who have fought, the ones with skills and experience, those American motherfuckers will send in their army. They say there are Russian troops over there, but there is no proof yet. If all that comes out, the foreign states are all going use it as an excuse to take action."

This kind of acknowledgment is widespread among civilians, too: nurses, morgue workers, and bureaucrats. They plead with the relatives to try to understand "the political factors."

A POST WAS going around online, "Photos of dead Russian scum, rated age 18+."

It'd been put up on May 31 by a Ukrainian blogger with a warning about it being a "disgusting spectacle." I quickly scrolled through the introductory text, but it didn't matter to Lyana. She identified Zhenya in the sixteenth photo. She looked through the rest of them, too, demanding we count: fifty-six dead faces total. "These are probably the ones that they didn't bring back. Some people must not even know that their loved ones have died."

We went back to the picture of Zhenya.

"It doesn't look like him. That is his necklace, though, or it looks like it. . . . His ears don't stick out like that. The head is totally different, the face. But the tattoos. Look, these are so sharp, his are faded and old. No, those aren't his eyebrows. His are thinner. . . . He's really gotten so hairy. Shit, it is probably him. I think so. The chain. He had a necklace like that. The chain. The nostrils, the nose. Yes. It's him. It is him."

IT IS EXTREMELY HOT OUT. We're standing next to a roadblock a bit to the left of where the family was standing the other day. In the morning, one of the veterans got in touch with a surgeon from Hospital 1602 who promised to get us a pass into the facility.

He told us not to go through reception: they've recently changed the rules so that only people with special permission from the head of the hospital are allowed into the morgue, and the head of the hospital doesn't allow anyone in.

The surgeon is out, we're waiting for him. Lyana and her friends Dasha and Igor pace. Dasha is updating her on the news: Andrik ended up with a lot of cars from people who left, but he doesn't want to let go of Zhenya's until they "figure everything out."

"I don't care," Lyana says. "The most important thing is to get Zhenya back."

The surgeon returns, along with an older man in a uniform and a badge that says "Rudin" on his chest, who introduces himself as the officer on duty. Lyana barely stirs. As though we didn't just talk this morning, the surgeon asks, "So what's going on here?" Two guards watch us talk from afar.

"My husband was killed. I need to see him for myself to be sure."

"We one hundred percent do not have him. Have you checked the forensics division?"

"I asked them and they also told me that they didn't have anyone," Rudin replies to the surgeon.

"We want to see the lists."

"I don't have any lists."

"We need to get into the morgue. Please."

"You mean to go right into the morgue? You're asking me how to get in there?" The doctor feigns shock. "Who can issue permission to get in the morgue?"

"To get in the morgue," Rudin repeats.

"Well, you know. It would probably be the department head. But he's not in right now, one hundred percent. There's nobody there right now. I've asked."

"The morgue only has people who died in the hospital. Sick people, regular sick people."

"I am not a pathologist," the surgeon says. "I don't have any information about the dead. If they had been wounded, I would have known."

"But they are dead," Lyana says, biting her lip.

"There's no lab tech right now, I called him at home. He says that they don't have anyone."

"Can we go see?"

"I can't just get you a pass, miss. The head of the hospital . . . If they give you his phone number, go ahead, call him and ask."

"Let's go in where it's cooler," says Dasha.

WE GO INTO the reception office and sit Lyana down in a chair. We call the CRDD, the head of the hospital—silence. An old lady next to us asks to get into the church on the premises. The guard tells her, "All of the rules have been changed due to the situation with Ukraine. We don't let people into the church from outside anymore, that's the new regulations."

"What if we just climb the fence?" Lyana asks quietly. Madness begins to gleam in her eyes.

"They'll ask for a pass at the door to the morgue. They'll lock you up, Lyana, and you'll never find the body," Dasha tells her.

Two guards approach the officer on duty, casting glances at us. They have a brief talk. One of them naively asks Lyana, "Why were we told not to let you in under any circumstances?"

"Bitches!" Lyana screams. Dasha wraps her up in her arms, attempting to cover her mouth.

One of the guards has another quiet chat with the woman on duty.

"Are you girls from Donetsk?"

"No, we're locals."

"I'm going to give you the FSB phone number. Call them and figure it out with them. Because we were told—they said don't let anyone through. Here, call this number."

"How can you treat people like this?" Lyana shouts. "If he is already dead, what do they need him for?!"

"Just calm down and explain everything to this FSB officer. He'll issue orders to the head of the hospital, and then you . . . If it were up to me, but it's not. I was told: don't let them in."

The piece of paper has a four-digit extension through an internal line. Kuznetsov, Stanislav Aleksandrovich. We try to calm Lyana down.

She isn't crying anymore. In a calm voice, she's talking into the receiver, saying that her husband has disappeared, that she has information his body is here, that she needs to bury him. Or at least see him. But the head of the hospital is determined to not let her in.

I overhear the voice on the other end, "And what do you want me to do? I'm not even military, what do you want from me? Goodbye."

The officer on duty says, "Your biggest mistake was saying 'the head of the hospital.' It's not the head keeping you out, it's the officer on duty."

We call the FSB officer back in delusional hope. Same response.

But three hours after we took our places in front of Voenved, ten minutes after we called Kuznetsov, Lyana receives a phone call.

The man introduces himself as Sergey.

"Your husband is dead. His body is hidden somewhere—"

"At Voenved?" Lyana blurts out. "I'm here right now."

"Yes, it is here. But they're not going to let you through, Lyana. It's a classified military secret now, do you understand? Tomorrow we're getting another body out. And we can get yours, as well. Someone will call you about the funeral and we will help you with everything. Only the casket is going to be sealed."

"But I need to see him."

"The casket is going to be sealed. I promise it's definitely him. We verified the tattoos from the photos you sent."

TWO HOURS LATER, "Sergey" calls back and says that he can get the body out as soon as today. Lyana wants to go get it immediately and put it in any available Rostov morgue while she makes the arrangements for the funeral. Lyana also wants to open the casket and identify her husband.

Not a single one of the morgues in Rostov, not even the two private funeral parlors, agrees to it. At first, the conversations are business as usual: they name their price, ask about documents. "Sergey" told us that Zhenya's death certificate had been issued in Ukraine. Once the funeral homes hear that, they instantly change their tune, "Oh, did he come off that truck? We can't take him."

Some are sympathetic.

"This is a Russian citizen who died in a combat operation," Lyana says.

"But our country is not involved in any combat operations. Listen to me, I've been working in this industry for twenty-five years. You need an official identification, with a certificate. Do not attempt to open the casket yourself. You don't know who's in there. What do they say? 'We haven't got any bodies.' You should just bury what you have now. We won't keep it here, that would be extremely risky for us. The FSB could appear out of nowhere if we were to do something like that. It could even be considered a provocation."

A woman from one of the city morgues gives Lyana the phone number of a man who is working today and tomorrow. You can try to get him to bury the body without any documents. Another advises us to get in touch with a friend who works for a funeral home in Azov: they might not yet be aware of the situation.

Oleg, another funeral home agent, calls us himself. "Unknown people" have paid him and told him to organize Zhenya's funeral, promising to drop off the body with him. Lyana asks him to unseal the casket.

She is immediately called by somebody who identifies himself as a "commissar."

"There are bodies that have been lying outside of the airport since May 26 and we can't go get them. We managed to get Zhenya out and bring him back to Russia. And now you want to unseal the casket. Do you really think that that would be ethical toward your husband? I don't think so. They used heavy ammunition out there, do you get that? This way, you have your red velvet casket, everything's packed in neatly. You have a death certificate, officials identified the body. Yes, all of that happened in combat conditions. But he was identified.

"You're an adult. You know that Russia is not engaged in any combat operations. Your husband voluntarily went under fire at the address where he died.

"In terms of the body and funeral, we'll help however we can. We have sponsors in Russia who will facilitate burial. You must understand that we don't receive government support. But we will take care of your funeral."

(Here the "commissar" pauses, apparently for an expression of gratitude. Lyana says nothing.)

"Goodbye, then," the "commissar" says. "I'm sorry this happened."

"OF COURSE I want everything!" Lyana shouts at her friend. "I want an expert examination, I want to identify him, I want to be sure that it's him. But how?"

There's nowhere to keep the body. Nowhere to take it. Nowhere to open the coffin. It's ninety-five degrees out. Oleg was told by "Sergey" that they will receive the body immediately before the funeral.

Another one of Lyana's friends is searching for someone who can guarantee that the body will really be handed over to them. They get in touch with a general, who promises that if the body isn't given to them after all, he will personally accompany them to Voenved. "But only one body, you got it?" the general says. "Don't ask me for any more relatives. I can only get one body out!"

The funeral is supposed to happen on Monday. Lyana and Dasha are getting ready to go get a wreath. Lyana watches a video from the volunteers' group page. Tree branches strewn with rubble, a wounded man being dragged by his jacket, a woman with her legs torn off trying to stand. "It's not like he only saw these things on TV. He knew what this looked like. He couldn't not go."

I leave to meet somebody in another city. I come back at night.

The wreaths—there are two of them, black ribbons and roses—stand on the balcony.

Lyana sits on the couch, her face like raw meat.

"They're not giving me Zhenya. They called me this evening. They said they won't give me the body because I talked to a journalist. You."

I CUT OFF all contact with Lyana.

I wandered Rostov for two days, not talking to sources, not doing interviews, not making plans, not going out to the border. I was afraid to spook the people hiding the bodies. I couldn't leave. I ate berries at the market, dodged children on skates, there were thunderstorms.

In the roofless remains of the Paramonovsky warehouses, springs had broken through the foundation, and teenagers dove off the walls of the building into the water, then lay on the girders to dry.

Men at an antique stand were saying that even after Petro Poroshenko's inauguration, they kept getting slammed. They said it was like a rat getting eaten by worms after it grows sick and weak. "That's how it'll be with Ukraine, just like Darwin said."

Refugee women from Slavyansk, each with a child in her arms, on a city bus, "When I talk to my mom on Skype, I keep hearing this buzzing—*bzh-bzh-bzh*—and that will go on for sixteen hours straight."

"Your house is high up, it's just how the sound travels."

"No, it's because they've gotten all the way up to the gas station."

"Who?"

"The people shooting. They've blown up the gas tanks."

Women in church said the stars were in Putin's favor for two more years and that America knows that for two more years, it won't have the power, so they are giving Ukrainians weapons and bulletproof vests but no money.

Two days later, I learned that they gave Zhenya's body back.

He was buried.

CHAPTER 10

MEMORY (ERASURE)

SEPTEMBER 1 IS a holiday and I've always loved it. It's the first day of school. Children arrive dressed in their best and line up in the schoolyard while their parents admire them from the sidelines. The children have flowers in their hands for their teachers. The tallest upperclassman carries around the smallest girl in first grade while she rings a bell, and that's the first bell of the new school year.

September 1, 2004, saw the worst terrorist attack in Russian history. The terrorists took over a school in Beslan, a small town in the republic of North Ossetia. Children, parents, and teachers were led into the school: 1,128 hostages. They were herded into the gym and the gym was wired with explosives. On the first day, the terrorists killed 23 men. They stopped giving the hostages water, people were forced to drink their own urine. On the third day, two explosions went off, setting off an FSB siege of the school. The storming brigades fired grenade launchers and flamethrowers at the school, they shot at it with their tanks. Three hundred ten people died in the siege, 186 of them children.

Anna Politkovskaya flew to Beslan as soon as the terrorists took the school. She'd had a lot of experience working in Chechnya and wanted to try organizing negotiations with the terrorists. On the plane, she lost consciousness. She had been poisoned. The plane made an emergency landing and Politkovskaya was saved. My other colleague Elena Milashina flew to Beslan on her heels. The authorities were lying, claiming that there were only 354 hostages. Milashina was the first to report that there were actually over 1,000.

Novaya Gazeta opened a press corps office in Beslan. Our staff took turns working in the city for years to come. Our work slowly revealed the contours of what had actually happened. It turned out that on the night between September 3 and 4, before the investigators had started their work, bodies were taken out of the building; shrapnel, clothing, and body parts were transported to a dump. Chemical analysis was unable to establish the actual cause of the explosions that set off the siege. Explosive ordnance disposal specialist and Parliament Committee member Yuri Saveliev determined that according to the pattern of building damage, the explosions that set off the siege were caused by thermobaric and frag grenades launched at the gym from outside. Later, locals would find grenade launcher shells on the roofs of the surrounding buildings, where FSB snipers had been positioned.

The materials of the Beslan criminal case are still classified; there is no way to see them. My colleagues were able to obtain some of the documents from the criminal proceedings, the court materials from the trial of the single surviving terrorist. They interviewed every one of the hostages who survived. It became clear that the purpose of the siege had not been to rescue hostages—police only wanted to kill the terrorists.

This was later confirmed by the European Court of Human Rights.

We still do not know who gave the orders to storm the school, but it's unlikely it could have been anybody but Putin himself.

I remember the days of the hostage situation. A siege never crossed anyone's mind—only negotiations, only saving the children's lives. But there were no negotiations. Putin said Russia does not negotiate with terrorists, it eliminates them. I remember the images from the siege—Western TV networks broadcast it live. I remember the children running out of the school, into the cross fire. They would run out and fall over. I remember this and I'll never forget it. The siege bared the true essence of Putin's Russia: you can kill children in order to destroy the enemy, their lives are not too high a price.

The truth of this stood before your eyes, filling your whole field of vision.

But the government did not want us to remember. According to state-run media, because the special forces of the FSB had stormed the school, suffering losses, they were now heroes. The street that the school was on was renamed the Street of the Heroes of the Emergency Forces. The state's version of the truth was inscribed onto the map. People began to speak of Beslan as a tragedy nobody was responsible for, aside from the dead terrorists. Then they stopped talking about it entirely. People forgot about Beslan.

Novaya Gazeta was the only place that continued writing about it. We considered it a turning point in our history. We knew that forgetting and indifference always came at a price. Every year, one of our correspondents would travel to Beslan to write about the city that had lived through the unbearable, to commemorate the events of those three days in September. On the twelfth anniversary of the attack and the siege, it was my turn to go.

I walked through the city and talked to people. The city lay still in the August heat flushing through the streets. I was writing about the dreams of the hostages and the relatives of the deceased. In Beslan, dreams are more than just dreams, they fill in the gaps of a ruined world. I wrote my story and turned it in to my editor. My work was done.

But the people in Beslan kept asking me, Will you stay with us through those days? On the first three days of September, in the remains of the school, in the ruins of the gym, the relatives of the dead gather and they are joined by the whole city. What they were actually asking me was, Would you share our grief, or are you just doing a job here?

I asked for permission to stay in Beslan. My editor granted it.

On September 1, I went to the school. The gym was full. The walls were covered in hundreds of faded photos of children; every adult tried to stand in front of the picture of theirs. Red carnations covered the ground, rows of candles burned along the walls. People brought toys and open bottles of water so that the souls of the dead could finally quench their thirst. The TV cameras stood on the edges. They were awaiting the official delegation, authorities bearing flowers. Muscular men walked through the gym in button-down shirts—plainclothes security.

Suddenly, I noticed movement in the crowd, and the security all rushed over, forming a wall. I went up and looked over their shoulders. I saw five women—I knew most of them, I'd talked to them. The women had taken off their coats and sweaters, revealing white T-shirts on which they had written, "Putin is the Butcher of Beslan."

The officers pushed the women back toward the wall. The women said nothing. The cameras began their sweep of the room—the head of the republic and his retinue had begun their procession. The cameras swerved to avoid the women in white. They must not get on television.

I want to name these women.

Emilia Bzarova. Her two sons, her husband, and her mother-in-law were in the school during the siege. Nine-year-old Aslan was killed.

Zhanna Tsirikhova. She was a hostage along with her two daughters. Eight-year-old Elizaveta was killed.

Svetlana Margiyeva. She was a hostage with her daughter Elvira. Her daughter died in her arms.

Ella Kesayeva. Her daughter Zarina was held hostage and wounded, but she survived.

Emma Tagayeva, Ella Kesayeva's sister. Her husband, Ruslan, and her sons, sixteen-year-old Alan and thirteen-year-old Aslan, were all killed.

One of the officers quietly said to Emma, "You are embarrassing our republic." Another one said, "You are filth." There were more and more of them gathered around the women, trying to push them out of the gym. Ella Kesayeva started to scream, "Who are you trying to scare? Me? There's nothing worse you can do to me."

Other parents of murdered children began to gather around the women. Zhanna Tsirikhova said she had witnessed something flying into the gym from outside, with her own eyes, "That's how my daughter died." The officers hesitated, not wanting to arrest the women in front of everyone.

They were arrested outside, after they'd left the building. The women were beaten as they were arrested. Svetlana Margiyeva was hit so hard in the back, she threw up. Alongside the five women wearing the T-shirts, they also arrested Zemfira Tsirikhova for refusing to move away from her sister as she was being dragged on the ground by the police. Zemfira had been held hostage with her two sons. The younger one, Ashan, was killed by a fragment of a rocket-propelled assault grenade. He died in her arms. He was eight.

I was arrested as well, while I was trying to film the women being arrested. They also arrested my colleague Diana Khachatryan, who refused to stop filming.

We were released and the women were taken to court. They were charged with holding an unsanctioned rally and resisting lawful requests from police officers. The women asked that instead of a fine, they be sentenced to compulsory public service—they didn't have the money to pay the state. Svetlana Margiyeva hoped they would send her to work at the cemetery where her twelve-year-old daughter, Elvira, was buried. Emma Tagayeva calmly answered the judge, "I didn't think that I needed to ask permission to come to the school and take a stand there. My whole family died in there. They were the most precious thing I had in the world."

I sat in the courtroom and couldn't believe my eyes. That somebody could possibly pass judgment on these women. But the trial proceeded to its conclusion. The women were all found guilty. After they were released that night, they returned to the school to stand in front of the photographs of their loved ones. To talk to them.

The next day, I walked through the city again, but now it felt unfamiliar. Policemen, civil servants, and FSB agents kept intercepting me. They explained to me—slowly, meticulously, almost syllable by syllable—that I needed to take a more positive perspective, that the women were deluded idiots or provocateurs, that they were bringing shame on the republic. And, most importantly, that the only appropriate feeling for them to have after so many years was a tender grief.

"But what if they feel differently?" I would ask.

"They cannot feel differently."

Every person I talked to advised me to leave the city "as soon as you can."

I didn't leave. The next day, while I was at the school with the women, men in plain clothes came up to me and seized my phone and my notebook, pushing me out into the street. There, a young man in a T-shirt that read 'Anti-Terror" poured green dye on me. That's how they mark enemies of the state in Russia. They took my colleague Diana's phone away, too.

The police pretended not to see the people attacking us. They recorded statements from us and released us. We went straight to the cemetery, where there was a mourning ceremony for the dead. We couldn't get in, though—another man attacked us outside, someone whose daughter had died in the school. He didn't know us, but he had been told that we had organized disturbances at the school, insulting the memory of the deceased. Someone had pointed us out to him.

He hit me in the head, in my temple. The injury turned out to be serious, but I didn't realize that until the next day, when I couldn't remember who or where I was. I managed to get back to Moscow—the editor in chief had called me and told me I needed to come back immediately, it was now dangerous for me to remain in Beslan.

Before our flight, Diana and I were approached by policemen who gave us our phones back. They had erased all of the data from them.

"We're sorry you're left with such bad impressions of our city," the youngest one said. "Please don't be too upset. Come back again sometime."

I never went back to Beslan. But I can't stop thinking about those women; I remember them every single day. Emilia Bzarova, Zhanna

Tsirikhova, Zemfira Tsirikhova, Svetlana Margiyeva, Ella Kesayeva, Emma Tagayeva. My country murdered their children and called them criminals for refusing to forget it.

I'll also always remember the journalists who turned their cameras away from these women. I don't want to, but I can't forget their faces. They were so focused, just focused. The faces of people doing their jobs.

DREAMS OF BESLAN

September 2, 2016

Beslan is a black hole. A rend in the fabric of the world.

The completely impossible happened here, and it remains.

One thousand one hundred twenty-eight people showed up to the first day of school at Public School No. 1 on September 1, 2004.

Three hundred thirty-four of them were brutally murdered.

One hundred eighty-six of them were children.

Seven hundred eighty-three were wounded.

Nobody was left untraumatized.

Twelve years went by. The hole remains. The wind blows through it.

It blows through people's lives.

They plug it up however they can.

Most of us do it with blindness. Habitual tears, once a year. We try to move around it, feeling our way forward, risking great danger.

The government has more options. It covers Beslan in golden walls, millions of rubles, state-sponsored programs and events.

Beslan itself uses photos and dreams.

Dreams have become another dimension of Beslan's reality. They come up in every conversation. They warp in their retelling, intensifying. There are stories of classes at Beslan schools—after—being canceled because of children's dreams on the eve of September 1.

Each of these people told me theirs without my asking, unprompted.

Here are their dreams.

The School

You can't see the gym anymore.

It looks like an amphitheater. A museum in Europe. School No. 1 has been sheathed in a golden metallic shroud that is scored with perforations.

If you step back, the little holes form cherry blossoms.

The architects had envisioned this resembling a funeral wreath.

Locals call the golden sheet "the sarcophagus."

THE SQUARE IS littered in reddish debris with long-stemmed grass growing through it.

"So what are we doing? We're tossing out the empty bottles, sweeping, and that's it?"

"Are we wiping down the photos?"

It's a subbotnik for all the schools in Beslan. School No. 1, too.

The mayor, who is very young, is painting the leaning gate a dark blue.

Women are sweeping the floor of the gym, pouring out bottles of water on it. Their children are everywhere, in the photographs. A mother takes me by the hand and leads me up to her daughter. "She's the same age as you." The dead children age as though they were alive.

The gym floor is covered in bottles of water. Children look on from the walls. Photos, drawings, and posters cover the missing chunks in the plaster and bullet holes.

Plastic flowers rise up from the cracks in the floor.

The rest of the school has changed, too. Three years ago, they demolished the southern wing, which had been parallel to the gym. During the siege, the southern wing had been fired on by tanks. "All that was left was a bit of the first floor. People would come and ask, 'What happened here? Was it bombed, too?' It was all soaked in blood. Over a hundred people died there." They've also reconstructed the wall of the cafeteria, which had been riddled with bullet holes.

The parents were told that the necessary repairs were just superficial. They were promised that every crack and bullet hole would get filled in.

Every mark on the wall was a life cut short. None of that happened, of course.

"They wanted to take down the gym altogether. Or turn it into a chapel. I said I would lie down under the bulldozers if they tried to demolish it."

Rita Sidakova is extremely thin, in a dress down to her ankles. Her expression is always friendly and astonished.

Rita lost her only daughter, Alla. She was nine. In her photographs, she's posing next to a New Year's tree.

Rita can't not talk about her. She is shellacking the benches. The varnish doesn't want to soak in, you really have to work it. Then it's not easy to wash off the brush and the rollers.

"Just toss them, Rita!" Kazbek Dzarasov cries.

"We'll need them for next year!"

"I'll get you new ones! C'mon, Rita! It'll be your birthday present!"

Rita picks at the roller in silence.

"This is what humans are like," Kazbek says. "Other creatures couldn't take this much."

They've known each other for a long time. Their kids had gone to the same preschool, then been in the same class, 4A.

"Three girls and three boys remained here," Rita recalls. She recites their names in one breath, "Allochka Dudiyeva, Masha Urmanova, Alana Dogan, Asik Dzarasov, Sosik Bigonashvili, and Georgy Khudalov. And their teacher, Roza Timofeevna."

"Sarmat! Are you crazy?"

Six-year-old Sarmat, Kazbek's son, has pulled a couple of bricks out of the doorway. He hides behind his father's back, laughing. Sarmat's head is already bandaged—he was goofing around and got banged up.

"Little brat," Kazbek says.

He left behind his nine-year-old son in this gym. Tossed his eldest, Zaur, out the window; Babushka managed to save herself. Aslan, the youngest, didn't make it out.

"He had shrapnel wounds in his back, his neck, and his head. He was already dead. Or practically dead," Kazbek says, taking his camouflage hat off, then putting it back on. He talks quickly and smiles a lot. He rocks on his feet. It feels as though if he stops, he'll fall over.

"They called him number 299. Then the DNA results confirmed that it really was him."

Kazbek has had two sons since Aslan's death. Sarmat, the little brat, and six-month-old Artur, who is waiting for them at home.

Rita's husband died eighteen years ago. All Rita has left is the school.

"You know, Lena, people come here at night, too. From all around the world, all over Russia. With children, infants. They stop here on their way through Krasnodar or out to the sea. If you add up all the visitors, it's so many!"

Some women peek out from the gym.

"Hey, Rita, we're gonna get going. I'll leave the rags under the safe."

"I gotta go feed my kid, there's nothing to eat at home."

"It's time you go, too, Rita."

Rita doesn't go. She weeds along the school walls, rakes the leaves. Tries to sweep the whole yard. Kazbek stops her, talks her out of it, calls other parents in front of her, makes them promise they'll come and do their shifts.

"I think the time has come for the Lord to reveal Himself. Just like when the Virgin Mary conceived Jesus Christ—let him show Himself to us again, exactly like that," Rita says. "And with a Beslan mother! Why not, Kazbek? Huh? Why not?"

"We still have the desks," Kazbek says. "They're stored in a safe place. There's this idea. We want to re-create one of their classrooms. Rita says, 'Let's restore one of the rooms, set it up like it used to be.' You can't restore the whole thing, but you can do that much."

Kazbek's Dream

I saw my grandma's little sister. She'd come to our house and was standing there in the doorway, looking at us. Mama asks her, "Why did you come here, you're dead?" But she just stands there and stares, looking right at my son. Suddenly she smiles, turns around, and leaves. They say that you should never tell anybody your dreams. And then one day I come home . . . The last two weeks, Aslan was doing this thing. He'd get on the floor and just lie there with his arms out, like a cross. It unnerved me. Mama saw him do it first and she panicked. "What's going on, Aslan?" He says nothing, then he is fine, and it's all fine. When we were taking him to school that day, he was resisting. "Don't make me go." Our house is three hundred meters away from the school. He grabbed onto my hand and wouldn't let go. Then he kept looking back, like "Don't leave me." "Okay, all right. I'll stay with you."

They have this sense of premonition.

Dreams are like an eternity.

Three days before the attack, I had this dream. There was this really big garden, huge, like our arboretum, and it had these really little trees and then more substantial ones. There were these loggers walking around cutting down trees and throwing them into this huge, enormous bonfire. People would ask them, Why are you cutting our garden down? They'd say, It's no longer needed.

Rita's Dream

I kept seeing myself in black. With Allochka. Imagine my baby—and there we are, in all black. Once. Twice. I kept thinking that something was going to happen to me. Who would take care of my little girl? I even dreamed I was sitting next to a half-extinguished bonfire, a cold fire. I was all in black and black stockings. The sparks kept flying up and singeing me, my stockings were covered in holes. And she was in black, as well. I thought, "Yes, definitely. Something is definitely going to happen to me. I have to prepare my daughter." One day, I even said to her, "Allochka, you know how Papa left? Do you realize that I could suddenly leave too?" She instantly broke into tears. I said, "Alla, please," gently like that. I said, "Do you know who you would want to live with?" She picked her father's sister Fatya. I thought, like, "Wow, not one of my sisters, not Luda, not Dina, but Fatima, her father's sister." And I thought to myself, "At least now I know, she's attached to someone." But then you see how things actually turned out.

The Courtyard

The courtyard between 37 and 39 School Lane is flooded with sunlight. The sunlight dances off the sarcophagus and crosses over the roof of the garage, leaving no shadow. Squealing and shouting fill the air. Five- and six-year-old children are running around like crazy. A small horde of kids is throwing sticks at each other, sword fighting; one of the little girls hangs upside down from the monkey bars.

Ossetian grandmothers are holding court on the benches. They're beautiful, wearing earrings, their hair done. They're discussing a tripe dish.

A girl with a gun runs right into me, then keeps running.

"We don't do anything to mold them at all. Nothing," one of the grandmothers says. "For three years, it was completely silent here."

Thirty people died right in this courtyard.

There's a khazar* in the middle. Like a long shed with tables inside. They're holding a wake. A year ago, Magomed Melikov died here, on the threshold of the gazebo. His heart just stopped. His daughter-in-law Marina is walking among the tables in a long black dress, limping slightly. She's an elementary school teacher. It took them two months to put her leg back together.

Smoke rises up from the fire. The head and neck of a slaughtered bull bubble, engulfed by flames. The men raise glasses of vodka and "corn juice"—a local moonshine that smells like burning—and it spills on the tables. There's a special, traditional order to the toasts. The first one is

* An Ossetian hut.

always "to the great God." The hostages are included in the seventh one, "to those who never returned from war."

Not a single apartment in buildings 37 and 39 was untouched by the attack.

Four men smoke on a bench: Partizan Ramazanovich Kodzayev, Ruslan Gappoyev, Elbrus Tokhtiev, and Taimuraz Koniyev.

All of them ran into the school at the outset of the siege, under fire from both sides. All of them carried out people who weren't "their own."

Partizan Ramazanovich's wife was killed. He lives alone in a three-room apartment. Ruslan Gappoyev's wife managed to fling herself over their sons right before an explosion, "and only one of them's wounded. The eldest are huge now." Her name was Naida. First they buried her leg and then, later, "all of her." Elbrus's son burned and his wife "went insane, left me and took the other one with her." The four rooms of his apartment stand empty; he tries to spend all of his time out in the courtyard. "He was fifteen. But he was already taller than me, y'know? Captain of the volleyball team, y'know? He would have been such a beautiful boy now, y'know?" he tells Taimuraz. Taimuraz is silent. Eleven of Taimuraz's relatives were inside the school. All of them lived.

"It's not how it used to be around here. You should have seen this courtyard! Rusik would come home from work and shout up to my wife, 'Got anything to eat?' And she would say, 'Come on over, we'll scare something up.' Now everyone's jealous of one another—who's got more survivors. Who got wounded but not killed. Who got a free apartment. Who had grandchildren."

"Politics has eaten our children alive. Our sisters, our mamas, our wives."

Even those who get free apartments rarely leave the neighborhood. Only three families have moved out in the past twelve years.

"Some of my neighbors got two, even three apartments. I have two-hundred square feet to live in. First, they told me they owed me a three-room apartment. But the certificate at the bank is blank and expired. What did they do with all that money from Moscow?"

Vladimir Tomayev keeps his hands in his lap. His curtains go down to the floor, gray wallpaper, bare walls. The apartment feels unoccupied.

"I went down to the Ministry of Housing the other day. They said, 'We don't have any money in our account, but as soon as we get it, we'll get you a flat.' Nobody listens to anything that I tell them. I was right there holding the paper. Look at it!"

He takes out the documents.

His wife, Lali, comes in with some tea.

A little girl with a shaved head lies in the deep dent worn in the couch, her eyes as blue as the sky.

In 2009, Vladimir Tomayev remarried. Kristina was born. She has epileptic seizures; sometimes she runs fevers of 102 degrees. They don't have a diagnosis for her.

"It was scary getting remarried. It hasn't really worked out for us," Vladimir says unabashedly, even though Lali is sitting right next to him. "We're living together for the sake of our girl. For her sake, we have to keep living."

The victims of terrorism were promised apartments immediately. The law regulating the distribution of housing for them wasn't passed until 2011, seven years after the attack. The federal government allocated 1.097 billion rubles for this. They spent 737 million and bought 580 apartments. Where the other 360 million went is unknown. Two hundred eighty families were left without housing. The district administration calmly explains that while they did receive the funds in full, the republic's budget had already "borrowed" some of this billion and was then unable to pay it back. They also say that Moscow and Beslan counted the square footage owed according to different standards. They say: we're talking to Moscow. But Moscow says they've already disbursed all the money and there are no plans to give out any more.

Vladimir survives his wife and his daughter, Zinaida and ten-year-old Madina.

He shyly asks if I want to watch a tape. Around here, they still call everything that has long ago been migrated onto CDs and flash drives "tapes." Almost everyone has them. A montage of childhood photos, news reports, and videos of funerals.

"I don't watch the tape in front of the girl," Vladimir says, casting a glance at Kristina. But then he puts it on.

Madina in a red dress with mischievous eyes, at a relative's wedding. "They are sweet and they are nice," she says. She hesitates, she laughs. The video is choppy, the photos change quickly. "In her Snow Belle costume—that's 2003 already." Vladimir jumps up, starts fast-forwarding. Terrifying footage flashes by on the screen. "That's us lowering the coffin. That's my sister. That's me kissing the cross."

Three girls walk through the school gate.

"That's them going to school that year. So pretty. See that girl behind Madina? She died, too. She lived on the fifth floor."

"Is that my sister?" asks Kristina, who was born six years after Madina's death. "Papa, is that my sister? That one?"

He found Zina quickly. "Zina didn't have a skull, there was a hole in her chest, you could see through her." Zina was four months pregnant.

"Madina, I mixed her up with another girl. I ended up burying the neighbor's daughter, Aza Gumetsova. A month later, when they did the DNA tests, it turned out that my daughter's body was at a morgue in Rostov. They dug Aza up and brought Madina back from Rostov."

Vladimir raises a handkerchief to wipe his completely dry eyes.

"When they told me it wasn't my daughter I'd buried—do you know how terrifying that was?

"After what happened, ever since then, I haven't recovered. Take a look at those documents that they sent me. I'll move right away, I swear. I don't want to live here. From the very first days afterward, I've said that living here is impossible, all I want is to get away. Maybe to somewhere else in Beslan, maybe a little farther. Just so I don't have to look at that school anymore. They covered it up in gold—that makes it even harder. Before, you couldn't see it from the balcony, and now you can. If I could,

I would tear it all down, to be honest. Take down the photographs. Maybe if I lived somewhere else I would feel differently, but it's really hard for me to look at the school every day.

"And September 1. Everyone goes there. I'll go. What can I do? I'll go, too."

Vladimir's Dream

I wanted to pick a plum off a tree. One second, I say, I want to bring a ladder up to the tree to get the plum. Then a little girl standing under me says, I'm not your girl. I ask, Where is my girl? She says, She isn't here, I am another one. She lay there in the grave next to my wife. I'm not your daughter, she says. Don't pick me any plums. I say, Where is my daughter? She says, I don't know, go look.

Fatima

Fatima Dzgoyeva's first coma lasted seventeen days.

Her younger sister Zalina (age eight, she was starting third grade) burned in the gym. Zalina was quicker-thinking and always protected Fatya. In the gym, she told her, "Don't cry or they'll kill you." Fatima says that Zaya didn't cry, she didn't cry at all, not once, but she died anyway.

Fatima got lucky. Fatima got outside—she doesn't know how. A shard shattered the right hemisphere of her skull. When Fatima came to, they baptized her. But until they unbandaged her face, her relatives couldn't be sure that it was really her.

They reconstructed her skull out of bone cement and implanted a titanium plate into her forehead. At first, Fatima could only speak with her hands. Then she learned words. Then how to walk.

Then she got meningococcal encephalitis.

On the second anniversary of the attack, Fatima was in a coma for three and a half months.

"Fatya, how are you?"

"Fine and dandy!"

She's twenty-two but she looks fourteen. A miniature icon dangles from a red thread around her neck. She wants to put on Natasha Koroleva and gets upset that there's no internet.

First, baby bottles and a blender appeared in their home. Then a walker. Then the alphabet. Now Fatima's apartment has been reequipped to resemble a gym. There are wall mountings, an exercise bike, step machines for the arms and legs, a running machine, a posture corrector.

Three years ago, she got a phone call from the Ministry of Education. They asked her to take her Unified State Exam for finishing high school.

So Fatima went to take the exams. She almost passed.

After her second coma, Fatima was operated on at the Charité Hospital in Berlin. She got a shunt behind her right ear. Now extra liquid drains out of her skull through the shunt.

The shunt runs under the skin and leads down to her stomach. It needs to be serviced, which means once a year, Fatima needs to get to Berlin.

One trip to Germany costs 17,500 euros. "We'll go and then we'll start fundraising for the next one immediately." The longer this goes on, the harder it is to get money for it.

This year, they were supposed to go in May. They got a visa. But then they couldn't find the money.

Right now, the shunt valve is clogged. The pressure inside her head keeps building and her arterial pressure keeps dropping. Fatima shakes, she's in pain, she can't sleep.

Ossetian neurosurgeons have refused to take her on as a patient and put that in writing.

"They've refused, but they told us, 'Go figure it out. Get the shunt changed out for a Russian one.' We asked them, 'Can you guarantee that she will survive that changeover?' They said, 'We can't, but that's still what we recommend.' How could they say that?"

Her aunt Lana says that the head of the neurology department at the

Beslan medical center, Fatima Kazbekovna Dzugayeva, told her, "I'm so sick of you and that head of yours." Lana says (and asks me not to write down any names, although, of course, I have to) the minister of the republic called their trips to Germany "your little hobby." That was a year ago, when Lana brought Fatima to the minister's office and threatened to leave her there until the end of the day. The minister called a meeting and found the money to send her within two weeks.

But Fatima doesn't really do well with these visits to the minister's office.

"We sold everything that we had to sell," Lana says. "We didn't ask for anything when we still had the money. We sold Fatya's apartment. We don't have anything left."

Lana explains with horror that the shunt will need to be extended—Fatima is still growing.

There's not even a point in asking for help with the rest. Fatima can't accept any travel vouchers for sanatoriums or rehab centers because Lana always has to go with her. That means two travelers, which is hard on the budget.

"These four corners are her sanatorium. That's where this child got back on her feet, she did it herself, thanks to all this equipment and the fact that we live on the fifth floor. The courtyard is like a resort for her. I go to see the officials and they ask, 'What else do you want from us?' As though they're the ones who got her back on her feet."

"As though they're the ones who got me back on my feet," Fatima repeats. She thinks it's funny.

"She used to be a perfectly healthy girl!" Lana's now yelling at the imaginary doctors and bureaucrats. "All of these years, you've never called, you've never asked how she's doing!"

"Has Fatechka died? Has Fatechka died yet?" Fatya is laughing.

It's getting closer to noon. That's when Fatya may start feeling unwell. That's when the ambulance may have to come and help with her pain.

Fatima knows which of her school friends burned and which of them married and had babies. She can go on about that for hours. Madina Tokayeva, who was operated on alongside Fatima, got married and had two kids.

Fatima can only sleep with her eyes bandaged shut. She brings me the cloth, it's thick and white. Fatima's mother, Zhanna, has slept next to her for twelve years now, holding her hand. She says, "I'll never forgive myself if she stops breathing."

Fatima peeks into my notebook. She motions for a pen.

"Don't circle anything, you'll ruin it," her aunt warns her.

Fatima carefully circles her words, the ones about "died yet."

Then next to them, she writes, "The girl wants to live."

Fatima's Dream

I went to the school with my sister Zaya, I wanted to learn. When we went up to the school, there was a terrorist there. Just standing there. I started crying. I'd never seen any army men by our school before. When we came in from the courtyard, we went into the gym. I fell asleep in there for three days. Fell asleep for three days. Then I got tossed out, like by a wave. It was just like a wave. And that's it. That's it.

On the Other Side of the Tracks

Ella Kesayeva and Emma Tagayeva live on the other side of the tracks from the school.

It smells strongly of livestock. They have goats and chickens and a vegetable garden—health is very important to them. An Ossetian pie is cooling in the kitchen. The house looks nothing like a center for resistance, but it is the headquarters of the independent investigation of the Beslan terrorist attack.

They've gone through 130 Russian courts. In 2008, ninety-five pounds of documents traveled from here to the European Court of Human Rights in Strasbourg. There were 447 plaintiffs. Now there are 346. At first, the plaintiffs were the parents of minors, Emma Tagayeva explains. Now the kids have grown up and can speak for themselves.

"This is where we recorded their statements, transcribed them, translated them. Each of them testified for an hour, two hours. Then we wrote in a lot of things—additional evidence, everything."

The court is going to determine whether the government did everything possible to prevent the terrorist attack, minimize losses among the hostages, objectively investigate the causes of the tragedy and, most importantly, the deaths.

Seryozha, Emma's adopted son, lies on the couch. Sometimes he sits up and listens before falling back asleep.

Emma's husband, Ruslan, was killed on September 1. Emma's two sons were also killed. Alan and Aslan, sixteen and thirteen.

Ella's daughter Zarina managed to get out.

Now the boys' former bedroom has been transformed into an office and war room. Bookshelves, files from the floor to the ceiling.

Last year, the sisters created a poster holding the president responsible for the bloodshed. Photos of charred bodies. They made the poster out of fabric—they didn't want anybody to tear it. They made it in secret. Emma brought it with her to the first-day-of-school memorial ceremony. She hid it under her shirt.

"But they already knew what we were up to. They surrounded us almost instantly. I said, 'Are we getting in the way of your balloon release? We're not doing anything. We just want to stand here.'"

The police twisted their arms behind their backs. They asked them to hand over their "poster about the president." They told them that they were embarrassing the victims and creating a circus. The head of the District Internal Affairs Directorate, Ibragim Dulayev, questioned them, asking whether they had permission to hold a rally in front of the school.

"We're in a very strange position," Emma says softly. "People from law enforcement died in the siege, as well. They did. But that doesn't mean that they're not responsible for what happened. Some of them were rescuing people, but others were just shooting at the school, setting off grenade launchers. The terrorists led the hostages into the cafeteria, but they were the ones who shot at the cafeteria with tanks.

"If our boys had survived for three days, if they were still alive and then died because of the siege itself, why should we still blame the terrorists?" Emma says. "Are we just supposed to shut our eyes and ears? My daughter told me that before the siege, they were both alive. The people who shot at the school, they probably still have their jobs. And now they're just living easy after having killed all those children. They may have even committed more crimes, because that's what happens when crimes go unpunished."

Emma leaves the room to put Seryozha to bed. Ella says, "I know that Alan got out. When I compiled all those witness accounts for Strasbourg, I met a girl who told me that Alan had run out and made it to the garages. There is a narrow path between the garages, he got down on the ground and collapsed. The people who had to escape down those paths were forced to jump over him. They shot at him from out there. I mean, they were shooting at him, he got shot from the same direction that he was running in. Not in the back. He was still alive. The girl was older, she remembers. She looked at him and he looked at her. And then another boy testified that Alan had gotten out of the school and was still alive. We studied his body ourselves. Two wounds—one in the knee and one in the stomach. These little bullet holes. Not a single burn, not even the smallest one. Then we got an expert report saying that 60 percent of his body was charred and that the holes were from shrapnel from the explosions."

There's been no news from Strasbourg.*

* In April 2017, the ECHR found the Russian government guilty of violating the human rights of the Beslan hostages. The court determined that although Russian authorities knew of the plans for the terrorist attack, they had failed to prevent it; that they had failed to organize a sufficiently effective counterterrorism operation; and that they had failed to take advantage of all opportunities to free the hostages.

The court determined that FSB special forces used flamethrowers, grenade launchers, tanks, and a huge amount of artillery during the siege of the school. This indiscriminate use of force by the government was in direct contradiction with the central mission of the siege: rescuing the hostages.

The ECHR concluded that the Russian government also failed to conduct an effective and definitive investigation into the Beslan tragedy.

"I'm really waiting for it. We're waiting for it. Maybe it will make things easier to bear."

Ella's Dream

A month before the attack, I started having this nightmare. There were armed men with machine guns, in masks, right there, right under our two front windows. Me and the boys fled deep into the garden. And I kept having this dream every night.

Right before the attack, I had this dream that I was in a little bus riding up these small mountain roads. Higher and higher. The bus was full of children and I was with them. Then suddenly I realized that we were headed to the village of Lesken. The boys are from there, that's where their father lives. It's not way up in the mountains, but the road goes up pretty high. Suddenly, the bus falls off the edge of the cliff. I felt that instant of death. I jumped up. It was scary! I jumped into the bathtub, turned on the water. They say that you have to say your dream into water so that it doesn't come true. Later, when we were taking the eldest boy to be buried up there, I clearly remembered that feeling of going up that road from the dream.

Birthday

It's Milena Dogan's birthday. She's turning thirteen. Sixteen kids have come over to celebrate. On the door, there's a list of their names in multicolored pen, and next to each name, a careful plus sign. Handmade paper hearts taped to the doorknobs.

Milena is wearing a pink dress with a matching sparkly pink belt. She is an anchor for the school TV station and knows a thing or two about the function of beauty.

The guests are going wild. Daniil is bouncing on a ball. Zaur is reading a poem about a donkey who's gone swimming. They want batteries, big ones, three, hand them over. They want her blue hairbrush that's shaped like an angel.

A pretty clutch of balloons hangs down from the ceiling. Milena decorated herself.

There's a hand-cut and painted paper garland on the piano. It encircles a portrait of Milena's older sister, Alana. Alana was nine.

The younger Milena has now outgrown Alana by four years.

"Happiness is illusory, grief is real. Here it is. There used to be happiness, now it's all gone," Aneta, Milena and Alana's mother, says. She speaks quietly, the party is still going on in the kitchen. "The world is ruled by evil. I don't see any rhyme or reason in anything, if I am being honest."

The three of them were in the gym together. Milena was one and Alana was nine. On September 2, the terrorists let Ruslan Aushev* lead women with infants out of the school.

Aneta asked the terrorists to let Alana take Milena.

They refused.

Aneta took Milena out herself.

Alana remained in the gym. She died.

"If only there was something I could have done. See that wall? I used to beat my head against that wall to try to stop thinking about it."

Aneta wipes her tears with the heel of her hand.

"I have another child who wants me here. You try to adjust to it but you can't. You don't want to do anything, all you want to do is remember. And then there's this feeling that if you forget, you'll betray them. All of us lead double lives without ever really living either one.

"Lots of people had other kids or adopted afterward, but for me, it's unthinkable. I have to be positive and loving. I can't. It's unimaginable. The other day, Milenka was fooling around and it made me so happy. Then she said, 'Mama, you were never excited about anything that I did

* Ruslan Aushev was the president of Ingushetia from 1993 to 2001.

when I was little. You were always crying.' 'Do you remember that?' I asked her. 'Yes, I wanted you to appreciate me so much.' I couldn't appreciate my own daughter."

There's a quote under the photo of Alana, from Sigmund Freud, "Extreme grief after the loss of a child will subside, but we will remain inconsolable, and will never be able to find anything to take the child's place. Even if something can fill the void, it will remain strange and foreign. This is as it should be. It is the only way to hold on to the love that we are incapable of renouncing."

Aneta says that Milena follows all of the stories about the school very closely.

But they have yet to have the conversation about those three days that so irrevocably shaped their lives.

"She doesn't want to yet. She hasn't come up to me and asked, 'Mama, what happened? What was it like?' She isn't ready yet. Not yet."

CHAPTER 11

THE DARKNESS HAS NO HEART

IGOR DOMNIKOV. I have a photo of him—his hair is a mess, he has a cigarette in his teeth and a cat in his arms. The cat is stretching, euphoric. I love his articles so much, I've read them all. His kind humor serves as a cover for his unforgiving gaze, which makes the things he describes a little more bearable. He started out as a reporter in Norilsk, then was editor in chief of the independent newspaper he founded there. Working in Norilsk kept getting more difficult and more dangerous, so he eventually relocated to Moscow. At *Novaya Gazeta,* he was the head of special projects—he fostered young journalists, taught them to write. My favorite piece of his is "Lipetsk Is Risen: Glittering in Economic Miracles." It's about the governor of the Lipetsk and his friends robbing the region blind and then bragging about its unbelievable economic growth. On May 12, 2000, two men called Domnikov's name as he was walking to the elevator in his building. When he turned around, they attacked him with a hammer, breaking his skull in. He never regained consciousness. Two months later, he died in the ICU.

The murderers were found. They were members of the Tagiryanovsky criminal outfit. The murderers said that it was the businessman Pavel Sopot who had ordered the hit, but it turned out that Sopot was actually only an intermediary. The real client was Lipetsk regional vice governor Sergey Dorovsky. He wasn't charged with anything for a long time. The case dragged on, closing seven times, then reopened. When it finally went to trial, Dorovsky started having health problems, and so he never saw the inside of a courtroom. He claimed that he'd never asked anyone to kill the journalist—all he requested was "help," he didn't realize that the criminals would have taken that as an order to murder Domnikov. In 2015, the statute of limitations ran out on the murder charges and the case against Dorovsky was permanently closed. He ended up living a long, full life. He owned a sausage factory, traveled to sausage conventions in Argentina and Germany. He said that the best sausages are the ones that you raise yourself. He died of a heart attack.

Yuri Shchekochikhin. In the photo he's smiling, his smile is sweet and bewildered. I remember he started out writing about teenagers in our collapsing country. He knew how to talk to kids and, really, to everyone. They say his front door never closed—he had so many friends, they were all welcome to drop by, embrace, stay awhile. He was an expert investigative journalist and head of the investigations division at *Novaya Gazeta*. He wrote about corruption in law enforcement and special services agencies, organized crime, arms dealing, and the Russian army. Whenever his articles came out, people were fired from the very highest posts, served criminal charges. In order to better access the truth, he ran for the State Duma and got elected a deputy. On the eve of his death, he was investigating the explosions of buildings in Moscow and Volgodonsk, as well as the Three Whales case, a massive luxury furniture smuggling operation that was secretly run by law enforcement. It later turned out that the same channels were used to funnel drugs into Russia. In both cases, evidence suggested the involvement of officials from the central apparatus of the FSB.

In the summer of 2003, Shchekochikhin suddenly got very sick and died very quickly. Our deputy editor in chief, Sergey Sokolov, remembers that "in a matter of two weeks, he turned into a very old man, clumps of his hair fell out, his skin fell off, almost all of it, his internal organs gave out, one after the other." The doctors diagnosed him with Lyell's syndrome, an allergy to an unknown allergen. *Novaya Gazeta* demanded an investigation into his murder. It proved fruitless. Blood tests taken while he was alive disappeared from his medical history, and then the medical history disappeared, too. Today, in light of the death of former FSB agent Alexander Litvinenko, we can hypothesize that Shchekochikhin was also the victim of radioactive poisoning. He was fifty-three when he died. At his funeral, police cordoned off the cemetery and wouldn't let anybody get close to the grave. People paid their respects from afar.

Anna Politkovskaya. She was the first person I saw when I came to the *Novaya Gazeta* editorial offices. Tall, radiant, with silver-white hair, flying down the hall. I didn't recognize her, I was just struck by her beauty. She was born in New York, her parents had been in the diplomatic corps, but she grew up and spent her whole life in Moscow. When she was in college, she got married and had a son and a daughter. For many years, she was just a mother. She started working at *Novaya Gazeta* in 1999, when she was forty-one. Right at the outset of the Second Chechen War. For the next seven years, she constantly traveled to Chechnya. The bodies of Chechens, the bodies of Russian soldiers, torture, rape, murder, ethnic cleansing, funerals, exhumations, mass executions, arrests—article after article. Every issue featured a piece by her, oftentimes more than one. She never said no to helping people just because she was a journalist. It was the opposite. She rescued ninety-one old men and women out of a forgotten retirement home in bombed-out Grozny. She would collect the personal belongings of soldiers killed in Chechnya and bring them back to their relatives. She participated in the negotiations with the terrorists who took over a Moscow theater, she brought their hostages water. She flew to Beslan to take part in negotiations with terrorists there but fell victim to poisoning midflight. You could always tell when she was in the office—there'd be a line outside of her door, a very quiet line.

On October 7, 2006, she was supposed to hand in a text in which she accused Ramzan Kadyrov, the head of the Chechen Republic, of torture. She was shot in the elevator of her building while she was bringing home groceries. Six bullets: one missed, two in the heart, one in the chest, one in the hip, one in the head.

Her article was never published—the disk with the file was seized by investigators. The murderers were found. They were the Chechen Makhmudov brothers, who'd done it with help from associates from the Ministry of Internal Affairs and the FSB. They went on trial. The person who ordered the murder was never found. He is no longer being searched for.

Stanislav Markelov and Anastasia Baburova. I knew them both. Stas was our lawyer, he and I went out to Khimki once to see a man who agreed to testify against Khimki mayor Vladimir Strelchenko. Nastya and I went to college together, in the journalism department. She had a job as lab monitor in computer class. She would let you use the computer for longer if you needed to. Both of them had been leftist activists and antifascists, they were friends. Stanislav had more time to get more done—he fought and fought for the investigation into the murder of Igor Domnikov and stood up for the people from Politkovskaya's stories, including the family of Elza Kungayeva, an eighteen-year-old Chechen girl who had been raped and murdered by Russian soldiers. He also protected Politkovskaya herself when she was being threatened by a riot police officer she had accused of torture and murder. He stood up to people who had been beaten by the OMON riot police in Blagoveshchensk; the family of Alexander Ryukhin, a murdered antifascist; human rights activists who helped soldiers avoid being sent to war; the families of former hostages; a former soldier who'd put down his weapons.

Nastya came to *Novaya* to tell stories from the Russian streets—skinheads, Antifa, unofficial protests. She wrote about the new Russian Nazi movement, she received threats. She participated in the protests herself—in support of migrant workers, against police abuses. She traveled to environmentalist encampments. She made her way through the barricades and got footage of people who had been kicked out of the

Smena factory dormitory, she was arrested, police took her camera away. They wouldn't let her out of the cage for twenty-four hours.

On January 19, 2009, Stas was giving a press conference, publicizing the crimes of Russian colonel Yuri Budanov in Chechnya. Nastya came to the press conference, she wanted to interview him. Afterward, as they were walking down Prechistenka Street, they were both shot in the head. Stas died instantly. Nastya died in the hospital several hours later. Stas was thirty-four, Nastya, twenty-five. The murderer was neo-Nazi Nikita Tikhonov. Evgenia Khasis and Ilya Goryachev, the neo-Nazis who helped him, are also now behind bars.

Three months before he was murdered, Stanislav Markelov spoke at a protest. He said, "I'm tired. I'm tired of seeing the names of my friends in police blotters. This doesn't feel like a job anymore, it feels like survival. We need protection from Nazis, from mafia, and from law enforcement agencies, who often assist them. We know all too well that no one will come to our aid—all we have is each other. No God, no tsar, no law—there's no one but us."

Natalia Estemirova. Bright red bob, huge green eyes. Her father was Chechen, her mother was Russian. She'd been a history teacher. She liked to dress up, she was a single mother. When the Second Chechen War began, she became a campaigner for human rights. She joined human rights center Memorial and began to investigate murders, torture, and kidnappings. She helped Politkovskaya work in Chechnya. After Politkovskaya was killed, she started writing herself. We published her articles under a pseudonym. We were afraid for her.

In July 2009, in the village of Akkhinchu-Borzoi, Chechen police beat and publicly executed a peasant who had allegedly given insurgents a ram. His son, who was also kidnapped by police, disappeared. Estemirova investigated the murder and found the murderers' names. Our editor in chief and her fellow activists insisted that she be evacuated from Chechnya. She agreed but wanted to meet with law enforcement officials first, in order to integrate the police's and activists' databases of missing persons. On July 15, 2009, at 8:30 a.m., she left her house and disappeared. Her colleagues located witnesses who saw Estemirova being pushed into a white vehicle—she managed to shout out that she was being kidnapped.

Her body was found eight hours later, near the Ingush village of Gazi-Yurt, on the side of the highway. There were gunshot wounds through her head and her chest, her nose was broken, her arms covered in bruises and traces of tape. Black flies swarmed over her body. She lay with her eyes open.

Her murderers were never found. The case went cold.

Photos of Igor Domnikov, Yuri Shchekochikhin, Anna Politkovskaya, Stanislav Markelov, Anastasia Baburova, and Natalia Estemoriva hang over the table where we hold our editorial and pitch meetings. Every time a new portrait goes up, we try to hang it so that there is no more room on the wall. When you can't protect yourself or your people, you get superstitious. But then, with every new murder, the black-and-white faces crowd closer to one another, and there is always room for one more.

RUST

July 14, 2020

1.

Our first day in Norilsk, the rain smelled like chemicals. Criminal proceedings had just been initiated against Mayor Rinat Akhmetchin for criminal negligence "demonstrated by a failure to fulfill his duties during an Emergency Situation." The Emergency Situation: 21,000 tons of diesel oil spilling and seeping into the Daldykan and Ambarnaya Rivers, the result of a ruptured fuel storage tank at Norilsk's Thermal Power Plant No. 3 (TPP-3), owned and operated by Nornickel. Yury Kozyrev, the photographer, and I froze in front of the city administration building for a few hours, then headed to Kayerkan, a neighborhood far on the outskirts.

Local scientist Zoya Anatoliyevna Yanchenko, the director of the agricultural and ecological research institute Arktika, had asked to meet us in a park. It was 9 p.m. and raining. The park was an empty lot with a plastic sign reading "I Love Kayerkan." We met in a gazebo. I knew what Zoya Anatoliyevna had already told other journalists: fish in the rivers surrounding Norilsk had strange mutations in their reproductive systems. I needed to talk to her about what had happened before and after the spill.

Zoya Anatoliyevna was beautiful, wearing a mask over her made-up face, a light-pink scarf over her coat. It was cold. Shivering, we began our conversation.

Zoya Anatoliyevna told us her institute was entirely independent of Nornickel. Then three policemen appeared.

"Good evening, ladies and gentleman!"

They asked for our documents.

"Oh, Moscow."

They asked us about our assignment.

"Follow us, please. You are required to self-quarantine."

Fresh Covid test results didn't help.

I told them we were in the middle of an interview and they could wait for us to finish.

Fine.

They surrounded the gazebo.

Zoya Anatoliyevna changed her tone.

The fish really do have strange mutations, there are articles about it, but she couldn't speak to that, not being an ichthyologist. She couldn't advise us about who else we could talk to. "Those scientists—they're not from here."

She said, "I think everything will turn out all right in the end. The company will provide funding. . . . As scientists, we are ready and willing to help everyone, arrange everything. The most important thing is not to stir anything up."

"We'll definitely work it all out!"

She repeated this several times.

They held us in custody for four hours. The policeman in charge kept saying, "If I had known you were journalists, I would have never approached you."

"What a stupid coincidence," Yury said.

And that's what we really thought.

2.

What is Norilsk? It is nearly the northernmost city in Russia. You can only get there by airplane; there are no roads, the only railroad goes to the neighboring town of Dudinka.

It is a border zone—when you arrive, you have to fill out a form as if you're entering a foreign country. Actual foreigners are only allowed in with special permission from the FSB.

Precious ores lie under the tundra. Copper, nickel, cobalt, palladium, osmium, platinum, gold, silver, iridium, rhodium, and ruthenium are all extracted here, along with commercial sulfur, metallic selenium and tellurium, and sulfuric acid. Nornickel produces 35 percent of the world's palladium, 25 percent of the platinum, 20 percent of the nickel, 20 percent of the rhodium, and 10 percent of the cobalt. Practically all of Russia's nickel and cobalt and half of its copper.

Precious ores have always been here, while the municipality developed slowly—first came the Gulag, then came the factory, and finally the city itself.

The Complex was built by prisoners. So was the city. Construction on the Complex began in 1935. This is considered the date of Norilsk's foundation, although the city didn't start getting built until 1951.

The Complex encompasses the city; they are fused together.

Pipelines, pipelines, villages—those dead and those still living, shafts and mines and smoke, and the rare larch, like a ghost.

In the winter, it's -49 °F; in summer, it wanders between 50 and 85 °F. Two months of night, three months of day. While we were there, the sun never set, it didn't even touch the horizon. The light felt theatrical. At night, which was indistinguishable from the day, people would walk their dogs, teens hung out on the playgrounds. Various smokes streaked across the sky.

One hundred eighty thousand people live here, and a third of them work at the Complex. The rest either work in the Complex's own service sector or serve those who work at the Complex. For the past twenty years, every mayor of Norilsk, including the current one, Rinat Akhmetchin, cut his teeth at Nornickel.

So when did the spill happen? May 29. Word didn't reach "the mainland"—Moscow and Russia—until two days later. "Good thing they found out about it at all," Norilskers laugh.

The largest fuel storage tank, number five, burst at its very bottom. The crack, eight feet long, is visible from behind the fence. All the tanks—the one that burst and the ones next to it—are entirely covered in rust. Nornickel blames the melting permafrost, claiming it "moved," but the people of Norilsk know that TPP-3 and the Nadezhda Metallurgical Plant are both built on a ravine, not on permafrost. Although, as everyone also knows, the permafrost really is melting.

There was simply no berm there that might have contained the spill.

The stream of diesel poured into the Daldykan River, flowed into the Ambarnaya, and from there into Lake Pyasino. The Pyasina River flows out of the lake and into the Kara Sea.

According to official statements from the Complex and the Russian Federal Service for Supervision of Natural Resources (Rosprirodnadzor), the diesel never reached Pyasino, Nornickel stopped it. However, the first of the containment booms—floating barriers to hold the spill—weren't installed until thirty-six hours after the rupture. The rivers flow fast and the lake is so close.

Officials claim that an offshore wind kept the diesel out of the lake. This wind allegedly blew nonstop for two days, holding back 21,000 tons—350 truckloads—of diesel as it surged down the river. This story's repeated over and over—they tell it so often, it seems like they might even believe it.

So far, four people have been arrested: the head of TPP-3, its chief engineer, his deputy, and Vyacheslav Starostin, the head of the boiler and turbine unit. The petition to overturn the arrest of Starostin, who had only been on the job for five months, has already gathered 66,000 signatures. "This isn't where we should be looking for who needs to be held responsible," "the people are very afraid," "anyone could have found themselves in his position."

3.

Our second day in Norilsk. We head to Dudinka, the port through which metals are shipped back to the mainland, to meet with the leaders of local Indigenous nations. There are five of them here: the Nganasan, Dolgan, Nenets, Enets, and Evenks. They consider Dudinka their joint capital.

We meet with them at the Department of Education. They step out to smoke, and when they come back, they ask us, "Are you having trouble with the police?"

At the door, someone calls out our names.

A young cop, clearly uncomfortable, requests that we explain who we are and what we are doing here in Dudinka.

Two hours later, he calls me.

"When are you planning to wrap things up? You really ought to hurry up and finish. To clarify, I have been given notice that you are required to self-quarantine. You must fulfill this requirement. So if you choose to proceed without doing so, we will be forced to take certain measures. In order to prevent these actions, you must . . . I don't want to give you a bad impression or get into any kind of conflict, I am not trying to instigate anything. I am just asking you—please hurry up and finish your work and go back to Norilsk.

"Elena Gennadievna, please try to understand and don't think of this as any kind of threat or anything. . . . I just wouldn't want you to run into any trouble here in the Taymyr."

4.

We call people, arrange to meet, and then they disappear. It happens over and over. Phones ring, unanswered; doors close. We reserve seats on a helicopter; a day before we are to fly, they call us to say that policemen are boarding the helicopter, something is happening, your tickets are canceled. We make arrangements with a boat captain, then FSB agents show up to his boat, saying, "We are looking for drug smugglers. Do you by any chance have any plans for transporting civilians?" The same agents talk to the captain's boss to make sure that he won't take us. The boss threatens to cancel the captain's contract with him if he does. The head of a private helicopter company tells us that Nornickel requested that he not do any flyovers over the spill, and without their business, there won't be any business at all, you must understand.

No, we still don't.

"You're getting stonewalled," our editor in chief says.

Local journalists—Norilsk has two newspapers, one owned by the Complex and the other by the administration—also know we are here. They remember and love Igor Domnikov, who had run Norilsk's only independent newspaper, *69 Gradusov,* before coming to *Novaya Gazeta.* They tell us to say hello to everyone but they refuse to meet.

5.

Ruslan Abdullayev, lawyer and head of the Moi Dom* Alliance, chooses his words carefully. But he is willing to speak. We meet with him in his office. Norilskers believe that his letter about the spill ended up on Putin's desk.

For a long time, he was alone on the battlefield. Abdullayev has been filing public grievances against the city and Nornickel and then defending them in the courts for seven years. His reason is simple: I am a lawyer, he says, I want to bring Norilsk back to the right side of the law.

He loves the city, but couldn't say why, "Something about it just gets to you."

There are no members in his organization, but there is a skeleton crew—eight lawyers. Labor rights, corruption, ecology. "You wouldn't believe how interconnected they are." Up until last winter, the roads here were covered in a granulated slag that the city administration would buy from Nornickel. After a yearslong battle waged by Ruslan, the slag was finally acknowledged for what it actually was: dangerous industrial waste.

"Norilsk is like a sanctuary for corruption. They brazenly took their waste—which they're supposed to dispose of—and not only sold it off but got money for it out of the city budget! I mean, goddamn! None of the oversight agencies, no officials could now try and say, 'Oh, we didn't know this was happening.' They all knew. They essentially facilitated it.

* My Home

"So then what happened? I started receiving texts like 'Be careful,' 'Don't carry anything on you,' that kind of thing, like someone was going to try to pin something on me. There were anonymous tips against me—I was a terrorist, a Wahhabist, a gun runner."

One of these anonymous tips got him and his wife arrested. "After that, I doubled down."

Ruslan doesn't have any pity for Vyacheslav Starostin or anyone else who got arrested from TPP-3.

"No matter which way you cut it, he was the one liable; it's in his job description. It was his duty to let people know! I tell everyone, everywhere, I implore them—cover yourself, file reports, write, talk, do everything in your power instead of just sitting there saying nothing, then suddenly turning into the fall guy. That's what he'll be if he doesn't talk. And that is his choice. That's what all this is leading to, unfortunately—the Fifty-first Article* and an attorney from Moscow. That'll be it! Why doesn't he testify?

"If he had shown up and said, 'Yes, I started the job in January, I did this and that, I talked to my boss, filed complaints, I told them, I evaluated the facility and reported the parts that weren't in compliance, I saw that there were these risks. I made the people in charge aware, took all the necessary measures. In other words, I was doing my job and did my due diligence to prevent a disaster.' There'd be no question! And yet he didn't do that! And not only did he not do that, he's also still keeping quiet about it. Essentially, he is aiding and abetting them. How exactly were you exercising your authority? How much control did you have over the hazardous industrial facility entrusted to you? I'm sorry, but you can twiddle your thumbs all day long but still not allow something like this to happen!"

I consider the roots of the word *corruption*: decomposition, decay, rust.

Ruslan Abdullayev was the one whom Vasiliy Ryabinin, deputy head

* The Fifty-first Article of the Russian constitution guarantees a person the right not to incriminate oneself.

of the Norilsk Rosprirodnadzor, came to when he decided to publish his video.

6.

Vasiliy Ryabinin looks at us and says, "I'm not talking to you."

He's fit, in a button-down shirt, sitting behind a completely empty desk. It is his twentieth day on the job at Rosprirodnadzor. He'd already handed in his resignation, but they don't want to let him resign. A younger colleague peeks in, sees us, and leaves. The button-down shirts of the investigative committee circle below.

"Try to talk to the head of Rosprirodnadzor," Vasiliy says, half smiling. "Arrange for an official interview."

In the forty-minute video known around town as "the suicide," Vasiliy Ryabinin told the story of how he was doing an inspection of the Red Stream (the pipelines are constantly leaking, and the most unusual seepages are given these kinds of nicknames) when he got word of the spill. When they went to inspect it, he and the head of the Norilsk Rosprirodnadzor were prevented from entering the site by Complex security, who were accompanied by the police. Then they walked down to the Daldykan and saw the stream of diesel gushing out "like a mountain river." They tried to take a roundabout way back to TPP-3 but a van of armed men was following them.

The following day, Nornickel security department associates met with Ryabinin to ask him for his assessment of the situation.

Then local Rosprirodnadzor leadership directed him to only do water tests, but near the booms. They started circulating the story that no diesel had gotten into the lake—there was that wind. Meanwhile, no one had taken water samples at the lake.

"I got a group of people from our department together and told them that I believed that all of this constituted gross criminal misconduct. And that I didn't want to deal with it like this. Give me my assignment in written form. To which they replied, 'You have been taken off this inspection.' They told me to write out a memo to the agency's leadership about how I was dropping out. They said, 'Just put what you are dissatisfied with in writing.' Like that. I said that I would definitely do that once they gave me the directive to put me back on the inspection.

"Because the reality is that this isn't merely white-collar crime, it's a crime against my children.

"It's hard having kids around here. Mine cry all the time, they beg me, 'Please, Papa, let us go play outside.' But there's gas out there, and I can't shake the feeling that all this is on my shoulders, that it's my job to take care of this."

We step out to smoke. He tells us, "I'm going to quit and leave town. I've done my part, I fought for what I had to." He says, "The most important thing is keeping my kids safe. They can play outside when there is no gas in the air."

The deputy head of the Yenisei Interregional Rosprirodnadzor, Aleksandr Aleksandrovich Ivanov, tells us, "I'd talk to you, but I'd lose my job. Now leave."

7.

"The Lord probably knows how to help us people down here," says Ramil Sadrlimanov. He's a believer, Orthodox. His car is old and it's filled with icons. He says that one time, his heart stopped, and he remembers that feeling. He says, "I have a son and a daughter. I need to lead an honorable life." Ramil tells us about how he was an election observer when Putin was voted in, and "everything after that got turned upside down."

He has a bath products store. Igor, his friend, keeps hoping he goes out of business, "so you can hurry up and run for deputy," but Ramil doesn't want to go into politics. He has his Sony camera and his car. Ramil, Igor Klyushin, Ruslan Abdullayev, and Andrei Vasiliev run the Norilchane (Norilskers) Facebook group. It currently has 7,000 members.

Igor Klyushin used to be the deputy editor in chief of the Complex's internal newspaper, but he says he was wrong about things back then. What was he wrong about? He heralded the coming of Vladimir Potanin,* fought corrupt labor unions, and believed that Nornickel would "build Western-style capitalism." He quit in 2006. He is proud to have gotten out with a golden parachute: he has an Israeli passport and can leave Norilsk anytime. But for some reason, he doesn't. "It's like a nonstop apocalypse around here."

Ramil hides his car by the side of the road, and Igor and I head to the Red Lake—the Nadezhda Plant's oldest tailings dump.† We walk along rusted pipelines for a long time. New lights shine over the pipes in the polar daylight. The ground all around us has been worked over—after the spill, before the visits from high-ranking officials, they got rid of all of the little red puddles, then went over everything with a bulldozer.

The road turns. This is where trucks dumped diesel-soaked soil into the Red Lake.

Smoke seethes from the reeking earth. An excavator tosses heaps of dirt over the red banks of the lake. Instead of answering any questions, the driver taps the badge on his Nornickel coveralls and smiles.

The guys got word that the contaminated soil was being siloed in an abandoned hangar across from Ground Transport Lot No. 5. We are surrounded by abandoned buildings. Ramil takes a panorama while Igor climbs inside.

Ramil can't climb around anymore, not since he was followed and beaten by Cossacks two years ago. His back bothers him. But tomorrow, all of Norilsk will see his post.

They only got real internet here three years ago. Before that, it was

* Vladimir Potanin is the chief shareholder of Nornickel, officially known as the second-richest man in Russia. In 1995, when he was the president of a bank, he proposed the idea of holding loans-for-shares auctions. The government would buy credit from commercial banks and back it with shares in state enterprises. The banks would actually provide this credit using funding from the Ministry of Finance, which would open an account in each of the banks and disburse funds through it. As a result of loans-for-shares auctions, state enterprises were sold off at significantly lower prices than they were worth. The auctions themselves were essentially rigged. Potanin ended up with a 38 percent share of Nornickel, for which he paid only $170 million when the company was generating $3 billion a year in profits.

† Tailings are the waste produced from the processing of mined materials.

just satellite that was so slow, it barely loaded text. No YouTube, no social media.

Nornickel did the internet, too. They started implementing an SAP operating system, they couldn't survive without developing the local infrastructure. The cable was laid from Tyumen, through the Yenisei River. With that, they planted a land mine under themselves.

The Norilskers group started out investigating corruption among local authorities, who have a penchant for buying greeting cards and bouquets for 40,000 rubles a pop. They build "parks" landscaped with Astroturf; 3,650 municipal apartments stand empty while people languish on waiting lists.

Then the Norilskers got to the Complex itself.

Under the group's name there is a line that changes color. This is "the people's" air quality and sulfur emissions monitoring system. "Green means it's breathable. Orange means you can breathe it half of the time and not everywhere. Red means run for cover."

The Norilskers group became a major source of information after the spill.

But membership in the group is public.

In addition to them, there's also an "underground" almost entirely composed of former and current Nornickel employees. They call themselves "the underground" as a joke, but their security measures are anything but. When we met them, we had to turn off our phones and be diverted into various cars. Many of them had already been "taken note of."

They showed me the threats they'd received and wouldn't let me quote them. The threats were all written in very similar language: good, literate Russian, peppered with philosophical musings. I thought to myself that apparently, someone was getting paid to write these. One was especially memorable, "There is no future. Those who worry about it are hypocrites. Think of the present. The present can change very fast, and suddenly, you can find yourself completely alone."

I'm grateful to everybody who helped us, even though I can't name you. Thank you all.

8.

Gas from the Copper Plant covers the city, and I am breathing it in.

The feeling is hard to describe. A flat, sweet taste coats your throat and sticks deep inside. You try coughing it out but it doesn't help—the sulfur dioxide is already inside your lungs.

It starts raining and I get pulled under an awning. When water makes contact with the gas, it turns into a low concentration of sulfurous acid.

The next time I breathe in the gas, it's early in the morning. The streets are crowded, little herds of kids stomping around. Everybody just coughs a little. A third of the town breathes this at work every day.

They say that it used to be worse. Back when the Nickel Plant was still operating on the other side of town from the Copper, no matter which way the wind blew, the air downtown had gas in it. It's been four years since the Nickel Plant was shut down. Nornickel tries to pass this closure off as environmental accountability. Former workers explain that actually, it was because the roof and machines were falling apart and the company didn't want to pay to fix them.

In summer, prevailing winds swirl in and everyone does their best to leave town or at least send their kids somewhere else.

A white company car drives around town measuring air quality. They've been producing less waste since the spill. Even though it is most likely because of the influx of important visitors, Norilskers are grateful to the Complex for this.

9.

Minister of Natural Resources and Ecology Dmitry Kobylkin, Rosprirodnadzor head Svetlana Radionova, and Governor Alexander Uss arrive in Norilsk. They are taken to the site of the spill, to a meeting with representatives from Indigenous nations (there was a tough selection process for who got to go), and finally to the cleanup site. They are accompanied by the "right," handpicked, group of journalists. We did not qualify for this delegation. Transportation was being provided by Nornickel, and they didn't let us on the bus.

Nornickel representatives declare that they've already cleaned up 90 percent of the spill.

10.

A Nadezhda worker, "It doesn't really matter where you work around here. Norilsk is the kind of place where no matter where you go, it's a total nightmare. It's truly a state within a state.

"Building and facilities repairs at the Complex—that's a whole separate story. Everything is falling apart. The tank that ruptured—it was a symbol of the Complex as a whole. That's how everything is. Take the Norilsk Enrichment Plant—there's a few areas there that are downright frightening. Like this one elevator bay, it's been in horrific condition for years. There's holes this big in the walls. All of that sways in the wind. In order to fix things, you need to stop work. But it's just impossible.

"Right now it's all cranking along at full speed. This past year, 2019, was pure profit. The entire Complex had insane numbers, Nadezhda produced more than it's ever had in its entire history! They were doing a crazy number of experiments in smelting, they brought in all of these different materials, shipped all this stuff in. Meanwhile, the machinery was just screeching and clanging along. Best-case scenario, they'd come in and lubricate, weld something up real quick, and that would be that, back to work. What's lubricating going to do when everything's crumbling on the inside? Naturally, they try not to stop the ovens. Stopping the ovens is a big no-no, because then you have to start them back up and that is a whole ordeal.

"Imagine, you got this drum spinning right here in front of you and there's molten metal just spewing from every crack. Until there's a half-meter shell of hardened, spilled metal and all the walls are crusted in it, people will try and get away with just sealing up cracks, putting patches on them.

"I doubt that any of the smelters would be willing to talk to you. But you can ask them to show you their arms. They're all covered in burns, going all the way up to their elbows.

"So many problems, but no one says anything. Some people have tried to talk to the guys further up, but they would just tell them that what they were saying couldn't possibly be happening. It was impossible. They put us through this training course at the corporate university, and some higher-up from the Polar Division was lecturing us. People started saying, 'What are you talking about? We were committing all of these violations on orders from our own supervisors literally yesterday.' 'You can refuse!' 'Then we won't get our bonus.' 'That is impossible! You have it great over there! Everything's wonderful! Your working conditions are perfect!'

"If anything ever goes wrong, it's your fault. There are various standards, like regulations for dynamic risk assessment. 'You didn't assess the risk properly. That is your problem. You shouldn't have done that.'

"There were completely absurd cases with that. Like five years ago, a man got out of his car around the Central Ground Transport Lot and was attacked by stray dogs. He walked out of his truck and got bitten. What could you blame him for? He got attacked by a pack of dogs. 'He didn't correctly assess the safety of stepping out of his vehicle.' They got him treatment, then penalized him. Bullshit, right?

"On paper, we do have a union. No one has ever heard from them.

"Ecology! You've seen the pipes, right? There's vertical ones and then there are horizontal ones that take the gas out of the factories. Sulfur, all of those chemicals, they leave behind residue. What do they get clogged up with? The same thing that gets in the air, sulfur dioxide. They need to be flushed. When sulfur dioxide mixes with water, you get sulfurous acid. The only way to clean them is by washing that out. And where does it go after that? Where does it run off to—do you think that anyone oversees that? Nope. It's only a stream of acid. This is a private enterprise. They pour it into the soil and bye-bye. This is how things have been since ancient times.

"Yes, I was born here. You don't get much choice about where to work. There's nepotism, and really, it's really bad, it's actually one of our biggest problems, at the Complex and everywhere else. A lot of the time, people get jobs that they're simply not qualified for. They buy their diplomas, then somebody gives them a desk to sit at. The fact that they are responsible for other people's lives doesn't occur to them. They're just working and doing their job. Then they go up the ladder. As a result, our leadership is completely unqualified. It gets ridiculous: people don't understand the processes, they don't know how the equipment works.

"Not many people talk about the spill, they avoid bringing it up. Everyone knows that it's just the tip of the iceberg. That tank kind of represents the entire Complex. Like, everything around here is that rusted and corroded. The spill—what are they gonna say, that it's the Complex's fault?

"Right now, they're sending in people to clean up the spill. They've finally started doing the reagents. They pour those reagents into the water and that will supposedly restore it. Everybody who could have possibly been sent out was assigned to it. And everyone knows that what they had them doing for the first several days was just total nonsense. I mean, not total nonsense—picking up trash, cleaning up because the big bosses were coming, that's good. But when you're on top of a true ecological catastrophe and you're just walking around picking up bottles, it's . . . I don't know.

"They aren't scared of anyone else, but when Potanin is coming, you better clean up."

11.

"The people here are so beaten down that the only problem that they can see is the price of fish going up. What are you supposed to do with these people? Every nation deserves the government and conditions they live under."

We meet Vasiliy Ryabinin the day after our first failed attempt to interview him. With our phones off, almost at night.

He started working at Rosprirodnadzor on May 20, as the deputy head. He and his boss started by planning their first inspection together, of the Red Stream, which runs by the Red Lake and into the Daldykan River.

The prosecutor who they were planning the inspection with told them, "You're aiming too high. They won't let you work."

"I thought that if they're going to put pressure on me, I could leave after six months, at the end of my trial period. But that isn't how it shook out."

He says, "My decision has cost my family around 400,000 rubles of my six-month salary—not enough to sell out your motherland." He laughs.

One day later, he quits. They'd refused to fire him, so Ryabinin was forced to remind them that he was on his trial period. He understands perfectly well how the system works, and that is the greatest source of his strength.

Ryabinin is a company man. His first job was at the Mining and Metallurgical Research Center, a scientific institute owned by Nornickel. Then, when the plant didn't need science anymore and the scientists were "optimized" away, he went over to Rostechnadzor, the Federal Service for the Supervision of Environment, Technology and Nuclear Management, where he levied fines against Nornickel. Then he got hired at Nornickel's Security Department. He says, "They wanted to get rid of me at Rostechnadzor, so I got rid of myself." He says, "I was following the money." Six years later, he was told that they no longer needed him at the Security Department, so he quit. Would he have quit if they hadn't suggested he leave? It's unclear.

"Why am I quitting now? Because I've been relieved of all of my duties. [Rosprirodnadzor head Svetlana] Radionova said, 'Thanks to you, I'm a YouTube celebrity. If you're so smart, why don't you think of something to do and do that?' I told her, 'I want to do an inspection of the left bank of Lake Pyasino.' She says, 'You'll need a helicopter. We'll get you one; go and take samples.' I prepared in earnest, planned out the route, the sample capacity. Then they told me, 'We don't have a helicopter, take a watercraft. You said you'd be willing to go on foot, so then go.' They dropped me off there, I walked six miles through those swamps. A helicopter flew over me. . . . The truth is that other people's opinions hold sway over you, even if you're convinced of something. You start doubting yourself. I had to find that diesel, to prove it was there, first of all, to myself. It smelled like it, but a smell isn't enough.

"Then, when they were taking me back up the left branch of the river, I stuck my head out of the boat and I saw it. Now I'm sure I was right. I managed to get a few photos. That's Lake Pyasino in the one on the right, the left bank, with the tributary from the Ambarnaya River. Along the shoreline, it's covered in a ten-centimeter-thick layer of diesel. That's on the other side of the booms. If the diesel passed through there, that means it's long gone downstream.

"All sorts of people do the inspections. Really, all kinds. You couldn't say that everyone is taking bribes. Although of course I know people who do. They don't really get anything good out of it. Because it's the Complex. One wrong move and you're on the hook. If I hadn't done anything, I'd be on the hook, too. We spilled so much diesel, it's unbelievable. So where were you when that happened? It's not like they don't know the legal bylaws and ins and outs. They'll say that if you don't want to do it our way, some random guy will file a complaint and they'll start checking out how well you've been doing all your inspections. 'You signed off on that thing, remember?' They'll run an audit and it will turn out that you weren't doing your due diligence after all."

I ask him how he feels about the people who have been jailed, taking the fall for this spill. He says, "I'll tell you a story. Then maybe you can tell me how I'm supposed to feel. I oversaw gas at TPP-3. They have a gas distribution station. You have to open these flues there, little pipes with knobs on them, for venting excess gas into the atmosphere. The flues are supposed to point up from the roof. I got there and there were no flues. I said, 'What the hell, guys? What's going on here? Gas is accumulating—a spark goes off, God forbid, and all this goes boom.' I wrote out a directive. Then I came back to see whether they had complied. They're like, 'Yes, yes, of course, we did everything!' This was the director of TPP-3, understand? Not just some gas service supervisor but the director himself! He goes, 'Let's have some coffee. You can see everything out of the window of my office. We'll take a look from up there.' I tell him, 'I don't think so, pal. That's not going to work on me.' So we climb up in there. I look up from below—yep, there's the flues. . . . I climb the ladder up to the third story. The director is climbing behind me.

"Then something got into me and I reached out and jerked on a flue. It came off in my hand! Understand? They had just stuck them into the snow! They'd soldered some legs onto them and stuck them straight in the snow! Can you imagine how I felt?

"I wrote out the maximum fine, the highest possible amount for that violation. What am I supposed to feel about that guy now? I don't know! Can you imagine what would have happened if I hadn't checked? If I had said, 'Okay, let's have some coffee'? How are you supposed to trust these people? I'd be the one charged with negligence. When there's a gas explosion, it rips away all of your clothes and only your body flies up in the air. You end up a naked corpse on the ground."

Vasiliy slaps his hand on the torn-up wall. He says, "I don't know if I'm doing the right thing talking to you. You're going to turn me into some kind of hero. I haven't decided whether I want to be one. People are scared of heroes. No one around here needs them."

12.

The Security Department, or SD, is a small special services division within Nornickel. It used to be called the Directorate on Economic Safety and Order, and the old acronym, DEBiR, is what people still threaten each other with in Norilsk.

The department has eighty people. Most of them are former FSB or police. Sometimes there'll be more peculiar personnel. Like when the wife of the deputy head of the local FSB used to work there. "She'd always get very good bonuses."

Although the Security Department is supposed to be concerned with the protection of the facilities and the prevention of theft, in reality, it does just about everything. There are a lot of different departments within the SD. For example, the department for "monitoring the situation"—it's a factory town and nobody needs a revolution. The department for internal regulation, hunting for bribe takers and embezzlers. There's a department for the safety of technological processes, monitoring production errors.

SD associates monitor social media and forums, making sure no one posts photos from the facilities, punishing people who do.

There are also two mechanisms for external monitoring.

Friends from the FSB and the Ministry of Internal Affairs (MIA) inspect mail and tap phones. The SD works closely with law enforcement. They also join forces with them to provide security for visiting VIPs.

Armed men from this department were the ones who kicked Vasiliy Ryabinin and his boss out of the spill site.

This department is also responsible for approving all water- and soil-quality tests before they can be transported out of Norilsk. I'm told this multiple times by multiple people—geologists, policemen, former SD associates. They explain how it works: you go to 4A Ordzhonikidze Street, where the department is headquartered, hand in your samples, get back a stamp on your documents and special seals on the bottles, then, after that, the transport carrier police will approve the shipment.

No way, I think to myself.

They say, "You still don't understand where you are."

13.

The city says: Foreign interests lie in the Arctic. Russia has already messed up so bad, they can't wait to take advantage of that. Better not draw more attention to the spill.

The city says: Our wildlife sanctuaries are doing well thanks to Nornickel. Why would anyone want to bite the hand that feeds them?

The city says: Those who aren't friends with the Nickels aren't friends with common sense.

The city says: If there is no Complex, there is no us.

The city says: Why did you even come here?

14.

A cramped little apartment with homemade furniture. Vasiliy Ryabinin's wife, Irina, is delicate, blue-eyed, wearing an orange shirt that says "Mama." She picks up the walkie-talkie and says, in English, "Arseny, Vsevolod, *come home now*!" Two young boys, seven-year-old twins, run in from the courtyard, which is filled with pipes gushing fountains of water. Two-year-old Adelaida is playing doggy and Papa is scratching behind her ear.

"They're still so little, they don't know anything. They think I'm a hockey coach."

I ask Irina how she is dealing with everything and she says, "I'm fine. For better or worse. I took a vow to support him."

Vasiliy quit. He had lasted a month. In the morning, he has a fever, but he still asks, "So, are we going?"

We get to the railroad juncture by the Oktyabrsky mine and, climbing under the pipes (they are everywhere), we trail off into the bushes.

A man stands on the roof of his car like a black signpost. He looks in our direction but doesn't see us. He doesn't move. Next to him, a blue hut, the first security checkpoint. Behind him, the road that leads to the tailings dump of the Talnakh Enrichment Factory (TEF). The dump has only been operating since 2017, but it's already surrounded by lakes of every color imaginable, from azure to yellow. We've seen them on Google Images. Vasiliy believes that liquid is seeping out of the tailings dam. We are trying to walk to those lakes.

The man on the roof of the car raises his hand with the binoculars.

We were expecting security, but not like this.

"This isn't normal," Vasiliy says.

We turn to penetrate deeper into the tundra. There are three of us: me, Vasiliy, and his sister Maria—Masha. She came from Achinsk to take the kids but came out with us because she didn't want to leave her brother alone. She's two years younger than him, her hair is in braids, she laughs easily. Vasiliy's temperature's rising and she is making sure he doesn't forget to drink water. We have five miles to go through the forest and tundra.

The Complex feels far away. A partridge flies out from under a larch and we see its nest blanketed in colorful feathers. A rabbit hops over a clump of ore.

The tundra is carpeted in flowers. Very strange plants—like flowers from the temperate zone, but with very short stems, and then completely unfamiliar ones. Long-tailed blossoms twist out of hairy green stems, blue forget-me-nots, menacing wild rosemary. Chartreuse polar poppies. Mosquitoes swarm us, blocking out light. We trudge up and down hillsides, bushwhack through underbrush, jump over streams. Masha sticks a landing and says, "That's how I'm teaching my kids to do grand battements." She's a fitness trainer; she teaches cheerleading and tells us about the tricks.

We pass three more security checkpoints. Vasiliy's mood deteriorates. "There didn't used to be so many." He pulls a gray cover over his orange backpack and quickly mumbles something into his walkie-talkie.

We advance along the right bank of the Kharayelakh River.

At a certain point, we turn into the woods and walk along a strange, murky stream pouring out of a lake.

The lake is dead. Trees stick out of it like telephone poles—no branches, no bark. A strip of dead bushes along the shore; dead and dying trees, leafless, but with their bark still on. A milky slick shivering on the water.

We hear engines but can't tell where the sound is coming from.

We screw Vasiliy's camera into the drone. And in a clearing, we release it. It quickly becomes invisible in the low blue of the sky.

Vasiliy laughs.

The sound is coming from a black jeep on the road. It's very close—a couple hundred yards away—but the thick underbrush would make it quite hard to get through to us. We run, away from the car, away from the road.

We finally catch our breath half a mile from our destination. We laugh.

A couple of hours later, Vasiliy writes to me, "Come right away."

We look at the photos together.

And then we see it.

15.

What we see is three ramps on the edge of the tailings pond. Little booths on two of them—one yellow, one orange. Hoses threaded through both of the booths. One end of each hose is rising up from the mirroring surface of the pond, and the other is trailing over the edge and across the road. The road is dug up, covered in heaps of turned-over dirt. We see the car that had scared us.

There are white bursts where the hoses touch down on the tundra. The bursts birth a stream that pours down into the dead lake. And out of the lake into the Kharayelakh. Which flows into Lake Pyasino.

"That's waste. Fuck, shit! That's waste," Vasiliy says. "They're dumping *right now*, after everything!"

He goes through the photos. "The resolution is bad, we can't prove anything."

He opens the Nornickel *Atlas of Raw Minerals, Technological Manufacturing Products and Commercial Production*, muttering, "incredible book," and reads aloud, "Concentrated waste tailings are comprised of 0.068 percent copper, 0.53 percent nickel, 37.7 percent iron, 0.021 percent cobalt, and 18 percent sulfur." He says that when they are exposed to oxygen, these elements change into their ionic forms and could intermix with water.

He opens *Metal Production Beyond the Arctic Circle*, finds the chapter on the TEF, and reads, "The following substances are used in flotation processes for concentrates: aerofloat, pine oil, sodium bisulfate, xanthate, and active surfactants that are mixed with tailings in tailings storage facilities."

And then they leave the tailings pond through a hose leading into the tundra. Into the dead lake, the murky stream, the Kharayelakh River, Lake Pyasino, and the Kara Sea.

He says, "We have to go back there."

16.

Who is we?

We have to get back to the dump site. Three people are really, truly not enough; just one car from the SD could stop us.

There is the underground, which Vasiliy doesn't trust. "Someone will blab. As soon as word gets out, they'll switch off the pumps."

Vasiliy meets with Ruslan Abdullayev next to his building. The sprinklers on TPP-1's pipes are spraying Dolgoe Lake water into the air. Wet young women stroll down the pipes filled with industrial-process water. Vasiliy wants help writing up a report, and Ruslan wants to know, "What report? What did you find?"

Vasiliy says, "I'll tell you later. But I need support."

"You'll get it."

He goes home. The children are sleeping, exhausted from running through bushes. "They have a whole army down there," Masha says.

Vasiliy bends his fingers back, silently moving his lips. He writes the plan out on a sheet of paper.

"We need time. We need people."

"Goddamn revolutionaries," Masha says. "I'm coming with you, brother."

Irina's eyes become huge. She nods, saying nothing.

17.

The Greenpeace activists fly in early in the morning. Yosef Kogotko, Lena Sakirko, and their photographer, Dima. Yosef collects samples. He's from Saint Petersburg, he studied forestry. He's almost forty but passes for twenty because of his smile and his shaggy curls. Everyone calls him Yos. He's a raw-foodist, doesn't have a car or smoke. He says that Greenpeace is his family.

Lena Sakirko studied to be a translator, she knows three languages. She got involved with Greenpeace after translating for the activists who were held in custody in Murmansk. She's been a volunteer firefighter, putting out wildfires. She's soft-spoken and does her eye makeup even for going out in the field.

They pack in a rented apartment. Respirator masks, yellow protective coveralls, gloves. Yos instructs us, "We take off the caps, rinse the bottle three to five times, fill it up to the top, and put in the foil stopper. Then we screw the cap back on over the foil. Meanwhile, we're taking photos and videos. The samples from the bottom are taken from the bow of the boat. For soil, we make a square with five points on it with a meter between them. We dig everything between the five points into one heap and mix it together. Remove the rocks and root fragments . . ."

To choose our testing sites, we look at satellite images, studying the rivers, the lake, and the wind. We choose eight: where the Ambarnaya River flows into Lake Pyasino; a creek off the Pyasino River; and eddies and points that have "visible stagnating matter along the stream." The most distant point is a fishing outpost called Kresty. There are 112 miles between the first and last sites. We also need to take a control sample out of the clean tributaries that flow into the Pyasina. The rest of the water and soil will be compared with it.

"The amount we need to get done takes my breath away," Yos says. "These will be the first samples ever taken from the Pyasina, the very first ones. We're going to find out the truth."

18.

We are already loading onto the boats when a car drives up. Our captains are led away. Then they come back with people who introduce themselves as the transit police.

There are two of them. One polite and one intentionally rude. "They don't have a license to operate a small craft. No permits or pennant numbers. How did you find these so-called operators?"

"We have everything," the captains' boss says while continuing to help us load in. "I don't understand what kind of country we're living in here."

"Respected citizens, you seem discouraged, you've traveled here from another region and came across such dishonest people. If only just one of *you* could have aided the investigation . . ."

The policeman cracks up.

The captains are held for six hours and fined. Afterward, they refuse to take us.

19.

But we go anyway. It's like a movie.

We meet a man in a grocery store and agree on a time. We "go to bed" for a while, then silently pack our bags and get in the right cars with our phones off. All of our stuff gets tossed onto the boat in under a minute.

"Hurry, hurry." The men push the boat off the shore and wave to us with their giant hands.

20.

The lake is right by the city—nine miles, ten minutes on a hovercraft. When you see those miles, you realize there's absolutely no way that the diesel didn't get here during those first thirty-six hours while they were putting the booms out.

Nadezhda and the Copper Plant wave farewell to us with their smoke. A lens of smog envelops the city. The captain tells us, "We got out just in time. As long as we make it into the river, they won't touch us. Their luck has run out."

Blue, sleepless eyes. He knows that the other captains were fined, that they were threatened, but he is still taking us. Why? "I love these places. And I know them very well."

They say Lake Pyasino is dangerous. The depth ranges from thirty-five feet to sixteen inches, the wind meanders over it freely and easily capsizes boats during storms. But we get through.

The captain says that at the time of the spill, there was ice out beyond Golyj Point. And that the diesel reached Golyj Point.

We enter the Pyasina River behind Chayachy Island. The river is quiet, the water barely sparkling. The tattered forest gradually gives way to true tundra. Hunters' and fishermen's shacks dot the shore.

We pass a barge from Ust'-Avam. The captains wave to each other.

We breakfast at an abandoned hut. Behind it, reindeer bones bleach in the sun. There used to be thousands-strong herds here. They've changed their migration routes; the authorities blame the poachers, but the hunters say it's the Nornickel pipelines and gas residue on the tundra mosses.

Finally, we reach Kresty.

21.

Kresty stands on a steep ravine. At one point, there was a weather station here, a hunting, fishing, and gathering management (Gospromkhoz) hunting outpost, and a store. Abandoned buildings—by all appearances, former homes—and crumbling hunks of ice line the shore. Ice caves in the permafrost, so much rusted metal. The weather tower is covered in low grass. Only two of the buildings look habitable. Fishermen slowly emerge from them. No Russians here—only Dolgans and Nganasans. Sleepy, distrustful faces. They light up their cigarettes in unison, looking us up and down. They don't invite us in and answer us monosyllabically.

No, they didn't see any diesel. There were some oil spots on their nets, but who knows what those were?

No, the water doesn't smell like anything.

And no, there are no fish. No fish at all. Not since the spill.

22.

Sergey Elagir is a Dolgan, the master of Senkin Point. Zhenya Bogatyrev is a Nganasan, his former classmate. They grew up in Ust'-Avam and went to the same school. Now they fish together.

Sergey is a fisherman. He says he would have moved to the city a long time ago if it weren't for his adoptive father, whose dying wish was that he not abandon their homestead.

Their homestead: a house that looks like a ship, the fishing nets, and his crew. The house is warm. The children are still asleep. His wife, Nadezhda, puts a loaf of bread in the oven and quickly goes out.

Sergey pours out some tea and says, "Don't worry, the water's not from the Pyasina. We haven't drunk that water in a hundred years. Because of the Complex."

He goes on a long monologue about the government and the relationship between man and state. Then he asks that I don't include anything he has said "about politics." "I can answer for what I say. But there are people that I am responsible for who I can't protect."

Their cooperative usually manages to bring in three or four tons of fish a season. They sell them to the supermarkets in Norilsk.

They catch vendace, round-nosed whitefish, muksun, peled, taimen, grayling, pike, and the endangered Siberian salmon, which can't be fished. "These used to be wealthy places."

"For the Taymyr, this is going to be like . . . like Chernobyl. For the Pyasina River and therefore the people who live on and around it. That's just how it is."

Sergey and Zhenya go check the nets they put out the night before. The river worries, beating against the sides of their boat.

Sergey stops the engine. Zhenya runs his fingers gingerly through the net.

The first one is empty.

The second one, empty.

A little pike is tangled up in the third. Sergey picks it up and releases it.

"God, it's never been like this," says Zhenya.

Sergey turns away and spits in the river. Unthinkable. This river is holy and alive. Only now, it is dead.

23.

There are no fish at the outposts of Korennaya, or Tsentralnaya, or Kosmofiziki. The fishermen say: They killed the river. After that, they just curse. Victor from Tsentralnaya says that if the fish don't come back, he is making a noose. He laughs and his laughter is frightening.

24.

The captain wants to go down a creek to hide our boat—you never know who is coming. But rivers of fog creep over the tundra. We spend the night in a hut called Kurya.

25.

The sound of the helicopter wakes us up. It's a bright red like nothing else in the tundra, it lands on the shore. Four people step out. A uniformed policeman, another one in camouflage, with a mosquito net over his head, and two silent types in civilian clothes, "members of the public."

Later, the Norilskers identify them as "FSB Sasha" and the head of Nornickel's investigative department, Vladimir Sazonov. The "civilians" openly search the shore, Sazonov getting up close and photographing us with a high-quality professional camera.

The policemen say, "We need to search the boat for weapons." But they don't touch anything. They need the captain.

We tell them the captain went out for gas.

The policeman asks Yos what his nationality is.

"I don't know," Yos tells him.

At a certain point, the policeman decides to enter the hut. He checks under the bunks, under the bench in the sauna, asks us to unroll our sleeping bags.

Sazonov examines the bathroom.

FSB Sasha drones that it's no good to lie and they're going to find the captain one way or another.

"Well, look for him."

The policemen step away to make a call on their satellite phone.

Then they confiscate the hut owner's diesel.

They untie the rest of our gas from the boat. And they steal the key out of the ignition.

"You're going to strand us in the middle of the tundra without any gas?"

"We'll call in a rescue squad. You can get back to town on what you have."

"We're confiscating it! The captain doesn't have a license to operate, the boat isn't registered, and you didn't register with the Ministry of Emergency Management!"

They wave around a warrant for yesterday's captains. Sazonov continues taking photos.

They write out a warrant for searching the site, "In order to halt and prevent the group's advancement, we confiscated canisters presumed to hold diesel fuel."

But the fuel doesn't fit in their helicopter. They have to make two trips to carry it all away.

They spend a long time circling over the woods in search of the captain.

He finally reappears after the helicopters are gone for good. Angry and jubilant. "Shameless cunts," he roars.

At the next huts we pass, the people give us their fuel, which is like gold here. They say, "The helicopter has been looking for you for two days."

"They killed the lake, they killed the river, and now they're flying around looking for you, those fuckers. Whatever you do, get those samples, get them and take them out of here. And *you*—write, write about how things are around here, what's going on here right now, write about all of this."

26.

Yos gets the samples. Which isn't easy. You have to wash the bottles out really well. Then the river bottom is rocky and the special scoop that clamps shut when it's struck keeps getting snagged on the rocks and coming back open. We have to get doubles of every sample—we don't know which of them will make it out of Norilsk or how. Moscow is trying to figure out how we will ship these little containers of soil and water, but Norilsk isn't Moscow—we know that now.

Lena stands at a distance in yellow coveralls with a leaking bag. According to the rules, Yos needs to be decontaminated—washed down with clean water, and only afterward can they take off their coveralls.

The captain smokes angrily. He is afraid now and keeps grumbling,

"Hurry up, hurry, or else I'm letting you out here. You'll have to walk back with those test tubes of yours." Watching the low sky for signs of red.

A storm starts up on the lake. Mean little waves charge our propeller, making it impossible for us to get out to the final site where Vasiliy first photographed the shore covered in diesel. We turn back toward the city. Our precious samples are packed away, numbered, and secretly marked to avoid being traded out for fakes.

We are quickly unloaded into our cars. The boat, which doesn't have a key, is taken away to be hidden on its last bit of fuel. The captain nods goodbye. Then he leaves town.

27.

Nadezhda and the Copper Plant exhale their regular smokes.

Moscow City Duma deputy Sergey Mitrokhin arrives sleepy.

He is followed from the moment he steps off the plane—a cheerful, blue-eyed young man in blue gloves "recognizes him" and offers to help him, asking why he is visiting. Mitrokhin laughs it off and deflects; the young man offers to give him a ride but ends up in his comrade's jeep by himself and immediately starts making phone calls.

Mitrokhin has come to attempt to take the samples back with him to Moscow.

Before he returns to the airport, the ecologists ply him with tea and plan out what he should do if they try to confiscate the samples.

"Let's not even call them samples," Lena suggests. "It's just some soil."

The plan falls apart as soon as the first bag goes through the X-ray.

"Samples? You got permission from Nornickel?" an air transit safety officer demands. Then, into her walkie-talkie, "Hurry! Second entrance!"

Police appear with a man in a long trench coat and safety inspector Natalia Vasilievna Abramova.

Everyone openly says that Mitrokhin will need permission from Nornickel. Alexander Gennadievich Stebayev, shift supervisor for air transit safety, explains, "The only rules are that you can bring no more than five liters of liquid onto the plane and it can't be combustible. Otherwise, there is no problem. But we are not free people here, we're acting on orders."

"And what is your relationship to Nornickel?"

"Well, we are Nornickel. The airport is Nornickel. We're a subsidiary."

He steps away to talk to the police and the man in the trench coat and comes back laughing. "They're trying to figure out how to make you our problem."

Natalia Vasilievna isn't laughing. She leads us into a conference room and asks us to open our bags. Then she asks us to open the samples. After some back-and-forth, we agree to open one bottle. Natalia Vasilievna bends down low over it.

"But it really does smell like diesel!" she says, inhaling the scent of the Pyasino water.

They bring in a spectrometer. It reads green, indifferent to the samples. No restricted substances.

Stebayev returns. I am surprised by the change in his face. No trace of his former friendliness.

"Orders from above. We're seizing the samples for analysis. They're unidentified substances."

"But you just examined them!"

"We got a tip. From the police. Just now. An anonymous phone call. About an attempt to smuggle fuel and lubricants onto this flight."

"So are you going to search everyone on the flight?"

"Yes."

"Then we won't take the flight. And we'll take back our samples."

"Only with police authorization," Abramova says, and sits down to write out the seizure protocol.

In that tiny space of time, while they are crossing their t's and dotting their i's, we manage to get the bag with the samples out of the airport.

Mitrokhin flies back without any luggage.

28.

There is no rush anymore. We have time to go out and confirm our worst suspicion.

We leave for the Talnakh tailings storage facility at night.

There are more of us this time, the hike takes longer. We already know where the security checkpoints are, and we run through the clearings. We climb up the mountain and make our descent through the bushes and over streams. The Kharayelakh River has flooded, we have to maneuver around it. Our feet get wet.

The tundra sparkles with dew. Seagulls cry out overhead.

"Those gulls are really glaring at us," Masha says. "At least some of these watchmen aren't asleep." But we make it without getting caught.

Vasiliy is the first one to hear the motors.

We quickly eat in a little field by the dead lake, typing out texts we will send once we turn on our phones.

"Let's hoof it," Vasiliy says.

We walk along the lake to the road.

We hear the water. And the hum of the pumps.

Finally, we come out to the dump site.

29.

No, it isn't exactly like in the drone photos. In the photos, they were little white bursts, a spot, some pixels.

In real life, the pipes are twenty inches wide and spewing white slurry at a terrifying rate. Foam and spray. The liquid booms down a well-worn path. The larches on either side of the white stream are yellow.

"And it reeks of xanthate," Vasiliy says. "Fucking hell."

He gets out a tracker and marks the coordinates.

We turn on our phones and cameras.

At our signal, Yos, who stayed behind in the city, calls the police and the Ministry of Emergency Management. Then he calls Ruslan Abdullayev. He calls Igor Klyushin and a post titled "DUMPING!!!" appears on the Norilskers Facebook group.

Masha goes on Facebook Live. She doesn't have many followers, but what matters is that the video will stay up if they confiscate our phones.

The slurry keeps gushing. The pumps drone, the pipes breathe in and out with a whistle. We get out onto the road and go up to the walls of the pond. I need to be completely sure, so I look for myself and I see: the pipes are coming out of the tailings pond.

Vasiliy calls the police. He says, "Hello. This is Vasiliy Ryabinin. I want to report a crime."

But it's the Nornickel Security Department that's first on the scene.

Three men. One of them mechanically shakes Vasiliy's hand.

They don't take our phones away, they just ask that we stop filming. Workers begin to file in behind them. At a certain point, one of the workers and a security guy run to the pumps and shut them off. A few minutes later, the Rescue Service, a subdivision of the Ministry of Emergency Management, arrives. The pumps have already been shut off, but we show them our videos. The men grab their heads.

The police arrive. Frightened workers are already dismantling the pipes, but the police aren't concerned with that. "Everything has already been documented," a young policewoman says. Her partner climbs down the hill to collect a sample of the milky liquid.

"Alexander Victorievich Gorovoy, chief criminal investigator."

"Do you know what those guys just told us?" says Dima, the photographer. "They said this isn't a natural area, it's Nornickel property."

"As far as I can tell, they think that it's all Nornickel property."

An hour later, we are surrounded by people and machinery. Men in suits and uniforms crowd around the machines. Police write out warrants and reports.

The machines hurry to dismantle the pipes. People from the prosecutor general's office come in from the city. A Nornickel bulldozer backs into the police car that brought in the prosecutors, crushing it.

The people inside manage to jump out, unhurt. The driver of the police car stands on the side of the road. He keeps repeating, "I hope that he just didn't see us. I was ready to die."

The Emergency Management colonel gets on the phone. He says, "They're not talking. They just nod at each other. The police can't question them. No, Mikhailych, we're doing reconnaissance. There's a whole lake here that they have been dumping into continuously."

The colonel introduces himself, "Evgeny Alexandrovich Savchenko. I hope you're capturing what's really going on here."

The Emergency Management crew congratulates us, "Good work."

Emergency Management major Denis Makarov says, "One of my old classmates says they've been dumping in there since 2017. You know where else you should go? Oganer and Talnakh, their waste treatment facilities. They're not afraid of anything."

"Why don't you go?"

"How are we supposed to do that? There's been no complaints. Who would file a complaint against Nornickel?"

Another one says, "Ryabinin's with you? Wow. You guys, that's Ryabinin!"

30.

"I know of a hundred places actively dumping waste. We'll work two days on, one day off. How do you like that?"

It's night. Ryabinin and Abdullayev have just completed their letter to Putin. Both of them shake from exhaustion.

"I love it," Ruslan says. "I'll make it my entire practice. How much longer are you staying in town?"

31.

Meanwhile, scandal has broken out on the Nornickel board. The financial oversight department has delivered its own report on the spill and the state of the ruptured tank based on the company's own internal documents.

Here is what was in that report:

Although Nornickel management had known about the deteriorated state of the tanks, they had not replaced them for almost fourteen years.

The most recent inspection, in December 2018, had detailed the "limited functional capacity" of the walls, foundation, base, and equipment, as well as the existing risks of continuing usage.

The project to rebuild the tanks had been postponed three times since 2006 and never got past the planning stages. The projected expenditures had been optimized by 25 percent. At the same time, there were frequent repairs of the tanks' individual components.

The inspectors laid out the systemic causes behind the disaster: budget cuts and the failure to prioritize the maintenance projects necessary to fulfill the requirements of supervisory government agencies, as well as those related to industrial and ecological safety. They noted that the annual failure to complete Nornickel's general investment plan has been at about 30 percent for the past several years, equivalent to $600 million a year.

According to the department, the permafrost melt under the TPP-3 tank's foundation may have been localized. It stemmed from anthropogenic causes.

But the immediate cause of the rapid and widespread rupture of the tank wall was the degree of its deterioration.

Rust.

The inspectors included a list of potential locations for subsequent spills of the same nature: TPP-1 at the Norilsk-Taymyr Energy Company, and the Norilsk, Kayerkan, and Dudinka petroleum storage facilities.

In response, the inspectors were accused of bias and incompetence. There were also rumors that the report itself was just a new round in the war between Nornickel's chief shareholders, Vladimir Potanin and Oleg Deripaska.

32.

This whole time—three weeks—I had been trying to get in touch with Nornickel. I got a lot of help from many of its staff members, but no one wanted to talk to me on the record.

But after they wouldn't let us take our samples out, after we managed to document the dumping at TEF, I finally got an interview. The director of the company's Polar Division, Nikolai Nikolayevich Utkin, agreed to talk to me.

I arrived at the interview with sand in my hair. I'd gone to the area around the Lebyazhie tailings dump to see what would happen if they didn't stop the dumping at TEF.

It will turn into a colorless desert filled with dead trees where the wind chases the dust.

The dead Kupets River flows through the desert where reindeer had once rambled along its shores.

Ruddy, rusted, oxidized metal sticks out of the gray, pulpy soil.

I don't know how to put what I realized there into words.

The Nornickel Polar Division headquarters are in Norilsk's most beautiful Stalin-era building, on its most central street, in its most important square.

Nothing inside resembles the Stalin era. It is all light panels and high-speed elevators. Bottles of Evian stood on the table in the director's office.

Andrei Grachev, the head of the Department for Cooperation with Government Agencies from the central office in Moscow, sat in on our interview. He was the one who'd arranged it. He looked at me from across the table and said, "Whenever you need a justification, you will always find one on hand."

"I have nothing to justify," I replied.

"I'm not asking you to justify yourself. Sometimes, when tragedy strikes, there are people who show up and make things worse."

"The tragedy" is what he called the spill.

Nikolai Nikolayevich Utkin was energetic, fit, and amiable. He arrived with printouts of his answers to my questions but hardly looked at them. We talked for an hour.

"What happened is very painful. For me as an individual, and not to mention how painful it is for Nornickel.

"What you saw there wasn't corrosion. It was waterproofing. That was, once again, done during the maintenance repairs in 2017 and 2018, which we can provide documentation of. The surface shows wear from rain and extreme temperatures. After a year or two, it simply becomes discolored. That's what you were seeing."

I ask him about Nornickel's intervention in the return of our samples to Moscow. "I've heard all about this," he says, "and I can assure you that no Polar Division agencies, no security department, had any part in this."

I ask about the dumping. "I am confirming the fact that, in violation of all rules for the utilization of tailings storage facilities, the leadership of the [TEF] factory made a decision in aims of preventing . . . Yes, there was rain, high water, and a decision was made to dump—not tailings but standing water, which is now being reverse-drained back into the factory. This was an alarming situation for Nornickel, a serious incident. And we will take very serious measures to resolve it. This is not what we do here at Norilsk Nickel. What happened was an exception.

"When it comes to the city, in ten years' time, what you will see here are brand new, modern buildings with contemporary technologies, analogous to those being built in Finland and Canada. That's how I see Norilsk in ten years. It will be green. A city where you can't smell the sulfur in the air. And most importantly, it will be filled with the happy faces of the Norilskers.

"I wish for us all to turn over a new leaf. And most importantly, to remember that the company really is doing a lot right now. This accident will have no effect, it will in no way limit the functioning of our enormous ecological program."

In parting, Nikolai Nikolayevich gifts me a book called *The Nature of Taymyr Peninsula.*

33.

"Mama's calling," says Masha. "We're both about to get it."

The Ryabinins have just stripped the wallpaper off one of the walls in their apartment.

"You've completely forgotten about your parents," their mother begins.

"Did Papa catch any fish?" Vasiliy asks.

"A whole barrel."

They're silent.

"I hope that you're done with all that."

"We have a few more things to take care of. You are my parents, you have to support me."

"I support you, but . . ."

"Say what you mean."

"Your life is more important."

"Come on. You can't jump over your own head. You can live in shit or in a swamp, but you still have to fight for a better life."

"How's the apartment coming?"

"We're stripping the wallpaper little by little."

"No point in doing it little by little, you have to do it like you mean it. Just stay out of trouble. Where are you going to find a job now, smart guy? Quit fooling around, you all have mamas and papas."

"I am the way you raised me, Ma."

"But try to think of your family."

"This is for my family."

34.

Rosprirodnadzor assessed the cost of the ecological damage from the TPP-3 diesel spill to be 148 billion rubles. A fine unprecedented in Russian history.

"The overall damage to Arctic natural resources is unprecedented. The fine reflects that," said Minister of Natural Resources and Ecology Dmitry Kobylkin.

The company was offered the opportunity to voluntarily pay these damages. Nornickel responded that it would dispute the fine. "It is the company's opinion that the assessment of the damage to the water and soil made by the Yenisei Interregional Directorate of Rosprirodnadzor is based on principles which skewed the resulting numbers and therefore require correction."

Six days after this statement was issued, a pipe full of jet fuel burst near the village of Tukhard. Forty-four and a half tons of it spilled into the tundra. The pipe (we have photos of it—it's rusted and coming apart at the seams) belonged to Norilsktransgaz, whose parent company is Nornickel.

CHAPTER 12

IT'S BEEN FASCIST FOR A LONG TIME (OPEN YOUR EYES)

It was March, the end of March. Vera Drobinskaya, mother of seven adopted children, posted some photographs on her blog. They were blurry. A cemetery, just-melted snow, low, tender grass. The graves were nothing but unmarked heaps: no crosses, no tombstones, no names. Vera claimed that these were the graves of the children from Raznochinovka. "Some of them seem to be mass graves," she wrote.

Raznochinovka is an internat, a live-in facility for children with mental disabilities. An investigation by the prosecutor general's office showed that forty-one children had died there in the course of a decade.

I think I asked to go there myself.

Astrakhan is in the very south of Russia. Steppes, feather grass growing taller than you. The Volga here runs at full strength and spills into a hundred arms. The sun is so bright that you're always squinting, searching for shade.

Vera lives in a small wooden house. It's filthy and cramped. I see all of her children at once. Nadya, Roma, and Masha are reading. Tavifa is changing into a new dress. "She's such a coquette," Vera says. "If she doesn't change clothes four times in a day, it's all been in vain." Misha is sitting at Vera's feet, watching us anxiously. In the yard, Kolya and Maxim are taking turns on a skateboard.

All of Vera's children are said to have neurodevelopmental disorders.

Nadya, Roma, and Misha came from Raznochinovka. Kolya, Maxim, and Masha came from a regular orphanage but were about to be transferred there when Vera saved them. Vera took Tavifa to Germany for surgery, then adopted her.

Vera is a doctor, a neonatal specialist. She says that she first found herself at Raznochinovka nine years ago. She went with an Italian woman who hadn't managed to get her adoption papers together in time, so the child was sent there. "He died that same night. They were so happy to tell her. . . . The nannies took us on a tour. It was a Saturday, no one in charge was there—they were still fearless back then. The ward for the bedridden. Children lying on the floor, on plastic sheets. Some of them tied to their beds by their feet. The nannies said, 'So they don't run away.' But aren't they supposed to be bedridden?"

That was the first time that Vera saw Misha. He was tied to a bed with nylon stockings and chewing on his hands. Vera adopted Nadya and Roma along with Misha. "The nannies said that they didn't understand why they were there, they were totally normal."

"It was so hard at first. The children could only communicate in a mixture of swearing and gestures. They didn't want to go to school, they would shout, 'We are retards, we don't need to!' You'd raise your hand to caress them and they would cower, expecting that you were going to hit them. They'd never known anything but cruelty. Misha didn't walk back then, he could only crawl. One time, I asked Roma to help get him into the kitchen, and he started kicking him in the stomach, to kick him out of the room. I grabbed Roma and shouted, 'No! You can't do that!' He was so shocked!"

Vera keeps talking and talking, telling me how a Polish priest started her on volunteering, how at the hospital where she worked, infants would die for lack of the right formula, how she had been planning to adopt an eighth child from Raznochinovka, but child services rejected her application, how Misha had been injected with Thorazine and when she wrote to the prosecutor general's office about it they said that the Thorazine was to treat epileptic seizures. "Thorazine doesn't treat epilepsy. They inject them with it just to make them lie still." My pen runs out of ink; I get out the next one to keep taking notes. The children are watching *Harry Potter.* I think to myself that this can't all be true, everything she is telling me, it is too wild, too dramatic. On the other hand, she is a doctor, doctors are reliable, but then, she no longer works, now she is just the mother of seven children with disabilities—nobody sane would have taken that on. Was she getting revenge on the children's home for not letting her have an eighth? Anything seemed possible.

I talk to Nadya. Nadya was seventeen and finishing the ninth grade. She started going to school when she was eleven, after Vera adopted her. They overturned her diagnosis of "mental retardation." Nadya tells me about the orphanage. The schedule was simple: In the morning, they would "get dressed, line up for attendance, eat breakfast," and then they would be put in the playroom. That's where they usually spent the whole day, though sometimes the nannies would take them outside. "The yard had a big gazebo, that's where we sat." She says, "I was illiterate. But they did teach us embroidery." She talks about how one of the nannies slapped her for bringing a kitten inside. "They also hit you when you went in your underwear . . . or if they thought you stole something. One time, one of them yelled at me, 'You stole my pen!' and pushed me on the floor. . . . If you attacked a nanny, they'd give you pills and tie you down to a bed, then you slept all day. But I never did that. It was too dangerous. By evening, a lot of them were already drunk." She says, "One day, they turned out all the lights before we had time to make it to bed. One nanny was in a hurry, they were having a party. She picked up a stick and started swinging. She got my head and my fingers. But it wasn't her fault! She didn't even see who she was hitting, the lights were all out. Maybe she was just clearing a path for herself through us all."

Vera sits back down with us. "The regional psychiatrist would say to me, 'But they're not normal.' He'd go, 'Compare one of them to a regular child, you can tell right away.' I'd say, 'Take a regular child and send him to Raznochinovka for nine years. Then try comparing them.'"

Vera puts the kids in the van and we head down to the Volga. The kids run straight to the water. Masha splashes by the shore. I remember how when Vera brought Masha home, it turned out the girl had a short frenulum that made it difficult for her to talk. "And that was the whole reason why they decided that she was mentally disabled. The main determining factor for landing in there is random chance." How can that be? I sit on the shore thinking and thinking. I end up with a sunburn. I am on fire, I want to throw up, my skin is bright red, I can't touch it.

I don't remember how I found Svetlana. Svetlana had her son admitted to Raznochinovka herself. "I had no choice. It was only because I didn't have a choice. Everything in our house was broken, he destroyed everything. Three times, he dropped this dresser on himself. He'd try to run out onto the balcony." We walk through her trashed apartment while she explains how she took him to a rehabilitation center in a neighboring town, how she worked nights doing the books for a salon so she could watch her son during the day. She wants me to know that she's a good mother, that it's not her fault. In Russia, there's no support for families with children like this. When Svetlana would go and see doctors, they'd tell her that her son was incurable, that all she could do was have him admitted to an internat.

At Raznochinovka she was told that she could only have him admitted if she signed over her parental rights. "That's why I'm legally no one to him at this point," she says. She visits him.

"He's lost weight, he's like a skeleton. All covered in bites and wounds. They tell me they bite themselves. But he'd never bitten himself before. All he does is hug everyone. Maybe that's why they bite him? He's changed so much. He turns on the lights everywhere. He is afraid of water now—before, you couldn't get him out of the tub. He has stopped crying, he doesn't cry anymore. How can I find out what's going on with him in there? He doesn't talk."

I went to Raznochinovka. It's in a village twenty miles from Astrakhan, the road is just hardened, burned clay. The village is Russians, Cossacks, Meskhetian Turks, a lot of mixed marriages. There is a livestock cooperative, but it's very small. Someone in every family works at the internat.

Raznochinovka feeds the entire village.

The locals don't want to talk about it with me, "It's a job, except that it doesn't pay well." They say, "They want to shut down our internat because they want the land. It's right on the Volga, there are a lot of resorts around here. That's why they bad-mouth us." "Andreyevna, our director, is like a mother to them. And the way that they feed them—we don't feed our own kids that well. Beat them? Are you crazy? Who would dare lay a finger on a sick child?"

My next stop was the cemetery. I'm sure that I went, but I don't remember it. In my mind, in the place of a cemetery filled with children's graves, there's just a hot, white blank.

The children's home was a long building along the Volga. The sun burned down on the empty yard, not a child or a shadow outside. The fence was low, you could see right through it. I walked through the gates, doing everything that I could not to get kicked out. Smiling, smiling, smiling.

Director Valentina Andreyevna Urazalieyeva said, "I've worked here for thirty-four years. The first nurse here was my mother. My brother built the main building. My sister worked in the kitchen. My whole family worked for the internat.

"In Soviet times, there was a clear line between the teachable and the unteachable. There was no law demanding you try to educate everyone. Rehabilitation has a broader meaning now. Over a hundred of our wards have been adapted to labor. The older ones work, they sweep, they clean. They dress themselves—they can take off their shoes, most of them can make their beds. All of the children are difficult, with diagnoses ranging from mild mental retardation to severe. A significant portion of them have cerebral palsy. Fifty of them are in intensive care, they are bedridden. I'll show you them."

The room had fifteen metal beds with high headboards. They were colorful and stood right up against each other. There were children sitting and lying on them. Huge or overly small heads, deformed faces, unbelievably thin bodies. The director looked at me as I looked at the children. What could I possibly understand?

"Why are they so thin?" I asked.

"From illness. Their muscles are atrophied," a nanny told me from behind the director's back. "We feed them well."

"Do you know what their diagnoses are like?" the director asked me. "Sheer horror. It's the diseases that kill them."

"I know that you're being investigated at the moment."

"And the investigation will prove everything, you can be sure of that. These children are very sick. We recently had to take one of them to the hospital. They were amazed at how well the child had been cared for considering the stages of central nervous system illnesses and cerebral palsy."

"We don't allow volunteers in here anymore. They'd show up themselves. Ask to help. We showed them what it was like. They'd send diapers, chefs, books. Started getting information out of the kids. Handed out cell phones. Began asking them provocative questions . . ."

"Like what?"

"Like, 'Do they hit you?' These children are sick, they'll say anything. But the volunteers just take all of their stories at face value. They believe them, you know? We used to let them talk to the kids one on one, but now there have to be staff present. Because the staff understand the kids' diagnoses, they know how the kids will behave in those situations. When the prosecutor's office came here, I was present at all of the conversations. I'm their official guardian, I had to be."

"Can I talk to the children?"

"Of course," the director said. "Bring in Nastya."

A teacher brought Nastya into the office. The girl's eyes were round and staring with big tears streaming down from them. She didn't sniffle or wipe the tears away. Was she in pain? Was she scared?

"Why are you crying?"

Nastya stared at me and then smiled from ear to ear.

What should I ask? Should I ask anything?

"Do you like living here?"

Nastya gave a thumbs-up. She began quickly gesturing with her hands. I know some sign language, but I didn't understand a word. The director tried to put her arm around Nastya, and Nastya broke out of her grasp, went off to the side, and froze.

"Take her away," the director nodded at the teacher. "There. You see for yourself. The girl is seventeen years old. She's mentally ill. Families are lucky not to have children like this, that this tragedy has passed them by. But you always have to remember how close it is! Most of our personnel understand. The children are well taken care of, it's comfortable here, and beautiful, too. It's cozy. I believe that you should work so hard that when you leave this life, you can know that you've done everything that you could have for them."

Then she showed me the embroidery. "The children sew everything themselves." She showed me the vegetable garden. "We have very fertile soil here, we always have parsley and dill and salad."

All I could think was why is it so quiet here, two hundred children live in this building, where are they, why don't I hear them?

"What happens to these children afterward?"

"What do you mean? They go to the PNI."

"What is the PNI?"

"It's an internat just like this but for adults. They can't live independently."

I went to a PNI. A volunteer told me the name of a girl who had just been transferred to one from Raznochinovka. Her name was Sveta.

I walked in and smelled how it smells. It wasn't until many years later that I'd understand what that was. I didn't manage to take a single step forward before one of the guards ran up to me—a large woman in a robe. "Who are you here to see?" I said Sveta's name. "All visits are held in the gazebo, out there to the right. You can go wait out there." She waited for me to go back outside. Another woman led Sveta out. I worried that I would have to explain who I was, but Sveta pretended she knew me, she came up to me and took me by the hand. When the nurse left, she asked me, "Who are you?"

I introduced myself and asked about Raznochinovka.

"They beat us, mostly the boys. There was this one girl, they punished her by pouring boiling water all over her. She died. But that was a long time ago, before I was there."

"What was her name?"

"I don't know. Are you going to start visiting me? Did you bring any food?"

"Are you hungry?"

"I wish I had coffee and candy."

Around twenty young men suddenly poured out of the building. They were dressed strangely, their clothes didn't seem to be theirs. Half of them ran up to the gazebo, surrounding it, sitting down next to us. Every single one of them wanted to talk to us. Sveta changed the subject. She started talking about the amazing workshops they have, that you can do woodworking there, or draw, that she'd just performed in a concert.

The woman in the robe watched us from the porch.

Sveta moved closer to me and said, "Guys from the village sleep with the girls. Some of them have to get abortions. Some of them are sterilized."

"What?"

"It's a kind of surgery. So that you can't have kids. Will you write about that?"

"I will."

"How will you prove it?"

I don't know how I will prove it.

Sveta took down my phone number and went back into the building. The woman in the robe followed her in.

The prosecutor's office investigation showed that all of the children at Raznochinovka died as a result of their own illnesses and were buried in accordance with all regulations. They found no other violations.

I never wrote the story.

Director Valentina Andreyevna Urazalieyeva peacefully worked until retirement. But two years later, she found herself under investigation. One of the men from the village had kidnapped and raped a six-year-old girl from the facility and Andreyevna covered it up. She forbade her subordinates from calling in doctors. But the girl survived. She had a mother, and her mother found out the truth. There was a trial. The director was given four years' probation. She was also forbidden from working with children for two years.

Raznochinovka's next director built a ten-foot-tall fence around the perimeter. It is solid.

INTERNAT

April 30, 2021

Beyond the Wall

You get to the wall and halt at the wall. It's eight feet high. On the outside, it's painted a cheery sky blue with yellow diamonds. Cold, rough municipal oil paint. There are two cement boxes on either side of the entrance, flowers grow in them in the summer. On the inside, the fence is gray. But we don't know that yet.

Gray apartment blocks rise all the way up to the wall. In the windows, lights are on. Colorful curtains and shadows moving behind them. Cars and buses going by. A glowing shop sign.

There's a deep, wide trench in front of the wall full of meltwater. No one remembers how long the trench has been here or whether it's meant to be, but the trench serves a purpose, so there are no plans to fill it in.

Birch branches reach out from behind the wall. They've changed color already, it's springtime. On the other side—darkness, and their white trunks.

The building itself is farther back in the darkness. It has three stories and it is shaped like the letter H.

It looks just like a school or a municipal office, the kind you see in small towns.

This is not a small town, it's a city. But these outskirts, remote, industrial, feel like a separate place. Those who work in the building tend to live nearby.

If you go behind the building (not everyone is allowed to go there), you'll see several more outbuildings. A laundry, a boiler room. Soon you will hit a wall of sheet metal barring the way to the pond. You used to be able to go down there—not everyone, only some people could go—but ever since a young woman drowned herself, the pond has become forbidden, impossible.

Not everyone gets to see the birches, either.

The size of your world here is fixed by how others perceive you.

This is a PNI, a psychoneurological internat. The people who live here have psychiatric and neurological illnesses and have no relatives willing to care for them. They will live here until they die. Each medical record held at a ward's nurses' station has notes for the steps to be taken in the event of the resident's death.

I will be spending two weeks here, as a guest. I will be allowed to leave.

I am given the master key—a square metal rod with a plastic handle. It can open the windows and doors. You can use it to go between wards. Each ward is monitored by CCTV and has an assigned letter and number: 3-A, 2-D, 3-BG. In here, this key is the prime symbol of power.

The first thing that hits you is the smell—food, piss, oil, bleach, and human sweat.

Four hundred thirty-six people live here. Only forty-two among them are legally competent; the rest have been declared legally incompetent. They are referred to as "clients" or "residents." There is also the acronym PSU—social service recipients. Their names are written on the doors of their rooms. The staff addresses them all with the familiar form of "you." Between themselves, the staff refer to them by their last names.

The staff must all be addressed with the polite form of "you," using their given name and patronymic.

Because of the pandemic, the staff have to live here, too, working in shifts. Each shift lasts for two weeks.

The pandemic has reduced the life within these walls to a bare minimum. No more activities, no more dances, people living in different wards have not seen one another all year. Officially, the pandemic is now coming to an end.

Everyone is completely exhausted.

The coronavirus rampaged through here like a wildfire. There were three waves. The first one began at the end of April and lasted until midsummer. One hundred forty-one people fell ill, seven died in local hospitals. The second spike came in December, but they managed to quash it by CT scanning everyone: only eight people caught it in the end. The third wave arrived on the first of January. Fifty-seven residents came down with it, four of them died. The administration set up a quarantine ward.

The internat buried the dead whose families didn't come for their bodies. There were no final farewells. There's no provision for final farewells anywhere in the facility complex.

The Disco

"Oooh! Ooooh!" Someone is hooting beneath our windows, high and long like the cry of an exotic bird. It's Tasya, who lives on the hospice ward. She has a shaved head and blue eyes, the pad of her middle finger has worn down almost to the bone. She howls in short bursts, and the howls can be heard everywhere in the building.

It's the first disco in a very long time, everybody is overexcited. Life is returning to normal.

For the first time in a year, the men and women can see each other. There are only two coed wards: the rehab and the mercy ward—all others are strictly single sex, the doors between them locked.

In the least restrictive ward, rehab, they're busy picking out shoes. Elena Sergeyevna, one of the aides, brings these out, a gray-haired woman in a kerchief with a meek, kind face. It's Lent, she is fasting; she eats only black bread and salt and she reads to the residents from a prayer book.

They're choosing shoes for Nina Bazhenova. She's going to sing. She's already wearing a purple dress from the costume room, she looks like a princess.

The rooms overflow with whispers. "They don't have enough dresses, but the skirts are too small. . . . They won't go over my stomach." "Try eating less." "The tights all have seams! Should I wear them?"

The all-female Ward 1 is getting into black woolen dresses—it's like they're going to a funeral. Those who didn't get a dress are given new tracksuits instead.

Zul'fiya applies a stub of lipstick with an unsteady hand, and her lips become red. Lyuba puts on her own earrings, the ones with green stones a nurse gave her to keep. Pigeon-toed Sasha from 3-A, the strictest ward, maneuvers into a gray suit. It's too big for him, but it's a real suit, just like on the outside. They call the world beyond the wall "volya"—freedom.

Elena Sergeyevna is cajoling Anya to choose different socks. "Something cheerful for the party, something bright." Anya wants the striped ones, but Elena Sergeyevna is smiling and immovable. She makes a tour of inspection.

"I don't want to, don't want to," says Liliya. "This is the third one I've tried, they all look bad."

"We'll find you something," Elena Sergeyevna assures her, diving into the wardrobe. She knows where everything is because during the biweekly deep cleans, the aides go through the residents' things. Some of these things are thrown away, at the orderlies' or the nurses' discretion.

Elena Sergeyevna—like everyone else here—knows that Liliya used to date Slava but then he married a volunteer and left the home for good. No one holds it against Slava—what an opportunity. But they feel sorry for Liliya. She doesn't want to go to the dance. Elena Sergeyevna declares that everyone has to come to the scheduled events. Vera, who was planning on finally dyeing her hair tonight, is forced to go, too.

The hall was aired out, but it still smells of rotting floorboards. The rehab ward enters first. Rows of chairs. The walls are painted a yellow green, a paper garland spells out "Welcome Contest Participants."

One by one, other wards drift in. The aides roll up with people in wheelchairs from the mercy ward and park them in the front row. They all have clumps of hair behind their ears; they've been shaved, but sloppily.

It's easy to tell who is staff: they're the ones in the masks and lab coats.

The men start to mix with the women. They sit together holding hands, speaking quietly. "It feels so good to have you here," Olya tells Oleg.

An energetic blond with a stack of papers appears.

"So, does everyone remember my name? We're finally together again! Let's give ourselves a big hand!"

She takes a deep breath and launches into her opener, "Spring is in the air. And spring is in our hearts. But what is spring? It's a beautiful season of love. Love makes the world go round! Every last little thing loves some other little thing. . . . Have you missed dancing?"

There's still a long way to go before the dancing. First up is a talented orderly with a song, "This is the state-funded institution! This is the PNI! We are one great big happy family! Every girl and guy!"

After that, riddles, "Who sings in the morning? Birds! Who runs quick and bright? Streams!" You have to name the months of spring, say a tongue twister, guess what kind of insects live in hives.

Finally Princess Nina takes the mic. Her purple dress glows against the yellow walls.

> I've loved you for so long
> But you never hear my song
> You don't bring me flowers
> Or stop to talk for hours
> The rose blooms by the stream
> And like the rose I dream
> And bloom alone with love for you!

Another few performers and then, finally, the music comes on.

Half the assembly spills out onto the dance floor. The other half stays in their chairs; this is the time to be together, talk privately. One couple tries to go out in the hall, but the orderlies stop them.

People dance as well as they can. "Loving life, it's true! When I'm together with you!" A short young man is embracing a girl, weaving his hands above her head. Kissing her fingers.

"This pandemic has wrenched apart loving hearts!" calls out the blond. "Not everyone has a cell phone! Now for a slow dance!"

An elderly pair, the man unhurriedly leading. She's well made-up and in a blue dress, long earrings dangling down to her shoulders, holding herself like a queen.

One girl is whispering hotly into another girl's ear. A young man is kissing a woman.

A tiny young woman approaches me and takes me by the hand. "I love you. What's your name?"

The slow dance is over, but the couples stay where they are. They dance together, jerkily, to the faster beat. They have to be quick, the music is almost over. Single dancers gingerly avoid coming between the couples. Only the blond emcee jogs up and down and through the dancers, clapping enthusiastically into their faces.

A young woman with Down syndrome, wearing a red blouse, gyrates next to another girl who is dancing with her in her wheelchair. But soon her friend is wheeled away; the chair is wrong for her, her back is hurting, she can't sit anymore.

"Cut it out, Bunny," Sasha tells Yana. They're sitting down. "Don't be mad at me."

"Get out of here! Go dance!"

"Bunny."

The blond announces another slow dance.

"He's not my boyfriend or anything," Yana explains, getting out on the dance floor.

Dima is dancing with Anya, they have the same buzz cut. He can't take his eyes off her.

The disco lasts half an hour. Disco day is Wednesday.

Women's Ward 1

"Die! Why don't you go on and die! Die, die, you bitch!"

It's only Aglaya from the room opposite—an old woman with a crow's nose and bulging eyes. She wants everybody to go on and die. Everybody is used to it.

This is my ward—Ward 1. It's huge, divided into two wings, men's and women's. Forty-one women live in my wing.

The light switch is outside the room. There are no handles on the door, nor on the window. No outlets, either. Not here or in any of the other rooms. Actually, there's just one, by the TV, and it's monitored by the nurse. There's nothing to charge, though: there are only three cell phones for the forty-one women, and they are in the possession of the social workers. They give out the phones on Tuesdays and Fridays, after the late-afternoon snack, for half an hour.

Reveille is early—everyone is on their feet by seven. We all want to smoke. There's a smoking timetable tacked to the wall: 9:30, 13:30, 16:30. You get five cigarettes a day. The men get ten, but then they don't have their own hot water urn. Their hot water is brought in and then taken out, so if they want any after 7 p.m., they have to get it from the hot tap.

I make my way to the barred balcony and find Olesya there. She used to be a teacher, Russian language and literature. She has dark hair and ice-pale eyes. It's her birthday today. She has schizophrenia. She speaks in aphorisms and adages.

I'm getting shoved in the back. "Come on, hurry up! They'll see us."

I wrap my coat around me and edge farther out. It's cold. The other women are smoking in their housecoats. It's a catch-22: you can't smoke outside without a winter coat, but the coats are locked away and brought out strictly on schedule. Keeping outerwear in the bedrooms is not allowed. Unscheduled smoking is punishable by revocation of cigarette privileges, and not just for the offender, but for the whole ward.

I light up one of my own. Everyone else is smoking LDs, noxious things from a red pack. Not everyone has a cigarette. Several grannies are hanging around, hoping that someone will leave them a couple of drags. They're out of their own, it's too hard for them to ration. The grannies are roundly ignored. Everyone flicks the ashes off with their fingertips.

"We're like political prisoners," Olesya says. "We're in for life."

She squints up at the clouds and says, "I hope we get some sunshine on my birthday."

There is a menu taped to the door of the utility closet. For breakfast we're having "Friendship-brand kasha, glutinous, with milk."

The TV set in the tiled hallway is showing a cartoon about a kitten.

"When I grow up, I'll get a muzzle, too, just like him."

"Why do you need a muzzle?"

"So I don't bite."

Thirty minutes before breakfast everyone lines up in front of the closed door. We stand and wait. A woman with a shaved head and a lone tooth in the cave of her mouth crouches down and stares into the floor. I can finally get a close look at the women. Only Olesya has long hair. That's because Olesya occasionally performs at events—long hair is pretty, visitors like it. There are a couple of bobs and a couple of short cuts. The rest, including the grannies, are shaved.

The women study me, too.

"What nice teeth you have. I didn't think anyone could have teeth that nice," one of the women finally says.

Not everybody goes to the cafeteria. Eight of the residents have their meals in the ward—the bedbound, one blind woman, and those whose privileges have been revoked for bad behavior.

The doors open, the crowd hurries down the stairs. Three of the women press themselves flat to the wall and linger, waiting for men from the other wing. That door opens, the men stream out. Couples exchange quick kisses and walk to the cafeteria together. There's so little time when being together is allowed. This, the walks in the "garden" (if you get lucky and men are let out at the same time as women), and Wednesday discos.

Dating is called being "good friends."

Men and women pass parcels and notes. The parcels have coffee, an absolute treasure, and also the secondary currency of tea bags, which can be traded at an exchange rate of five for a cigarette. The couples look after each other as well as they can.

I'm trying to spread the butter on my bread, but the butter is not butter. I eat a second slice of bread instead, and chase it with a murky brown beverage. It doesn't smell like anything but it is warm and sweet. The kasha smells strongly of bleach. "That's the smell of health and hygiene," a passing doctor tells me. He seems offended that I'm not eating my kasha.

This particular PNI is proud of its cafeteria. A small rock-hard pear is included with breakfast, and I stab my teeth into it.

When I get back to my room, one woman after another will file in and leave me her pear on my bedside table. They're making friends with me. I am a good friend to have: I'm from the outside, I have smokes and a phone.

"Rosa, chew! Chew up the kasha first, then you can chew the meat after!"

Rosa is a fragile-looking, bedbound old lady with faded eyes. She is chewing obediently while Lyuba spoon-feeds her. Before she ended up at the internat, Lyuba had worked at a livestock farm. Lyuba lists off her lost treasures: husband, daughter, mother, father, in-laws, nephew, niece, rabbits, geese, Ferret and Lazybones the stallions, and five cows named Nighty, Marta, Dolly, Dawn, and another Dawn. Her current possessions are some trinkets given to her by nurses and a cassette player with dead batteries and five cassettes, including Zemfira's *Fourteen Weeks of Silence*. A photo of her husband and daughter. "I only have memories left, nothing else," Lyuba says, pushing another spoonful into Rosa's mouth.

"She's only got a few teeth, but she'll bite my fingers. You quit hiding it in your cheek, now!"

Lyuba pokes Rosa's bulging cheek.

"She stuffs it in her cheeks, then lies there chewing. I don't let her eat lying down, she could choke."

"I'll lead you down to your grave!" Aglaya is baying monotonously from across the hall.

"I would have been happier looking after my husband like this instead of a stranger."

Her husband died several years ago, after he came to visit her and gave her a phone. His friends organized the funeral. Lyuba only found out later. She's never been to her husband's grave. "Who's going to let me go and have a cry there?"

The nurse is here with the medication. The women line up. They open their mouths like baby birds. If you are caught not swallowing, next time, they will dissolve the pill in water. Refuse to drink and you'll get injections. Resist the injections, you'll get sent to one of the local mental hospitals.

One strapping woman goes straight to the head of the line. This is Nastya. Lively and tough, she's the top dog on the ward. She has the TV remote. Only she and her trusted cronies can change channels. She doesn't use her own shampoo, she chooses whoever's she likes. Just before New Year's she seized some of the more timid inmates' candy and traded it for smokes. But she's in good standing with the powers that be, and if anyone needs grabbing and holding down, Nastya is here to help grab and hold down. Nastya is strong.

I learn that because I am here, the aides have to wash all the floors themselves, instead of getting the inmates to do it for extra cigarettes—one extra smoke for a scrubbed hallway and bathroom. The aide is irate. She herds the women toward the TV set. "You want me to piss my pants?" snarks Lyuba as she hops across the freshly washed floor on her heels. "You're cruising for an injection!" an aide threatens a slender woman who didn't line up in time. The woman skitters into another room. She never watches TV with the others, she's a pariah.

At least there won't be an inspection by the head of the ward today.

Tall and booming as a grenadier, some time ago she was actually in charge of the whole facility. When we first met, she told me that Russia needs to defend itself against China, and that "that Zuckerberg has caught all in his network." You better hide your icons if she is around. She has something against them and is always looking for reasons to throw them out.

The icons tend to live on the windowsill. People pray on their knees in front of the window, with the door closed as far as it goes.

It is impossible to be alone. Each room holds three or four people. There are two stalls in the bathroom; both are usually occupied. The doors can be locked, but no one ever does, "We're used to it."

The women are anxiously waiting for cigarettes. "They forgot all about us, haven't they?" Finally, the head nurse arrives. The women circle around her, she doles out two cigarettes into each trembling hand.

There's a stampede for the balcony and the ashtray. There can't be any ash on the floor.

They smoke quickly.

The old women tear off the cigarette filters to make them stronger. "Mutilating those cigs," Olesya says.

Everyone knows that yesterday Olesya received a generous care package: chips, mineral water, soda, and coffee. Plus a real cake. Supplicants come to her for a bite.

Olesya has already split off a third of the cake for Zhenya, her partner of eleven years. "We sang a duet at a concert back in 2014," Olesya explains. "But never again since that time. He had a guitar. An orderly broke it and threw it away because a cockroach crawled out of it."

Not everyone gets treated to cake. The have-nots grumble and call Olesya a slag, but under their breath, in case she changes her mind.

It's getting close to the time when we can go outside. Will we? The head nurse decides. The head nurse dislikes precipitation and can't stand wet shoes and coats. It was raining this morning, but the rain stopped, but what about the puddles? What will she decide about the puddles?

We're going outside! With the men!

There's a small crush in the coatroom. There are as many overcoats as there are women, but not all of them are in good condition: some have broken zippers, others are missing buttons. There's only the one extra-large and three larger women, so one of them grabs it and walks away while the other two put on thin raincoats and hope that the nurse won't notice and lets them out anyway. There aren't enough hats, either, so a few women wrap kerchiefs around their heads.

Each item of clothing has "001," our ward number, tagged inside in white paint.

Olesya is torn between fancy white boots and comfortable black ones. She goes for the fancy white ones.

The key is applied to the door and we're on the stairs down to the "garden"—an enclosed courtyard between the middle and legs of the H-shaped building. The exit is fenced in and locked. There are two little gazebos, one for the smokers, and eight birches. One hundred twenty-four steps will take you around the perimeter. The ground is half puddle, half ice, it's slippery. The grannies immediately retreat to the furthest gazebo and sit down, stretching out their thick legs.

A few people opt to walk in circles.

We head to the smokers' gazebo, we are rich today. The men file out from their wing. With Zhenya nowhere to be seen, Olesya flies into a rage.

"You tell him," she says to his wardmate Yura, "I'm done with him. That coffee I gave him? I bet he's sitting around drinking it with the guys. What's he doing in there, jerking off? I thought he'd come out and get some air. I'm sick and tired of looking out at the world through these bars. Is he worried I'm gonna bum smokes off of him? I've got my own! He doesn't want to give up any of his cigarettes, he cares about them more than he cares about me! It's like Nastya said, April's for fools!"

Yura nods and turns away to kiss Marina. She has steel-gray hair down to her shoulders and rosy cheeks. The voices told her that she'd be well fed, that she would have baby after baby. The voices told her that yogurt and condensed milk would flow from her breasts.

Yura slides his palm between her thighs. Marina says, "Let's just smoke, okay?"

Yura nods and takes out two cigarettes—one is for her. I catch myself thinking that in here, just like out there, the men have more resources. I laugh to myself and Olesya tells me I shouldn't laugh for no reason or else I'll end up just like them.

Yura is squeezing Marina's breast. She blushes and sighs.

"They're practically fucking," Olesya says. "Come summer he'll be taking your clothes off and fucking you for real."

Marina and Yura make out. The woman sitting on the other side of them wants to know whether I saw the fight over the coats and tells me that there are plenty of new coats in storage but "they don't want to waste them on us." "They did give out new tracksuits before you came, some people even got dresses."

One old woman is trying to bum a smoke off another one, "I'll get you back. Honest to Christ, I'll get you back by dinnertime, just help me out."

"Zhenya and I have been together eleven years," Olesya says. "We've even had sex, he snuck in to see me when I was in group observation. He's a gypsy, a real gypsy! He knows gypsy language, he can go off in it. Listen: *Tu miro devel.* That means 'You're my god.' *Tu miro rap*—'you're my blood.' Nose is *nag*, eyes is *yagkha*. I have an ear for languages!"

Every bench is filled up with couples. Those without a place to sit promenade in circles, slipping on the ice. You have options: you can circle clockwise or counterclockwise.

"Okay, don't tell him we're splitting up. Yura, you hear? Just say: 'Olesya is mad that you didn't come out.' And there I was thinking about treating him to some crab stick with mayo—Nastya would get us the mayo. You think I don't have my own cigarettes? I don't need his right now. I gave him some coffee, and sausage, and tea. He's probably up there partying. Or maybe it's his arthritis? Acting up in this weather?"

Shouting from the door, fresh-air time is over. Our fifty minutes of the outside have run out. We stomp up the stairs. There's a man snatching a final kiss on the top landing, right by the wards; an orderly gives him a shove and he hurries away.

On TV, there's a psycho holding a woman at knifepoint; the grannies are laughing their heads off. Commercials. Coffee makers. Beautiful people. Jewelry. The news.

Bowlegged Katya (radio engineer, schizophrenia, twenty-six years in the internat, attempted suicide but only managed to break both her legs and get her legal competence revoked) has a question, "Lena, when Putin is speaking, is he looking at everyone? I feel like he's only looking at me. Is that a symptom? Or could it be real?"

We're released for lunch. Olesya collars Zhenya, "D'you have a bit too much of my coffee?"

"They gave us very cold kefir yesterday. It hurt my throat. Forgive me, my darling." Zhenya has gold teeth and looks nothing like a gypsy.

Lunch. Lunch is lukewarm soup, liver, salad, and pasta. The crushed liver, cabbage, and pasta shells are all heaped together. I pick at my bowl under the chief physician's reproachful eye. Everyone is eating fast, literally stuffing themselves. Eventually, I catch on to why they're all in such a rush: there's a phone booth downstairs, with a short, anxious line forming behind it. You can only dial local numbers. The aides drive everyone back after lunchtime is over, whether you managed to fit in a call or not. The doors have to be locked on schedule.

Now for the second washing of the floors. The female orderly works the mop in a silent fury. She'll have to do it again before she leaves for the night.

Lyuba is trying to feed Rosa quickly when someone pitifully calls to her from another room. A bedridden old woman is asking her to change her diaper.

"I'll stuff you full of your own shit, you fucking bitch," Lyuba grumbles as she thrusts a hand between the old woman's legs. "Where's it wet? It's not even leaking."

The bedridden are allowed three diapers a day. "I change them if they're really wet, or if they've shat them. And after dinner I change them, before bed. They're so dumb, they don't usually say anything. You have to check every time, morning, evening, and lunchtime. But she's all dry—why is she lying? Even if she's peed in it, she can pee in it again."

The girls are slowly assembling for Olesya's birthday coffee. Not everyone, just an inner circle of six. But there's a problem: the nurse left, locking the room with the hot water behind her. They have to use the hot tap.

"Can you open a candy for me, Olesenka?"

Coffee is served. The women sip it daintily, one mug per pair. The mugs are identical, so they use fruit stickers to tell them apart. They take turns pulling chips out of an open bag. The cake is long gone.

"The years gone by are weighing a bit heavy on me," says Olesya. But the other women are fixated on the food.

"Take garnet—that's Libra's birthstone," Olesya continues. "But I've got the best one: mine's diamond, or else rock crystal."

"The coffee is so aromatic, even in the cold water," one of the women replies.

"It's almost 300 rubles a can! Black Card."

"I've had it before."

"There's this ice cream called Glissé Angelica," Olesya tells them. "It's coffee with ice cream and then whipped cream on top. I've had it at Café Labyrinth so many times. They have these little private booths there, and ice cream. I used to go there and have coffee with cognac. Smoke and drink herbal liqueur. Quiet music."

"Line up for meds!" someone shouts from the hallway. All at once, the women get up and leave.

"Birthdays are sad," Olesya says. "And that's all there is to it."

After the meds you get two more cigarettes, so there's a rush for the balcony again. It's not as desperate as first thing in the morning, and the old women get a few butts to finish.

The talk is of suicide and how to do it. The consensus is that only hanging yourself is a sure bet; there's never been a single successful leap from the window in the internat's history. "Even if you throw yourself down headfirst, you always end up landing on your feet. Some people tried in the summer, that's what happened to them. Don't even think about it," says Katya, the resident expert.

The TV is playing music videos—a young climber cuts his own rope and plummets into a beautifully rendered valley.

Screams from the bathroom. A nurse jumps to her feet, but before she can get there, Nastya emerges, looking pleased with herself. Behind her is the fragile-looking woman the orderly was berating this morning.

"Paramonova again," the nurse sighs. "Paramonova! You wait, I'm going to go get the doctor!"

"She was squealing like a stuck pig," the old women laugh.

Nastya is laughing in a circle of girls.

"I was in the stall and that one started waving her hands in my face. So I popped her one! She was hanging around me earlier, too. I'm going to put you in the ground one of these days, you hear me?"

"She just started slapping me," Paramonova tells the nurse, crying.

"That's because you provoke everyone! And for crying out loud, nobody hit you," the nurse replies, even though you can hear Nastya bragging about it all through the hall.

"The black crows pecked the white one to death!" says Paramonova, making wings out of her arms.

"Go to your room," says the nurse.

She returns with another nurse, who is holding a syringe. Paramonova is about to get shot with tranquilizer for being "agitated." Everyone's file says what to inject them with if they get agitated. Paramonova is getting Aminazin, an antipsychotic.

"It's vitamins," says the nurse.

"I don't want a shot! I'm leaving!"

"Doctor's orders," the nurse says. "It's for your primary disorder."

"I don't have any disorder!" Paramonova runs to hide in the bathroom.

"Go get the orderly," the nurse tells an attendant, who nods and goes out.

The big and beefy orderly gets in front of the bathroom door and looks over at me. "You don't expect me to go in the bathroom and get her."

"She can't hide out in there forever. We can wait," says the nurse with the syringe. She goes over to the orderly.

"She was misbehaving in the cafeteria, too. Then she hit Nastya," says the first nurse. She turns to me, "And it's spring, so her symptoms get worse. She gets eczema, scratches her legs to shreds."

"It's like a preschool in here. You need so much patience to deal with them. Not everybody can take it. You feel sorry for them, I can tell. But we have to be strict."

Paramonova peeks out of the bathroom and scrutinizes the nurses and orderly.

"I'm going myself," she says. "I'll go."

She takes herself back to her room; the woman with the syringe follows her. The orderly stays by the door.

When I pass by her room, Paramonova is lying in bed, wrapped in her blanket, face to the wall. Motionless.

News from the outside world plays on TV. Dinner is carrot-and-potato mash with baked fish casserole.

I go back to my room, but there is no being alone. One woman after another comes in asking to call her relatives. They're nervous, they're not allowed to use other people's phones. The numbers are written on faded scraps of paper. The callers wish everybody good health, express sympathy at their troubles. Lyuba's brother was hospitalized. Lyuba cries into the phone, "Just don't let him die." Olesya is begging her daughter: you can have all my disability checks, just take me out of the internat. Her daughter says that she needs to sort out her work situation and debts before she can think about it.

"Won't you come visit for Easter, and bring Sonechka?" pleads Olesya. "I haven't seen you in two years."

A tiny woman keeps getting disconnected—call rejected—then asks me to send a text instead.

"Vanya, it's Mama, please answer."

"Can't talk. I'm at work."

None of the women get caught.

Seven o'clock means lights out. *The Voice: Kids* is on TV. Come evening, nobody feels like talking. I creep out onto the balcony, where several women are standing quietly. We smoke together in silence. The lights in the windows on the other side of the wall seem as distant as stars.

A nurse and an orderly barrel in, guns blazing. They seem to be competing for who can scream loudest.

"Half dressed!"

"Smoking off schedule!"

"What do you think you're all doing?"

"What if you catch a cold?"

"No cigarettes tomorrow!"

"Who's that I see? Standing out here with bare legs!"

A woman tries to duck out. "I was dressed!"

"Were you, now? This what you call dressed?"

"Who's that over there? In the housecoat? Wrap it up!"

"Off to bed!"

But the women are lagging. One asks me to leave her a cigarette butt.

"We're like caged animals."

"You can't go out for a smoke half naked! It's not like you don't know the rules!" The nurses haven't let up.

"The nerve! They've lost all shame, nothing scares them!"

"You could get corona or freeze off your lady parts! There aren't enough doctors or hospital beds! No one would take you crazies anyway!"

"I'll get Ekaterina Borisovna to come down here, she'll teach you what's what!"

"No cigarettes tomorrow!"

The women stub out their cigarettes carefully and sidle back in.

"This is the nice shift, they're not going to tell, don't worry," one woman is telling another.

"What an exciting day," says Olesya. She's fine, she got a whole pack today as a gift. She has plenty to smoke.

I wake up from the feeling of somebody's gaze on me. It's the dead of night. Someone is digging around in my coat, which I left on the windowsill. Shorn gray hair glows in the light coming in from the street.

I recognize her from the back. One of the grannies who wait for spare cigarette butts. She never says anything, she just looks.

I get up to touch her shoulder. She turns and startles.

"Forgive me. Forgive me. I forgot myself. I just forgot. Don't tell them. I forgot myself." She's tilting sideways, searching the air with her fingers, for something to lean on, for the edge of my bed. She won't leave.

I don't understand and I'm frightened.

Then, I understand and I'm frightened.

She is trying to get on her knees.

An Announcement Tacked Up on a Metal Cupboard

Attention: Due to the increased incidence of client escape attempts, male orderlies are to accompany female orderlies to the laundry during the morning shift. Clients are not allowed out of their wards unaccompanied!!! Infractions will result in docked pay.—The Management

You Ask

A boy whose face is disfigured by a gigantic purple hemangioma is writing in big block letters:

FOR CHRIST'S SAKE MOVE ME TO A DIFFERENT INTERNAT
OR I WILL DISSTROY YOU

ONE HUNDRED PERCENT FOR SURE

YOU WRECKED MY LIFE.

WRECKED, YOU ASK?

OF COURSE YOU WRECKED IT!

I DESPISE YOU FOR THAT FOREVER!

THE PEOPLE HERE ARE ALL STUPID.

I WANT TO BE FREE AND INDEPENDENT.

THE PEOPLE WHO WORK HERE ARE MORAL DEGENERATES.

I HATE THIS MADHOUSE AND EVERYTHING IN IT.

The boy's ability to write is considered amusing. His roommate can read from *Eugene Onegin*, though he can't understand it. Their room is included on every tour of inspection, to show off the talented youths.

Tyoma

This is the only ward that the master key doesn't open—it can only be opened from the inside (staff have to be let in and out). Ward 3-A reeks of urine. We're told that these are the most difficult clients: the runners, the aggressive ones, the agitated. They don't eat in the cafeteria, but some of them are allowed out on walks. We're advised not to turn our backs to anyone.

I'm with Katya Taranchenko, the head of Horizons, a volunteer organization working with internats. We approach a steel door, the first of many. A padlock hangs from the latch, open but threaded through the loops.

The door has a small plastic window.

Katya peers in. She unhooks the padlock and enters.

The stench is overwhelming.

A young man stands in the middle of the room, completely naked. He is thin, shaved almost bald, with bruises all over his butt from injections. He is looking through us, but strangely, I can't seem to make out his face. A thread of drool hangs down from his lips.

Along with the young man, the room has two beds, only one with a mattress.

In the corner, a bucket.

The young man goes to the bucket to piss, then returns to the center of the room. He wipes himself with one hand then runs his hand through his hair.

The nurse is quietly briefing us: Artyom S., a severe case, used to have a roommate, but he's in the hospital, so he's alone. "He rips everything up and eats it. He's been eating the windowsill, look!" The plaster has clearly been picked at.

"How often does he leave this room?" Katya asks.

"Artyom doesn't go out on walks," the nurse tells us after a beat.

"Where are his clothes?"

"Just a minute." The nurse scurries off.

Artyom is rocking in place. He glances at Katya, then looks up.

He goes to the cot, lifts up the mattress. Retrieves underwear and socks.

"Thanks, Tyoma. Do you feel like getting dressed?" Katya asks him.

Tyoma puts his clothes on and I can finally make sense of his face. It's the face of a starved wolf cub from a cartoon. Pale. Deep-set brown eyes. Protruding ears. He looks around fifteen.

The nurse is back with pants and a T-shirt. "We take them away because he tears everything up, even the bedsheets. Those are government property, you know."

"We'd like to take Tyoma out," Katya tells her. "When is the scheduled walk for this ward?"

"Only with the doctor's permission. I'll call him."

She dials and passes the receiver to Katya. I can make out, "He's acutely retarded. Currently under close observation. It's not endogenous, it's exogenous. Congenital mental deficiency. With long periods of remission. So that's that, I'm afraid." The doctor is saying no.

Katya hands back the phone.

"All right, then, we'll have a walk around the ward. Tyoma, do you have any shoes?"

Tyoma reaches underneath the cot for some plastic slides. Puts them on.

We're out. Tyoma heads straight for the ward doors. He tugs at the handle. He makes a noise, "Ugh."

"That's right," Katya tells him. "Unfortunately."

We walk around, past many cells filled with people. So many people. We find a room with tables, the lunchroom. Further on, there are more people, but they're in dorm rooms, not cells, for those who are not "under observation" and can enjoy more freedom. They assume that we're here to check on conditions, and one young man complains that his own plastic cutlery has been thrown away. "Because they were dirty!" the nurse says. "No, they were clean! What am I supposed to stir my tea with? My finger?" Later I learn that there's a prescribed list of personal items that may be kept in a special plastic box—these live on the windowsills. Comb, handkerchief, toothbrush, toothpaste, and toilet paper; everything else is superfluous and therefore confiscated and discarded. "They're always trying to sneak things through, though, to hide away some trinket: a used mask, a leaf they found on a walk, stuff like that. Just what they're like, I guess."

Tyoma is walking fast, he gets to the balcony doors in a few big strides. Katya has an idea.

But first we need to get Tyoma back to his cell and lock the door. Tyoma follows us meekly. He removes his socks and hides them under the mattress, then lies down on the cot and turns to the wall. Katya stalks out without a word, leaving me to put the padlock back on the door.

The next day we go to see Seven Wings, the doctor in charge of Tyoma's treatment. They call him Seven Wings because of his catchphrase, "You may be in charge of a facility ward, but I've got seven whole wings!" Each psychiatrist is usually responsible for one hundred patients, but because of the pandemic, they have had to take charge of four hundred. It turns out that Seven Wings started exactly one week ago. He doesn't know Tyoma at all. He reads out Tyoma's medical record, "Transferred from state orphanage to PNI. Mother stripped of parental rights, father deceased. Fell out of stroller aged eighteen months. Aged three, displayed a marked change in behavior: hiding behind furniture and under covers, running in circles, obsessively watching TV commercials. Started talking less, then stopped entirely, squeezed out the contents of every tube, chewed up every wire in the house. Ran around during class time, ripping his clothes, ate flowers, notebooks. Screaming, biting."

We plead for permission to take Tyoma out onto the balcony. The doctor is irritated. He wants to know why we're doing all this, attempts to ask several times but stops short.

Tyoma is waiting for us, fully dressed.

"Hello. Good job getting dressed, Tyoma. I'm so happy to see you," says Katya.

We go to the balcony door. Katya pulls Tyoma's coat on, he's helping, putting his arms into the sleeves. Katya hands him a hat, and he pulls it down almost over his eyes.

We walk out.

Sunshine. High-rises, trees touching the sky. An overpowering smell of meltwater.

Tyoma presses his face to the iron bars and breathes it all in.

He turns back to look at us—really look at us, for the first time.

"Do you want me to turn some music on?" Katya says. "You like music, Tyoma?"

She plays "The Green Coach"—a lullaby about the coming of spring—on her phone. Tyoma sits down on a bench, then lies down and curls up, arms tight around his knees. He is looking at the sky through the bars, breathing it in through his open mouth.

The next day we go back to see Seven Wings, to tell him that Tyoma behaved very well and they should try letting him go outside. We'd be right there with him, and the male orderly would be there, too, and the garden is gated and barred, anyway. We have more arguments to present, but Seven Wings unexpectedly says yes. "But you'll be personally responsible. I've told you what I think about all this."

Tyoma is dressed and waiting for us. He is as nervous as we are. "We're going outside," Katya tells him. "For a walk outside. Down there, where the street is. We'll go in a minute. But have some candy first, so you're strong enough." She hands Tyoma several chocolates.

An orderly brings some clothes to the cell. She is shaking her head.

"Would it be possible to air out the room while we're gone?" Katya asks.

"Yes, just a minute." She opens the window with a special key.

Katya turns to get Tyoma dressed, but he's already doing it himself. He's pulled the trousers on over his pajama bottoms and is working his way into the sweater. Katya shows him how to do the coat zipper and Tyoma remembers that he already knows how. He has long, slender fingers.

We emerge into the hallway and encounter a crowd of men in hats. They look like trolls—big, clumsy, completely unthreatening. When did I stop being afraid of them? Why? The orderly unlocks the door, and everyone proceeds down the stairs. We bring up the rear.

Tyoma is unsteady on the stairs, but he's going down fast, very fast.

The outer door swings open.

We face the 124-step walled courtyard.

Sunshine. The last of the snow.

Another patient, pigeon-toed Sasha, squints up at the second floor. Yana, his love, lives up there. She's in the window, and he shouts to her.

"You want some candy? What d'you want, Bunny?"

"I'm off to have a wash," Yana says, but she doesn't go.

"Go on, then!"

"I'm off to go drown myself," Yana says, and she doesn't go.

Sasha looks up at her, he's laughing.

"I'll drown myself! See if I won't!"

"Go on, go on, go, go, go!" the men shout up to her. Their raised faces are brimmed by identical black hats, pointy like gnomes' caps. "Hey, you, where you going with that cigarette butt?" the orderly barks.

Tyoma circles around the yard. And again.

He looks deeply disappointed. He pulls his hat farther down, almost over his eyes. His stride keeps getting longer. He stops. Turns to Katya.

"Ugh!" he says. "Ughughughughughughughugh!"

"I know. But look here, look at this." Katya takes him up to the fence. Beyond, the gray high-rises are like cliffs, almost pink in this light.

They stand together, looking. Then Tyoma takes Katya by the hand and leads her back to the door. They walk up the stairs. The ward door is locked again, but we have our own key.

Tyoma walks into the ward, back to his own cell. He gets undressed and gets into bed. He pulls his blanket all the way up over his head.

We sit with him for a while. Then we leave.

The next day Tyoma is waiting for us right at the door to his cell. He watches for us from his plastic window. He is dressed.

The nurse who opens up for us tells Katya, "You must be a hypnotist or something. Since you started coming, he hasn't ripped anything up or chewed anything he's not supposed to. It's incredible. You have a gift."

Katya's face contorts. It scares me. But she doesn't say a word, she just goes inside.

She unlocks the window and flings it open. A spring breeze cuts through the cloying stench of piss.

Katya turns back to us, already composed again.

"Hello, Tyoma. I'm so happy to see you. Are you happy, too? Are you ready? Let's try to go on another walk."

Tyoma comes close, looks her full in the face. Opens his palm questioningly.

"Yes, I brought you some," Katya assures him. "This is a Snickers. Have you had Snickers before? It has nuts in it."

Outside, Tyoma goes off the path and steps onto bare earth. The last of the snow is dry and crumbly. Tyoma sits down on a bench. "Look Tyoma, see how hot the sun is," Katya says. Tyoma squints at the sun from under the brim of his hat, swallows hard. I haven't seen him drool for days. He goes up to the gazebo and the men make room for him. He sits down next to them. Katya asks if she can put on some music.

The men nod. Katya puts on "Cardiogram" by Boris Grebenshchikov.

> The nightingales are singing too loud these days
> New words evanesce from the blue
> It seems like someone has got hold of my heart
> Sometimes I think it might be you
>
> My lips have forgotten how to form smiles
> My features grown hazy, it's true
> But something good's happening to my heart
> You know what, I think that it's you

"I think that it's you," Katya sings to Tyoma. And he smiles. Hesitantly at first, then for real.

"It's so nice to see you smiling," Katya tells him. They are both smiling.

The sun casts shallow light across the spinning, floating world.

The next day Katya leaves town.

Banya

Banya day—wash day—is once a week. Before you go to the baths block, you have to put on your flannel bathrobe. Women bring their own shampoo, if they have it.

You get undressed in the anteroom and then sent inside in small groups. The bathrobes and underwear all go in the same big laundry sack. Olesya doesn't want to give up her brand-new bathrobe, but it's taken away anyway.

We enter a tiled room, a nurse standing guard in the doorway.

"If you have washed, leave!"

There are only two showers, the naked women form a line. You have to get under the water twice: First you get yourself wet, then you go up to the orderly and hold your hand out for some herbal-smelling green liquid soap from an unmarked bottle. Then you pick up a sponge (these are communal and will later be disinfected), lather up, and lather your hair. Then you wait in line one more time for your second turn in the shower. We're up to our ankles in foamy, dirty water.

The women wash their private parts, lift up their breasts. I take out my razor and whispers spread through the room. Razors are forbidden. Those who have them conceal them. It takes an unheard of amount of nerve to use one so openly—nobody's ever done it before.

Bodies, bodies. Fleshy, thin. Shaved heads, protruding bellies. We study one another.

"Out you go! On your feet! Next five, get in!"

There's a bench for washing those who can't do it themselves or are going too slowly. They pour water on them from a black rubber hose. Normally, this is a job for the other residents, but because I am here, the orderlies have to do it. The orderlies are wet and pissed off. They might as well be scrubbing meat.

A woman gets soap in her eyes and she cries like a child. The orderly says, "Oh, come on now."

The ones in wheelchairs get moved to a wheeled plastic chair. After being doused with the hose, they are rolled under the showerhead.

"My chair, my chair!" a granny wails. "Give me back my chair! I can't get up! I can't walk on my own!" They just keep washing her.

Rosa has soiled herself, shit runs down into the common drain.

As you exit, you have to lift up your breasts to show that you've washed yourself well and you don't have a rash. A nurse inspects all the women. Everything will be noted down in a special banya-day journal.

They're handing out towels, bathrobes, and underwear. The underwear comes from a mixed bag. They're faded and gray from the laundry, all the wrong sizes, but the women meekly put on what they're given.

Back to the anteroom to wait to be taken back to the ward.

"Good bathing, ladies!" says Olesya. "Makes the soul sing, doesn't it?"

Sveta

I meet Sveta Skazneva on the mercy ward, which is on the ground floor. Everyone ends up here sooner or later—usually before they die. There are many bedridden and wheelchair-bound patients. The usual tiled walls and steel doors. This ward even has its own solitary confinement cells that lock from the outside.

Sveta Skazneva has been shaved bald. She has a single remaining tooth, which makes her face seem almost perfectly round. Cheerful brown eyes and a big smile. Sveta's body is racked by spasms, ceaseless convulsions contorting her limbs. Her arms are stuck behind her head, she can't lower them. She has cerebral palsy. Her parents gave her up long ago. She used to live with her grandmother, and then an aunt, but when Sveta turned thirty-one, the aunt got sick and their relatives turned them both over to the state: the aunt to a nursing home, and Sveta to a PNI. Sveta is now forty-seven.

To say even a short phrase, Sveta must overcome her own body's staggering resistance. So she speaks very slowly, and in the long pauses between her words her body writhes and warps. I listen. It's hard to watch.

"Is it hard for you to talk with me? Are you tired?"

"No. Let's keep talking. I want to talk."

Sveta's roommate and best friend, Yulia, is sitting by her bedside on a homemade set of wheels—a stool on casters. Yulia feeds Sveta, brings her the bedpan, helps her to dress. Yulia is classed as nonverbal, but Sveta can understand her just fine and translates for me fluently. "We are like sisters. Nobody talks to her," Sveta says, "or to me. No one. One nurse did. But then she quit. She'd write things down for me."

"What things?"

Yulia claps me on the hand and rolls up to the bedside table. She pulls out a plastic bag. Two notebooks inside.

The notebooks are filled with poems.

Our Father who art in heaven, will you not tell me what for
I suffer, unwanted and friendless, my fate has been sealed
evermore
My life is a hell, though I'm blameless, with no one to care if I die
In poverty, sickness and suffering, and no one to hear my soul cry

The world of poetry is wider than the internat walls. Wider than anything possible in the present.

There once was a house in a village.
Two streets and a hill in the air.
The village was full of hardworking, good people.
My granny and I once lived there.

Sveta once had love, too. He also lived on the mercy ward. But there was no happy ending:

They could not accept such a couple—the doctors and nurses,
not one.
In anger he lost all his reason—the young man decided to run.
He made it back home early morning, the guards couldn't find him
there.
But his ill and unhappy mother, she brought the escapee back
here.
He knew then that he'd been so foolish, he ruined their lives
in a day—
By leaving his dearest beloved and throwing their happiness
away.

The young man was sent up to 3-A, the ward for runners and difficult patients, an impossible two floors away. They would never be together again.

And everyone here knows this story—the tale of two lovers apart.
But never will they be together, for the doctors, they don't have a
heart.

"Did you dictate all that?"

"Yes. At first. Then. Got. Phone. I wrote it. I write."

Sveta braces her face against the mattress and wrenches a tiny Alcatel cell phone from underneath it with a gnarled hand. She jabs her left pinkie at the buttons. The draft folder lights up with lines of text.

"How long did it take you to learn to type like this, without looking?"

"Six months."

Later, Sveta sends me a text, "I'm very careful and precise about my poems. If there's a single typo, I insist it's corrected straightaway. A poem can be ruined by a single wrong letter or word."

"There's a poem here called 'Lullaby for My Daughter.' Do you have a daughter?"

"No. That's me dreaming."

Sveta's life is circumscribed by the edges of her bed. A standard-issue wheelchair is of no use to her, but that is what is prescribed in her IRP—individual rehabilitation plan—so that's the only kind she can be assigned. There's a TV set in the corner that hasn't worked in two years. "Yulia watches the one in the hall. She tells me. What's on. But I want to see for myself."

It's too far to the window. All she can see is the opposite wall. On the wall, there is a painting. Galloping horses.

> They run down the wide-open pasture, like arrows of lightning
> aglow—
> Their manes streaming bright in the sunlight, their hoofs raising
> dust as they go.

I go and see Seven Wings to talk to him about the wheelchair and the TV. And about the spasms. Is Sveta taking an antispasmodic? These things exist, don't they?

It turns out she isn't. Why not? "I have no idea, I've only been here a week." The doctor pulls out her medical record.

"Cerebral palsy, brain damage, severe retardation. Severe congenital dementia, to the point of oligophrenia. Nonverbal. Communicates by hand signs and facial expression. Responsive to simple instructions. Primitive. Demonstrable deterioration in cognitive function. Vegetative."

"That's Sveta?"

"Uh-huh."

"What does that mean, 'vegetative'?"

"When a person is only interested in food and physiological stimuli. That's it."

"She writes poetry."

"What do you mean, poetry?"

"She has these notebooks full of poems."

"Did you see her writing it? Listen, this is ridiculous. She's never even been to school. Pushkin had a vocabulary of twenty thousand words. She couldn't possibly even have a basic set of words to express her thoughts or feelings."

"I talked to her."

"And she read you her poems? All right, let's go and see her, then, let's go right now, so she can read me them, too!"

Seven Wings is really mad.

"You think we just write up any old nonsense in these records? I'm not even the one who wrote that. She was examined at the Serbsky Institute—they're specialists!"

"Let's go and talk to her together tomorrow."

"Okay, if you want to do it tomorrow, we'll do it tomorrow," Seven Wings grumbles. "I can't wait to hear what she has to say."

The next day, Seven Wings is already in Sveta's room when I get there. He's clearly perplexed.

"I was trying to puzzle it out last night. Tried talking to her myself. But it didn't work. Show me how you are doing it."

"Sveta, good morning. How are you today?"

Sveta braces her forehead against the bed, hunts for the phone with her curled left fist. She pokes at the buttons with her pinky, misses, tries again. Her spasms are worse today.

At last the drafts folder comes up, "I was born in the town of N. When I was seven months old, I got meningitis. Until I was nine, I lived in a village with my grandma and grandpa . . ."

"Who wrote that?" asks Seven Wings.

"Sveta, did you write this?"

A spasm. Another.

"Me."

"When did you write this?"

A lengthy spasm. The doctor studies the ceiling.

"Last night."

"Let's see her write something. Anything. A sentence."

"Sveta, could you write down how you feel? Please."

Sveta is racked by hard tremors. Finally she braces herself against the pillow and slides the phone closer.

I open one of the notebooks to "A Young Woman Asks God" and hand it to the doctor. "Please read it." He begins to read.

Sveta starts jabbing the phone with her pinkie. My hands are shaking. I hide them.

I look at Yulia. She's sitting up straight on her rolling stool, as straight as she is able to. The smile on her face is serene, proud, and confident. She gives me a nod.

Sveta gently nudges the phone to the edge of the bed.

I hand it to Seven Wings.

"I feel very nervous."

Seven Wings looks at Sveta. She looks back at him. Then at us.

Sveta says, "You picked me. Why?"

I mumble some embarrassing nonsense, something about her talent.

"There are others," Sveta says.

"Many others," Seven Wings says to no one in particular. "Not enough nuance in the system for them all."

Outside her room, he lays into me, "We are severely understaffed. In a good home like this in Spain, they have five thousand staff members for one thousand beds. We have one nurse for forty! The intellect is a complicated thing, we have to rely on psychological testing. Somatically, this woman is vegetative. In a hospice setting our job is to deliver care. She writes poems, okay, but her intellect and memory are impaired, and she has issues with self-agency. Her cognitive function, reasoning, mirroring, all are impaired. She's been stripped of her legal competence! Legal competence is a machine, a state-run machine, I'm not the one who stripped her of it. There was a panel, the Serbsky Institute, courts! You'd be more help using your connections to fix her wheelchair situation!"

What the Staff Say

"So I am a nurse, right? I should be monitoring the clients' condition, that's my job. Right? Want to know how many papers I have to fill out every day? Look. The rotation change log. The doctors' orders list. The privately-purchased-prescriptions list. Consultant appointments log. Banya-day roll-call sheet. Single-dose patient medication log. Haircut and shaving log. Prescription-only dispensing log. Doctor-prescribed neuroleptics dispensing log. Daily prescribed medication dispensing log. Disinfectant use and supply log. Fire safety log. Patient roll-call spreadsheet. Patient hygiene requirements spreadsheet. Patient outdoor access spreadsheet. Indoor temperature and humidity log. Doctors' daily notes sheet. A UV bactericide timetable and sign-off for the hallway, corridor, two bathrooms, the shower block, the duty nurse's office, and housekeeping—each logged separately. Staff hygiene spreadsheet. Client temperature log. The Visual Inspection of Sanitary Hygiene and Antiepidemic Measures Register. Timetable for charging the courtyard light. The "mens" log for tracking menstruation. Register of deep cleans, separate for every cleaned space. Pharmaceutical dispensary requests log. Epileptic seizures log. There's also a log for changing the filters on the Kront air-purifying apparatus, but luckily that's only once a month on the eighteenth.

"If I miss filling in one line, I get docked all of my pay. Now, I ask you: When exactly am I supposed to be monitoring the clients' condition?"

"**Fresh air is timetabled.** In theory this is on a voluntary basis, but really, the longer they spend outside, the less time they spend hanging around in here; the nurses can take a breather, everyone has a break, the doctors can have a break. So it makes sense to drag them out as much as possible. I never make them, but there's one aide here, Natasha, she just loves getting rid of them. One guy hid, he didn't want to go outside. So she starts poking him with a broom. Come on, get out. He grabs the broom away from her and hits her over the head with it three times.

"That was it for him. They shot him full of drugs and shipped him out to the mental hospital. Even though he apologized. Natasha had it put in her record as a workplace injury."

"**These kinds of** things happen, sure. I've seen it myself. We had S. strangling A. once, with a twisted-up bedsheet. . . . The orderly was making rounds and heard the wheezing from one of the solitary cells. He had him down flat on the bed, choking him with the sheet to keep him quiet while he was ramming him. They had to stitch A. up afterward, he was all torn up.

"It's easier in the rehab ward, there's both boys and girls in there. But they have no outlet for their sexuality, they're like animals. The girls go sex crazy, too. The other day, one of them was going around screaming, Take me to the mental hospital, I just want to suck dick. I guess they're not as strict in there. She wants a man. But she knows it's not going to happen here. So they start going at their roommates. Fingers in every hole. The men try to get at other men. Some of them even like that kind of attention, others fight it off.

"You get ones that don't mind, sometimes. We had this Sasha—everyone called him Dasha, like he was a girl. He didn't even protest. But he was always trying to run away. You take them to the cafeteria, but where is Sasha? He's in the cellar, hiding, waiting for the noise to die down so he can make a break for it.

"We get the doctor over if we ever catch them at it. The doctor decides what to do. If it is sexual assault, they will try and get them referred for treatment. If it's a mutual thing, then the doctor just has a stern talk with them: See that it doesn't happen again. Or else it won't be just a warning, there'll be injections so there's no more undesirable arousals."

"I FEEL TERRIBLE for them. I've boarded here for a year, doing shifts, and I really understand what it's like for them now. It's a real prison. It's actually probably better in prison. Everything here is timetabled: eat when you're told, sleep when you're told, take meds, can't go outside without a guard . . . You open your mouth, you get jabbed.

"If a patient dares to complain about anything, the nurses threaten them. Say one more word and you'll get shot full of drugs. They log it as a change of patient condition. They'll log whatever they want in there.

"Even if someone is shouting, even if they are waving their arms around, something drove them to do it. But who's going to take their side? Who's going to listen to them or believe them? The nurses can do whatever they want. They can smack you with a slipper or say nasty things to you. Just you try to talk back.

"There's one nurse who jabs you just for looking at her the wrong way. A mental case, honest to God. She's on maternity leave right now, thankfully.

"I don't do injections that often, only when someone's having an epileptic seizure or I can see they're about to have a psychotic episode. Or if a woman comes and says, Jab me, because she's starting to hear the voices again. But it's not always up to me. We have this one deputy head nurse—acting deputy—she goes around winding everyone up, and then she goes and winds the head nurse up. It's our responsibility, this wing, our decision to make, but she's always sticking her nose in: Jab this one, jab that one. I don't always do it, but she goes around checking, tattling to the management.

"That nurse, the same one, insulted Tanya just before the end of the shift. I was in the nurses' station and I heard Tanya saying, I wanna go home so bad. And then she says to her, in front of everyone, Who do you think you were back home? You were a deadbeat, a drunk. Tanya was so upset she was shaking. Then she goes to me, 'Jab her.' I said I wouldn't do it. What for? For saying she missed home? I called the doctor down. It was one of the good ones, he prescribed pills instead of an injection. Like there's any room to inject anything—all the butts are bruised blue.

"It has to come down from the ministry itself, a rule that we aren't allowed to beat them or talk about their past and remind them of their life before.

"We need staff who actually care about them. So that the residents don't live in fear of them. Some of the staff see them all as deadbeats, but it's their disability benefits that pay our salaries. They think our patients are all psychos, that they need to be drilled to obey. I've stopped having tea breaks with the other staff, all that shit-talking, calling them names: Those fuckers, how did they ever manage to live on the outside? Just bitching about them endlessly. Too pea-brained to realize that people can just get sick. That anyone can get sick. There's no compassion for them here, no pity at all."

Love

There was a woman who lived in an internat. Once upon a time she could walk, even if it was on crutches, but now she was in a wheelchair. Like everyone who lived at the internat, she was very lonely. But she was also lucky because she had her mother to visit her. Her mother was elderly. They'd go on walks, and not just in the courtyard but also around the outside of the building; they could even go all the way around it (this is usually forbidden). Sometimes the mother brought along a young girl from the same ward—she also couldn't walk. She had Down syndrome and funny little bald spots on her head. The woman would ask her mother, Why do you bring her along? And the mother would answer, I'll tell you one day.

Then one day, the mother told her: That girl is your sister.

"My real sister?"

"That's right," said her mother. "You're sisters by blood. First I had you, then her. You have different last names because you have different fathers. But she is your sister, look after her."

The woman began to take care of her sister. She fed her, changed her diaper, washed her clothes. She hugged her and kissed her. Then she started to care for the other girls, ones like her sister. She made a request to the staff, and they moved four girls with Down syndrome into the woman's room. Even though they were all between twenty-four and twenty-nine, none of them were any taller than a four-year-old. This was because children with Down syndrome need love to grow. The woman's room came to be known as "the preschool." And that was how her life became filled with love, and how the girls started, little by little, to grow. The woman looks after all four girls but loves her sister most of all because "she's all I have in the world."

The staff have seen all the paperwork and they know that the sister story is completely made up. But nobody says a word. You can't ask the woman's mother about it; she died—though not before leaving behind someone for her daughter to love. The woman couldn't go to her mother's funeral: first of all, she can't walk, and second of all, who'd let her out?

Sterilization

There are three of them. We're huddling together in a bedroom, scared of a nurse coming in. The women pull up their tops, pull down their pants and tights. White scars on their stomachs. One has a thin one, running horizontally like a C-section scar. The other two have wide up-down seams that have been stitched up roughly.

They were all pregnant. Their babies were aborted. The women were sterilized.

They are Alina, Vera, and Olya.

Alina and Vera were both five months pregnant. Olya doesn't

remember—her mental issues are more severe, it's harder for her to keep track of time. When they found out she was pregnant, Olya's relatives had her released on medical leave and got her sterilized in a neighboring town. "I wanted to look after the baby, but I didn't get to. There was a nice nurse there, Valentina Sergeyevna. She helped out in the hospital. My grandma came. My mom came, too, they looked after me in the hospital. There were nice people working there."

Alina and Vera were sterilized by the internat.

Alina in 2007, Vera in 2016. Alina was twenty-one, Vera thirty.

Pregnancy is forbidden here. The official reason is that the institution's charter does not extend to the upbringing of children. A mother-to-be must be legally competent and leave the PNI if she wishes to raise her child. But most of the women here have been stripped of their legal competence, they're not allowed to raise children. Any children they had would automatically be sent to state orphanages. Not that it would ever get that far. Children are always aborted.

How does the internat know a woman is pregnant?

None of the women have their own sanitary napkins. To get one, you have to go to the nurse, who will log it in a special menstruation logbook. The use of sanitary napkins is periodically monitored: an aide or a nurse will check the bathroom after a woman suspected of concealment has used it to see whether she actually disposed of a used pad.

Women who don't ask for pads for two months in a row get sent to the gynecologist for a physical exam and a blood test. Those who are found to be pregnant are referred for an abortion. The law requires the woman's written consent, but nobody ever asks them.

Instead, the women are sternly told that they have to get rid of their baby. This speech can be delivered by the woman's primary care physician, or the chief physician, or the head of the ward. They always make sure to mention that once-upon-a-time-in-this-very-facility a woman threw her own newborn out the window.

Alina's and Vera's cases were a glitch in the system. Their pregnancies were discovered too late and they were forced to get premature C-sections, with sterilization as an "add-on." Vera had her fallopian tubes cut and cauterized. Alina's medical records are vague—it just says "sterilized" and that's all.

Neither woman knew that she would be sterilized. No one asked their permission, neither at the PNI nor at the hospital. When they returned, the nurses informed them that they would never have children.

Alina says, "I wanted children. It's what any woman wants. It's a spiritual thing. I came here in 2005, and they found out I was pregnant in the spring of 2007. If we were home, we could choose for ourselves. But here it's the administration. 'It's hard enough as it is for you with your disabilities. You see it on the news all the time, kids getting abandoned. They all end up in orphanages, internats. Do we need more of that?' That's what the doctor told me. She is the one who said I was going to get an abortion. 'You weren't scared to sleep with a man, don't tell me you're scared of the gynecologist.'

"They took me to the hospital for an ultrasound, but they wouldn't even tell me if it was a boy or girl. One of the women goes, 'That's it, we're taking you in for an abortion.' The chief physician asks, 'You don't feel bad about the baby? The girl is still young. Are you sure?' And the midwife goes, 'Nah, they're all head cases over there.' She meant that about me.

"Nobody asked me anything. Nobody. I never signed a thing. They put something on my finger and a needle into my vein, then I fell asleep. Who knows what they did to me. I woke up with a stitched-up scar. I never saw the baby. Later, this nurse, very pretty, she told me that it was a boy, just like a regular newborn, wrapped up in the umbilical cord.

"That midwife came in to see me the next day. I said, 'Get out of here, I hate you.' I was so angry. What did I do to deserve that?

"When I got back to the internat they told me that my tubes had been tied, no more children.

"I love kids. I love looking after them. My friend had a daughter and I looked after her. My friend would rock her and rock her, but she wouldn't fall asleep. When I picked her up, the baby fell asleep right away. My grandmother on my mother's side, people would bring her their babies when they were crying and crying and wouldn't sleep. She'd read the Virgin's prayer over them three times and they would fall asleep, every last one of them. I don't think I've got her gift. Or maybe I do?

"The scar hurts when the weather changes.

"Is it okay if I don't say what I feel?"

Vera says, "I kept eating candy, craving everything sweet. And salty things too. I felt nauseous sometimes, but I figured that it was just food poisoning. I was working in the banya, helping to wash people, lifting heavy stuff, very late into my pregnancy, it turned out.

"We get a physical exam once a year. I was pregnant.

"We had a different chief physician back then. He said, 'Get a C-section, you can't have a baby in here.'

"So they sent me to the maternity hospital, with Tanya—she lives here, too—to take care of me after the operation. The doctors asked me, 'Are you going to deliver naturally or by C-section?' I said I didn't know. The lady in charge there says, 'Are you sure you won't regret this? Killing your baby?'

"But what could I do?

"Anyway, I was already almost under, I couldn't feel anything until I woke up in intensive care. The lady doctor in charge of the ward told me, 'You gave birth to a girl, five months' gestation.' I asked to see her, so they took me. She was lying there, so little. Covered in wires and tubes. She smiled at me with her little mouth. Waved her little hands at me.

"I didn't have time to think of a name for her.

"I was in there for a week, and when they came to sign me out, they told me she died. She didn't survive. I was hysterical. So they let me see her. All the machines were turned off. They let me say goodbye.

"They never told me where she was buried.

"I wanted to go, too. To kill myself. But they kept a watch on me.

"The other women in my hospital room kept saying, 'You will have more.'

"I only found out that I'd been sterilized when I got back here. That nurse Allochka said, 'Your tubes are tied, you can't have any more children now.'

"Can they untie the tubes, on the outside? No one in here will tell me.

"My scar isn't on my stomach, it's sort of underneath. So neat you can hardly tell anymore.

"My soul is in pieces. But I never show that to anyone. You can't. They'll ship you off to the mental hospital. That's where you'll end up if you scream and cry.

"How do I get out of this hell?"

According to federal law, only a court can rule on the sterilization of a legally incompetent person, and only in her presence. No one ever goes to court.

Appended to Alina's case file, there is a letter of request from the facility director, which cites an out-of-date set of guidelines from the Ministry of Health—a list of medical conditions that allow for the termination of pregnancies. Although the list includes psychiatric illness, the guidelines themselves say nothing at all about sterilization. This didn't deter the internat or the hospital. That list, coupled with a copy of the court document declaring Alina legally incompetent, was enough.

An orderly tells me, "If you take two schizophrenics, or, say, two retarded people . . . they have intercourse—and their baby will be just like them, a hundred percent. They'll fill up all the orphanages. It's not like we can forbid them, exactly, but at the same time—one is completely disabled, the other one is completely disabled, not one percent of normality there. One is mentally challenged and so is the other one. How are they going to make a normal child? I ask you."

A Letter

Dearest Sveta,

Please forgive us for not being able to come and see you. Our uncle is still doing poorly and only rarely gets behind the wheel these days. He's aged a lot since Ivan died, and no wonder, now he's the only one left of the family. Lida swapped her apartment for a smaller one. Katya got married and had a daughter, but her husband caught her with some Armenian and threw her out. Now she lives at her mother's, she and the baby. Lyoshka lives in N., his wife has a big house there. They have a son. He looks so much like Ivan. Taya is also not very well. She hasn't been well since she buried Sasha, two years ago now.

Lena and Katyusha, her daughter, from O., came to L. for the summer, but they are gone now. Katyusha is in her final year of school, she wants to go to dental college. Lyosha left O. for good and moved to P. He has two kids, a boy and a girl. Irinka had twins, daughters—Sonya and Dasha, they're nineteen months now. Tatyana's still on her own, working, she just got another college degree. She lives in N., doesn't come home very often.

So there is barely anyone left in the village, just the people who come to their dachas in the summer. Only old Granny Anna left now, out of the two villages, she's the only one who was born here. Lena comes, but she only goes to her dacha, she doesn't come round to see us. Doesn't come visit her mother's grave, either, or go to the village graveyard. We're looking after all of the graves ourselves for the time being.

Well, that's all the news, I think. Forgive us. If we can, we might come see you, but I won't promise anything. It all depends on our health. There's Uncle Volodya, Aunt Nina, and me. I've had two surgeries and a microstroke. Everything is on me, I'm not as strong as I used to be. Forgive us.

What Does It Mean to Be Legally Incompetent?

A legally incompetent person is a citizen who cannot through his or her own agency gain and use his or her civil rights, acquire civic duties, and perform those duties. This is what is written in the law. Children are legally incompetent. An adult whose psychiatric illness renders him or her unable to understand the consequences of his or her actions or to control those actions can be declared legally incompetent by a court of law. The court commissions a psychiatric report and almost without exception concurs with the report's recommendations.

Legally, the person in question is required to attend the hearing, but a doctor's note claiming that the person cannot attend "due to their mental state" is sufficient to decide their fate without their ever coming before a judge.

A legally incompetent person is assigned a guardian. They are divested of certain rights: the right to have charge of their personal property and finances, to vote, to marry, raise children, file government documents, will property to others or make business agreements, or to adopt. They may be divorced from their spouse, have their children adopted, and have their personal data handled—all without their consent.

Their other civil rights are unaffected.

So what happens to a legally incompetent client of a PNI?

The internat acts both as guardian and as service provider. The internat is the purchaser of its own product. This can create some truly amazing opportunities.

Let's start with the money. The 404 legally incompetent persons living here hold a combined total of 98,956,665 rubles* in their bank accounts. As a rule, they each receive a disability pension, and the pensions accrue. The internat retains 75 percent of their pensions for services rendered. The remaining 25 percent can be used to improve a resident's quality of life, but only with permission from their guardian.

So why doesn't Lyuba have any batteries for her tape player? Why must people scrub floors for an extra cigarette?

It's simple: it's the internat that rules on the needs of the people in its care.

De facto, a person declared legally incompetent is forbidden from going out into the world. One woman I met told me that her greatest wish was to go to the nearest market (three blocks away from the internat) to choose, try on, and purchase a pair of shoes.

A legally incompetent person may not leave the facility without another, outside guardian.

* $1.14 million.

The chief physician (he's new here and considered to be progressive) believes that the internat has the right to decide literally everything for the legally incompetent. Because the legally incompetent cannot be responsible for their actions, their guardian, in this case the internat, knows what is best for them.

A perfect example of this policy is encoded in every resident's medical file: a treatment plan, signed not by the patient but by the internat's director, who, "being fully informed about the nature of the psychiatric disorder, the aims, methods, and duration of proposed treatment, as well as its side effects, risks, and metrics of success," agrees to pretty much everything therein. This is against the law—patients must be informed, but this never happens. The patients don't need to know what pills they are made to swallow and what goes into those syringes. No one asks women whether they consent to an abortion or even bothers to inform them that they've been sterilized.

Many of them don't know, and are too afraid to ask, what their diagnosis might be. I met a young woman whose periods stopped when she was twenty-six. She had a physical exam and something was logged in her record, but no one told her what, and she's too afraid to ask. Why is she afraid? Because asking questions could be interpreted as complaining. Any complaint can and probably will be viewed as "deteriorating mental condition" and be dealt with by an injection, or a transfer up to 3-A or, worse, to the mental hospital, depending on the severity of the transgression.

And this is a whole other layer of hell: You can never be in a bad mood or be angry or tearful, never call nastiness nastiness or cruelty cruelty. If you want to stay safe, you must put a smile on your face, or at the very least be neutral—indifferent, docile, no matter what they do to you and those around you.

Nina Bazhenova lost her legal competence during one of her hospitalizations. "This man explained what legal competence is," she tells me. "And I realized that I'd lost everything. What is the point of living? I've lost all my human rights now. It was such a blow to me. I was terrified.

Terrified that I wouldn't count as a person anymore, that anyone could say to me, 'Who do you think you are? You are nothing.' That is how I understood it. And it all turned out to be true."

The Rehabilitation Ward

Forty-nine incredibly lucky people live here.

The rehab ward is the least restricted place in the facility. Its door is only locked at night, so you can go to the internat library (by yourself, without a guard) to use the computers, or to the gym to play tennis. The ward has its own shower, which anybody can use, and a kitchen. You can ask for pots and pans and cook. You get a whole pack of cigarettes every two days. There is a terrarium with three turtles, live ones, even if they do bite. The ward supervisor is a psychologist rather than a psychiatrist, you can talk to her if you want. The rehab ward residents take their walks outside the building itself, rather than in the 124-step courtyard. The building is long, so you get a real walk.

The ward is mixed, though the shared bedrooms themselves are single sex. You can sit on the sofa and cuddle, or kiss. You can even hide away from the nurses and "grab a personal moment" with your sweetheart.

There is a flip side to this happy existence: it is purchased by ceaseless and unpaid labor. The women wash floors here and elsewhere throughout the building and work in the laundry; the men load and unload crates, push the wheelchairs, and bathe the wheelchair-bound on wash day. Any ward can send staff down to requisition "a few pairs of hands." A few of the legally competent residents work for quarter pay; the others work—or rather, they "receive vocational rehabilitation"—for the right to live in paradise.

The rehab ward was opened by gubernatorial decree in 2001. Its purpose is to prepare residents for life outside the walls of the internat. In the twenty years of its existence, four people have made it to "the outside." One woman drank herself to death, one man went off the radar, and two more are married and have jobs.

Vanya has lived here for two years. He is twenty-six.

In "freedom," he was a trained welder and had a job.

I want to tell his story in detail, because the line that lies between freedom and the internat is impossibly, vanishingly thin.

Vanya was fifteen years old when his mother died. After his wife's death, Vanya's father began to drink, and he also died, two years later. Then his grandmother. Vanya was left alone. He inherited a share of his family's apartment, his father's studio, and his grandmother's two-bedroom. But not for long.

His maternal aunt—a real estate agent—took charge.

The aunt asked him to transfer his share of the family apartment to her—to help her daughter get a mortgage. To help the family. Vanya agreed. Then the two-bedroom had to be sold to fund renovations in the studio. Vanya agreed to this, too. There then was a complicated maneuver involving the purchase of a dacha, the sale of the dacha, the sale of the studio, and the resulting purchase of another apartment solely in his aunt's name.

Vanya didn't take much of an interest in these proceedings. Having lost his entire immediate family, he "went off the rails, smoked spice, snorted stuff." He remembers dancing wildly under the influence of something, totaling somebody else's car.

"Then I saw *Harry Potter and the Chamber of Secrets*, and I thought, What if the basilisk is real? I went off my nut, really. And ended up in the mental hospital. A few times. I kept seeing vampires, other weird shit. They decided it was schizophrenia. There was this doctor there, he knew my aunt. He told her, get him declared legally incompetent and send him to a PNI. So that's what she did. I ended up in 2-D at first. I took one look in there, and I said to her, What are you doing? Get me out of here. And she's like, I can't take that responsibility. What if you do something bad? I'll have to go to prison. She comes to see me sometimes. The apartment? She's rented it out, I think. Why do you want to know about the apartment?"

Now that Vanya isn't on drugs, he doesn't hallucinate. No matter, he still has to take his pills: Cyclodol, half a haloperidol, and a couple of sedatives every night. The medications make him blink uncontrollably, but he's "used to it now." The medical staff are not convinced by his diagnosis of schizophrenia but are in no hurry to review his case or appeal the court's decision—with Vanya as a ward of the institution, they too could sue for his property.

Vanya is seeing Nina, the girl who sang at the disco dressed as a princess. The one who "lost everything" when she lost her legal rights. She has been here forever—fifteen years. She lost a baby here—an abortion, but luckily without sterilization. It was an early-stage job, just a D&C, so "they didn't cut me open." Nina's dream is that one day, they will live together in their own house, perhaps the one that she left behind, "go away to our own garden and just live there. Fresh air, a house with an old-fashioned Russian stove. A bit of land, a banya. It's been fifteen years, so I don't know if it's still standing. You'd need a strong pair of hands, of course, a man. Vanya is too young, it would be too much for him. Or maybe you'd surprise us, Vanya?"

I find myself thinking that even here, people have the most commonplace, conventional dreams, just like everyone else.

But that evening, quiet Dima (he misses his mother and cries out for her in wheezy little sobs) is transferred to 3-A for calling one of the aides a bitch. He can't speak very clearly, but she still caught him saying it. This was Elena Sergeyevna, the pious older woman who was helping the girls get dressed for the disco. She called for the nurse, who gave Dima an injection, and, with the consent of the on-call psychiatrist (here to relieve Seven Wings), they sent Dima up to solitary, a locked, bare cell with a bucket in the corner. They didn't trouble themselves unduly about what to call it in his medical notes, they just put down "bad behavior."

As a devout Christian, Elena Sergeyevna is, naturally, unhappy with how things turned out. She says that she only wanted to scare him a little, she didn't expect the nurse to be so ready with the injection. But apparently, the nurse herself was already annoyed with Dima. Elena Sergeyevna says that she always prays for "Dimitry and all of the other orphans" and won't stop praying for him even though he insulted her.

There's no smoking schedule in rehab, and you can take any coat you like off the hangers.

Looking through the balcony bars and beyond the dark courtyard, I can see the backs of the cars receding down the gray strip of the road. I can see the lights of a store and the shadows of people inside it. I see the entryways of the apartment buildings. A man in a black overcoat comes out. He pauses and lights up a cigarette, smoking unhurriedly. He must be wearing headphones—he seems to be dancing to something. A wave of his hand, and one of the cars blinks its headlights. The man gets into his car. He drives away.

I know that for him, I am a darkness among the darkness. I am indistinguishable, we are indistinguishable.

What do people who end up at PNIs all have in common? Tyoma and Sveta, Vanya and Dima, the women of Ward 1, the women who can never have children? It isn't their diagnoses, which are all different and some of which are clearly wrong.

All of them have been abandoned by their families. Their relationships and social connections are severed, or else weakened to the point of disappearing entirely.

When human connection is lost, all that is left is the state.

My state is the internat. Not the Sputnik V vaccine, not the Olympics, not space shuttles. The real face of my state is right here, I can see it.

What do I think after two weeks in the PNI?

That I have only scratched the surface of hell.

I lived in the internat by special arrangement. I went behind the wall that faces the outside with cheerful diamonds by special arrangement. The agreement between *Novaya Gazeta* and the internat's management prohibits me from revealing the name of the facility or its location. The names of the people imprisoned or working here had to be changed.

This internat recently turned fifty. According to the volunteers who visit and the local ministry of social services, it is neither good nor bad. It is just average. Normal.

There are 155,878 adults currently living in PNIs across Russia. And 21,000 children in specialized-care homes, doomed to end up in a PNI. Every 826th Russian citizen will live out their life in a PNI and die within its walls.

CHAPTER 13

THE WAR (HOW IT BROKE THROUGH THE SOIL AND BLOSSOMED)

I AM FIVE, I am in preschool. It's winter. We're playing war. The big hill of snow is the fortress, it's full of Germans. We storm it. There aren't many, nobody wants to be one of the fascists, but they have the tactical advantage—it's a lot easier defending a fortress. Snowballs are flying in every direction. All of the boys are fighters. I also wanted to be a fighter, but they only let me play nurse. Because I'm a girl. I drag the wounded off the battlefield. The wounded are covered in snow and laughing.

I am six. Mama tells me that my grandfather fought in the war. That fascists attacked our country and he defended it. He volunteered to go to the front. He was in the artillery ("artillery," I repeat). He got wounded but then he got better and went back to fight more, this time with the Japanese. Because the Japanese were helping the fascists. The war was called the Great Patriotic War because people were fighting for our patrimony. Why was it great? Because almost all of the men and many of the women fought in it, Mama said. And eleven million people died. How much is eleven million? Mama moves her lips, calculating. It's like sixteen Yaroslavls. Imagine that nobody in our city was left alive. And then no one was left alive in fifteen more cities like ours. Not one single person. All of them killed.

I imagine all the dead cities.

I'm eight, it's Victory Day. We're visiting our neighbor Auntie Tonya. She fought in the war. We bought her a cake and red carnations. Auntie Tonya is wearing a blue homemade dress and a medal on her chest. She's happy to see us and our cake, she comes over to hug me. I don't like Auntie Tonya. She smells bad. She's also deaf and you have to talk very loudly and move your mouth very big to get her to understand you. Also, her apartment is very clean, everything's gleaming, there isn't a speck of dust. I'm afraid of it being this clean, it's not normal. Auntie Tonya loves me. She asks how is school (it's bad but you have to say that it's good). Mama pours out the tea. We raise our cups and toast. Mama says, "To peace."

I'm ten, I'm watching a movie. It's called, *Only Old Men Are Going into Battle*. It's about courageous young fighter pilots, they're very handsome, fighting the fascists up in the sky. The movie is black-and-white and every face in it seems to be sculpted from light. Some young men join an air force squadron, and the old hands don't want to let them into the fray, they want to protect them. But the boys are also eager to defend their motherland. After flying in battle, the pilots gather into a choir and sing beautiful songs. They die, but heroically, majestically, going up in clouds of black smoke. As he dies, one of them shouts, "We're going to live!" There's romance, too—with the girl pilots. When the girl pilots die, the boy pilots visit their graves and promise to come back after the war so they can sing their favorite songs together again. I'm not even thinking, I am all feeling: Wow, this is so great, what a life.

I am eleven and I ask Mama, What did Grandpa say about the war? She says, Nothing. Nothing at all? Nothing at all. One time, he said that they ate dead horses. No, he said "fallen horses." It was winter so they had to hack pieces of meat off of the horses. And that's all he said? That's all he said. Did he have any medals? Yes. But he never wore them. He gave them to me. I was little, I played with them, I would bury them in the sand. I ended up losing them all. It's too bad. Too bad. How did he die? His heart stopped. Babushka told him that dinner was ready, but he wasn't coming. He was sitting here dead, right in that spot.

I am twelve and I go over to Auntie Tonya's. She is so happy to see me. I say, Auntie Tonya, tell me about the war. She says, I can't hear you. Auntie Tonya, tell me about the war! I can't hear anything, Lenochka, I must be totally deaf. About the war! About the USSR? It was a good country, the USSR. ABOUT THE WAR! I can't hear you at all, my hearing aid must be broken. Auntie Tonya takes out her hearing aid and she tells me, I'm tired, I'll go lie down. Goodbye, Lena.

I'm twelve and I go to the library. I ask for books about the war. They hand me about five of them and I read them all. I take out five more. Then five more after that. In the books, the war isn't as cheerful as it is in the movies, but there is more heroism and you can read slowly so you can really feel all of it. In the Karelian forests, under the command of Captain Vaskov, the antiaircraft gunner girls take down the fascist spies breaking through toward the strategic canal. There are only five girls and sixteen spies. All of the girls die. As she is dying, one of them, the very best one, says, "Our motherland doesn't even begin with these canals. That's not where it comes from at all. But we defended it. She came first, and then the canal." I cry so hard, my tears are so sweet. Of course the canals aren't even the tip of it, my beloved motherland.

I am twelve and I think to myself, What if there is another war? What if our country's attacked? Of course I'll defend it. I'll be, like, a sniper. If only I could hurry up and grow up. I'll kill all the fascists. Why fascists? I don't know, that's the only enemy that occurred to me, fascists. Maybe I'll die. I'll die so young. And Mama will cry, but she'll be so proud of me. She'll have this quiet, dark, restrained pride. I have only two friends; when I look at my classmates, I think, Later on, you will tell everyone that we went to school together, you'll tell everyone what I was like. The only thing that gets in the way of this fantasy is that I am the smallest girl in my class, the runt, and a weakling. That's fine, I can carry a sniper rifle.

I am thirteen, there's a funeral on our street. A young man was killed—only yesterday, he was a schoolboy. They enlisted him, sent him to Chechnya, and he got killed. I ask our neighbor Lenya, Who killed him? The Chechens. Why? Because there's a war there. With whom? With the terrorists. Wow, I think. Killing terrorists is even cooler than killing fascists. Although maybe not, killing fascists is actually cooler. Or maybe terrorists? Poor guy, of course. He is, of course, a hero. But Lenya's exaggerating about the war. On TV, they call it a "counterterrorism operation." If there was really a war, we would know about it.

I am fourteen and I'm reading an Anna Politkovskaya article about Chechnya. Holy fuck.

I am fourteen and I'm reading the books of Svetlana Alexievich. Holy shit.

I am seventeen and I am a student in the journalism department. I'm sitting on the sidelines of an international rights strategy game. Teams from various colleges' journalism departments have come to participate in the game. The team from Chechnya is two girls, Asya and Malika. They are so serious and beautiful. I go up to them after the game and invite them over. We go to my dorm room, I make them tea. I really want them to like me. I tell them, Let me show you around Moscow! And just as I'm saying that, as if I'd planned it, fireworks start going off outside. Look, fireworks! Look! I look out the window and say, Here in Moscow, we have fireworks all the time. The girls don't say anything. I turn around and they're gone. Where did they go? They're under the table.

I'm twenty, Russia attacks Georgia. The president says that this is a peacekeeping mission because Georgia's attacked South Ossetia and Abkhazia. Three correspondents go down there from *Novaya*: Olga Bobrova, Arkady Babchenko, and Roman Anin. I'm especially jealous of Anin—he's only a year older than me. I could have gone, too. But me and three other girls are assigned to the news feed instead. I need to verify all of the information and write up briefs. I also need to follow the movements of our correspondents, receive breaking news from them, and report to them on the movements of the Russian and Georgian troops. I never let go of my phone. It's very scary to miss an incoming call. It's very scary deciding which information is critical and needs to be shared with our people on the ground and what I shouldn't bother them with. What if one of them gets wounded because of me? Or killed? I can't sleep for three nights. On the fourth day, everything starts to look transparent and crystalline. My legs stop being able to support me. The girls say, Lena, go get some sleep, we'll keep watch. I lie down on the office couch, cover myself with the comforter, and lay my phone under my cheek. I black out. Somebody touches my shoulder and I jump up. What happened? Irina says, The war is over. An invisible light fills the room.

I can never let go of my phone ever again. I'm scared without it.

A day later, Babchenko returns. He screams at the accountant—she's asking him for receipts and tickets for the books. He says, Go fuck yourself. Goes to his office. I follow him. He shows me photos of charred bodies, people without legs, without noses or eyes, people swollen out in the sun like bad dough, people perforated with bullets, dead and alive. He shows me a scrape on his head and a hole through his pants: shrapnel. Then he starts falling over. What, are you drunk? No, I haven't had anything. He leans into me and he whispers, Do I smell like dead bodies? Smell me. What? I feel like I smell like dead bodies, can you smell them on me? I rode in a truck full of them. No. You're lying to me, Lena. I'm not. Just a minute. I go to the deputy editor in chief. I say, Babchenko's not well. We need to get him home. Yes, says the editor, just a minute.

I'm twenty-three and the deputy editor in chief says, You'll never get sent to cover a war. You're a girl. It's a man's job. I think to myself, You're fucking crazy.

I'm twenty-four. I travel to Egypt to cover the revolution. I see people burning alive after being hit with Molotov cocktails. I see flying stones ripping off people's fingers and ears, breaking holes through their skulls. Then the shooting begins.

I'm twenty-six and the war in Donbas begins. The Donetsk and

Luhansk regions in Ukraine announce that they are now independent republics, the DNR and the LNR. Ukraine begins its own "antiterrorist operation," and the "republics" respond in kind. Russia says that it doesn't have any soldiers there, claiming Ukraine is fighting with its own citizens. I look for the bodies of Russian soldiers (they're being hidden). I find them.

I am twenty-seven, I go to Donbas. I call my mother from the plane, I was too scared to call her before. I thought that Mama was going to scream and cry. Instead she says, Have you written down my contact information in your passport? Cover your passport in plastic wrap and always carry it with you, but not in your purse, in your clothes. Try to get in touch with me at least once a day, even if it's only a text. Drink water. Seek warmth, stick next to hospitals, avoid army vehicles. Did you bring any antibiotics? You need to get your hands on some tourniquets.

I see war. Not a single one of the books I read told me that war means dirt. Heavy machinery breaks through the top layer of soil and light-brown mud rises up through the cracks. It covers everything: people, cars, buildings, dogs. So many abandoned dogs. So many sleepless people with weapons.

I'm caught in the shelling twice. I learn that I can run on all fours. I glide along in long leaps, like in a dream, my body is agile and limber, I don't believe that I'm going to die.

I went back to Donbas twice.

I wrote many articles. I don't want to reread them.

I'm thirty-one, I'm taking classes at the School of Journalism at the City University of New York. Alia Malek teaches us international journalism. She's Syrian, beautiful, untouchably smart and sharp-witted. I spend more time doing work for her classes than for any others. I really want her to notice me, but I have nothing to impress her with. I don't read much and think very slowly. Alia teaches us to write carefully and honestly. Alia teaches us attentiveness and humility. For our last class, she brings us thyme pastries and Arab sweets. We eat them. People take turns putting on their favorite songs. I go up to Alia and say, I'm going back to Moscow soon. Please come and visit me. Alia's face goes so white, it looks like the light has changed in the room. She bends close to me and quietly says, I will never come to Moscow. Your soldiers are killing the people I love.

I'm thirty-four, my mother has Covid, I've come to take care of her. We sit in front of the television and listen to Putin. Putin says Russia recognizes the independence of the DNR and the LNR. "How long can this tragedy drag on?" he wonders. "Thank you for your attention." I go out to smoke and quickly buy a washing machine. I think to myself, Good thing I managed to finish renovating my apartment. I think, I'm so fucking practical, it's disgusting. The ruble is fucked, I tell Mama. She asks me, What's going to happen? I tell her, They're going to bring troops into Donetsk and Luhansk, but now they will do it officially. More war. Mama says, But at least they'll defend the Russians. Do you know how many Russians live over there? I tell her, I have to go back to Moscow. What I mean is, I'm going to Donetsk. Mama says, Bring the photograph of your grandfather. Restore it and make a big print of it, okay? Okay. I tuck the photograph of my grandfather into my passport.

In Moscow, I sleep and I have very vivid dreams. They're too vivid, it's almost painful, but also so beautiful. I get up and smoke. Come back into the room. My girlfriend is sitting up in our bed looking at her phone. I can't read her facial expression. Why aren't you sleeping? They're bombing Kyiv. What? They're bombing Kyiv and all of the major cities in Ukraine. We're bombing them? We're bombing them.

I sleep for two more hours, I make myself sleep. I get dressed and go to the office. They ask, Are you ready? Of course I am.

But really, it is impossible to be ready for being the fascists. I was not ready for this at all.

MYKOLAIV

March 13, 2022

Mykolaiv spreads out around the silver mirror of the Southern Bug River. The bridge over the Bug is raised, lowered, raised again. Every day, buses full of women and children depart for Odesa, which remains safe for now, though some flee farther still, to Moldova or to those parts of Ukraine not yet subsumed by war.

There are Russian divisions twelve miles to the north and east. They are shelling the outskirts of town.

Mykolaiv operates in blackout mode, no lights allowed after nightfall. The city administration has warned that a single individual's failure to comply will result in the electricity being cut off for their whole building. Only the grocery stores and pharmacies remain open. Schools and daycares have been on break since the war began; no one wants to separate children from the adults. Many of the bus routes have been canceled; some of the buses have been requisitioned by the army and others deployed in the evacuation.

There are heaps of car tires sitting at the city's intersections, ready to be ignited when Russian troops enter the city. Some still bear traces of paint from when they served as decorative borders for municipal flower beds. "One useful thing about the war," said the mayor, "is that at least we'll get rid of the rubber swans."

The lines for humanitarian aid packages are orderly: grains, tinned food, butter.

Everyday life takes place between air raids. The trauma center has been converted into a field hospital. Patients are evacuated as soon as their surgeries are completed and their wounds are patched up. Beds are then quickly cleared for incoming patients. The medical staff lives on-site and have done so for the past two weeks, since the war began.

Humanitarian aid comes through Odesa. The bigger city watches Mykolaiv with awe: Odesans believe that Mykolaiv is the only reason Odesa has not yet been besieged.

"Mykolaiv is partially surrounded," says Yaroslav Chepurnoi, press officer for the Seventy-ninth Brigade. "There are seventeen Russian battalion tactical groups [BTGs] positioned around town," he says. "Say each one consists of approximately a thousand men: that means seventeen thousand soldiers and 1,500 units of military tech—weapons, equipment, vehicles. We don't know their command center's plans, obviously; we can only assume that some of these BTGs will go north, possibly to Kryvyi Rih. But some of them will stay back and storm the city. We know that the Russian command has been ordered to take Mykolaiv, that it's been ordered to take Odesa, and probably also to punch a land corridor to Pridnestrovie. So we are building up our defenses. Each day that goes by while they wait to attack Mykolaiv we use to build up our defenses.

"The Russian troops attacked a few times already. Four times, I think. The first three were just to gather intelligence. They came in small numbers, and we repelled them, blew up their vehicles. . . . But March 7 was a proper attack, with rockets and tornado missiles at first, then they threw two BTGs at us.

"Here's something interesting. They had plenty of weapons and carriers, but all it took for them to turn back and retreat was our blowing up a few tanks and a couple of armored vehicles. As soon as they took a bit of damage, insignificant damage, they turned around and retreated. We were surprised, frankly. When you launch an attack with tanks and armored vehicles, you expect to lose a few of them in the course of fighting. That shouldn't prevent you from pushing on.

"According to the official count, there are three thousand captured soldiers across Ukraine. I trust those numbers. Even here, there are dozens and dozens. A couple days ago, we had twelve people surrender after some fighting. The fighting was over, even.

"They're shelling the city with Grads and Hurricanes and Tornadoes. Grads may be only 122 millimeters, but Hurricanes are 240 millimeters and Tornadoes are 320; these are all multiple-rocket launchers. At first they targeted military installations. On February 24, they shelled our military airbase at Kulbakino, but our planes were already gone, so no dice. On the evening of the 4th, they targeted the railway station and the fuel storage tanks. Then the bread factory—I mean, God knows what they're thinking. . . . And then, on the 6th and the 7th especially, they started heavily shelling the military units, as well as just residential areas. They've already hit the water treatment plants on the outskirts of the city a few times, so we figure they're trying to mess up the water supply for the civilians. They've stationed artillery in the towns and villages between Mykolaiv and Kherson, that's where they're launching from."

Shells rain down on Khersonskaya Street. This is Balabanovka, a residential neighborhood on the southernmost tip of the Korabelnyi district. The homes are so badly damaged they look half built. Slate tiles blown off the side of a fence, roofs sliding down into craters. The streets between the houses are strewn with the detritus of everyday life. A wall has shattered into bricks, though a little sign with the building number—22—survived. There's no glass left in the windows, which makes the buildings look abandoned. A crumpled GAZelle van sits stowed behind a green gate.

Beyond the gate, a vegetable garden, the earth recently plowed. A cherry tree, strafed to the ground, its branches scattered across the warm earth. There are three gaping holes in the attic roof.

Sasha is up on a ladder, clearing the shattered slate tiles off the roof. He seems not to notice the tears running down his own face.

"First the shelling. A big whoosh over the wheat, all our windows blew out. Then it seemed to get quiet. My wife was on the porch, I was in the kitchen. She sits down. I take a look out the window and see these two airplanes from who knows where, black like the stealth ones. My wife fell over, and then rat-a-tat-tat! Some kind of white smoke. I threw myself over my wife and we started crawling. I've been picking up all the shards. Look how sharp they are, you can cut a person in half with that."

His wife, Nadya, sits with her palms on her knees. "This is where I sat down. I was sitting right here. I'm sitting here, and there's no sound at all. No sound for me to be afraid of. These two airplanes, they were scary, black or dark gray, but I didn't even move from where I was sitting. I thought, They're not going to bomb civilians. And right at that second they started in on the ceiling. . . . I can't tell you how terrifying it was. . . . Look at the gate, all the holes. Another moment, and that would have been me. I'm still in shock, I still can't feel my legs. I'm terrified. Because the idea of leaving is terrifying, too. You still have to make it somewhere. This family I saw on the news, they were fleeing and they got caught in an air raid. The children died, and the parents, everyone."

THE MYKOLAIV ORPHANAGE was evacuated immediately after the war began. There were ninety-three children living there, aged three to eighteen, all "social orphans," children with living parents who cannot look after them. The children were taken to Antonovka, a village forty-one miles northwest. Five days ago, Russian troops assembled next to the village. On March 8, at 9:20 a.m., the troops fired on a car driving orphanage staff down the Kirovograd highway. Three women were killed.

Anatoly Geraschenko was the driver. He shifts anxiously from foot to foot. There's a piece of shrapnel lodged in his right leg. "The surgeon said that they'll operate if it starts to rot," he says, but for now they've left it alone. Masha stays close to her father. One of her eyes is blue, the other one brown. "I've got three sons and two daughters," Anatoly says proudly. He's visibly shaking now. "It's cold," he says.

This was his third trip to Antonovka. He wouldn't accept any money, only enough to cover the gas. He had stuck a red cross made of packing tape to his windshield. His van, a Mercedes Sprinter, burned along with the bodies inside.

"We made it past all the checkpoints, showing our passports every time. I had six women with me, two in the back. At one of the checkpoints, they said something had gone down in the night. They shouldn't have let us through!

"There was no oncoming traffic, just empty lanes. We made it about fifteen miles. My vision's not great, but a couple hundred yards out, the women spotted something, they tell me there's something up ahead, something military. I said, 'Ladies, what do we want to do?' I slowed down. Then came the machine gun fire, I didn't hear it or see anything. I only saw the gravel spraying out in front of me. Now I know why.

"I can't remember exactly how they shot at us. Either I'd stopped completely by then, or maybe the van was still rolling a little. I didn't see the blast, I only felt something shredding, dropping off of the van. A burst of light at my feet. I got out of the van, and they run over to me with their rifles. I'm lying facedown on the asphalt, screaming, 'There are women inside! Women inside!'

"The Russians opened the back door—there were four more people in there. The women came out into the field. They ran over to them shouting, 'Drop your phones!' The women, four of them, all tossed their phones on the ground by the soldiers' feet. I threw mine into the grass. I had a small one on me, in my pocket. My smartphone was still in the car, on the dashboard.

"When I go back to the van, it's gone. I start looking for it. There was a woman sitting by the door—she had no face left. Just her guts out. Her finger was lying on the running board. Her face was gone! It was gone! And the woman sitting right behind me was dead, too, but her I didn't see.

"The Russians were saying, 'We warned you! We gave you a warning round.' But I'm no soldier! Warning rounds aren't the kind of thing I encounter every day. One of the women was wounded in the shoulder. They lifted her up onto her feet. One of the soldiers, a Yakut, or maybe he was a Buryat, bandaged her wound. The other one was very young, a kid, really. He had the same sunglasses as me. I remember his face. My leg was bleeding from all the shrapnel. This kid, he drew back when he saw me. Maybe he got scared or something. I said to him, 'How do we get out of here?' He says, 'Take the fields. All the road signs have been taken down.' I said, 'We are going to walk on the road. If any of your men are up ahead, you tell them.' They said, 'We've informed them already.'

"They seemed completely indifferent, the Russians. They didn't even care that the car was on fire, that there might still be people inside. I said to them, 'Help me put it out, at least!' They just stood there.

"I saw someone in the back lying there when the van first stared to burn. I got inside. It was this woman, her husband had seen her off, kissed her goodbye. I pulled her out—another woman helped me. We laid her out on the road and her back was all bare. I'd been dragging her by her jacket. Her back was shredded with shrapnel. I didn't check her pulse or anything. Her husband called me today. I told him, 'She didn't burn, I pulled her out. . . . She's still lying there.'

"There were two bodies left inside, they burned with the van. That car really burned. My birthday is November 11. And now it's March 8, too."

The three women killed were Natalia Mikhailova, Elena Batygina, and Valentina Vidyuschenko. The director of the orphanage, Svetlana Kluyko, tells me about each one of them, "Natalia Mikhailova, she's been with us since 2014, a teacher. She used to work at a special-needs school so she was very experienced. She was the best sort of human being, kindness personified. If only there were more like her. She loved children, she was so wise, so good with her hands. All of my staff are excellent, but she in particular found a way to get on with everyone. She looked after the older boys. She would have been fifty on May 4. We were going to throw her a party. Elena Batygina took care of the little ones, dressing and changing them. Her children were always dressed so nicely. She had a big stock of different outfits and party dresses. The children loved her, too. She was so kind. Twenty years with the orphanage. She was sixty-four. Valentina Vidyuschenko, she hadn't been with us long. It was her second year as a teacher's assistant. She was working with the new intakes, one of the most difficult groups. . . . When the children first come to us, they're in tears. . . . They've been dropped off somewhere strange, it's so stressful for them. She was one of the first people they met. She helped them wash, dressed them, changed them, talked to them, made them feel better. That's the sort of people they killed. The children were inconsolable. They had been waiting for the teachers to come, we'd told them that they were on their way. The children screamed and screamed and wouldn't stop."

It was not possible to collect the bodies—or rather, what was left of the bodies, "We can't get to them." They remain where they were, fifteen and a half miles from the nearest Ukrainian checkpoint.

The wounded are in the Mykolaiv hospital: Anna Smetana, another teaching assistant, and Elena Belanova, a psychologist. The others, Galina Lytkina and Natalia Vedeneeva, have also been hospitalized, with "severe psychological trauma."

Ninety-three children and ten teachers await evacuation farther into Ukraine in a village encircled by Russian troops.

ALL THE DEAD pass through the office of the regional medical examiner. According to Olga Deryugina, its head, since the start of the war they have processed over sixty bodies of Ukrainian soldiers and more than thirty civilians. When I ask for the exact numbers, she replies, "What's the point? New ones arrive every day." Each body is examined by a team of investigators preparing to file documents with the International Criminal Court at the Hague.

"We've never had so many bodies at once. Shrapnel, bullet wounds, bomb blasts . . . shrapnel, mostly. We've had two corpses with unexploded munitions, the bomb-disposal technicians had to come out to defuse the bodies."

"That's right, there was an unexploded ordnance attached to the body, I removed it myself," says Yuri Aleksandrovich Zolotarev, one of the medical examiners. "It hadn't gone off because the fuse was damaged. I pulled out the casing to give to the bomb-disposal experts so that they could examine it. I told the women to stand back. . . . These had been soldiers. . . . I pulled it out very carefully and handed it over to the bomb-disposal technician. The fins were up inside the rib cage, but the fuse was inside the stomach—it hadn't blown up because the stomach walls are too soft. That was when they were shelling Ochakovo—these were mostly bodies from there. . . . The other guy, it was only a part of an ordnance. When the women came to identify them, the wives, the way they wailed, I haven't heard anything like that in my twenty years on the job. I was in the Bosnian war—I never saw such savagery. Two of our soldiers I autopsied—it wasn't enough that they finished them off with bullets, they also had to knife them in the back. . . . On March 6, two young guys went over to the aircraft repair facility, to try to torch it with Molotov cocktails. . . . The soldiers caught them, tied them up, shot them in the head, and then finished them off by stabbing them in the back. They had knife wounds, dagger wounds under the shoulder blade. It's barbaric, taking the wounded and finishing them off like that."

"First they shot them and then they finished them off?"

"I've been a medical examiner for twenty years! I know which of those wounds came first."

The bodies are piled up in two sections of the cold storage. But there isn't enough room in there, so the ones that have already been autopsied are stacked outside in the street, beside the wall. Eight of them, in black body bags. An outbuilding that was used as a shed before the war is now full of bodies, too—two rooms, each of them sixty-five feet across. There are bodies all over the floor. Five Russian soldiers lie in a corner. "We're keeping them while it's cold outside. Nobody knows who we should hand them over to, or how.

"These are all war fatalities, the burn victims are already body-bagged. . . . Step over them, don't be scared. I've got some others here, too. Once we've worked them over, we have to pack them up in these black plastic bags, because, to be honest, there's nowhere to put all the autopsied bodies, you've seen the state of the rooms."

There are bare feet and feet still wearing shoes. Here is a scorched, blackened young man on his back, arms spread wide, a charred black mess for a face. Half of a human body, flesh fused with grass, a jacket covering the head, and a man's hand hanging down from under the jacket. A naked man wrapped in a floral sheet. A Russian soldier with his hands behind his head; his camo jacket is riding up and you can see a clean undershirt and the yellow strip of his belly.

The bodies in the cold storage are stacked up in layers. Two girls lie one on top of the other. They are sisters. The older one is seventeen. All I can see in the heap of bodies is her hand, her slim, long fingers with neat pink nail polish. The younger girl is three years old and lies on top of her sister. She is blond. Her jaw has been tied shut with gauze, her hands tied together to rest on her stomach. Little red wounds from the shrapnel cover her body. The girl looks alive.

"Arina Butym and Veronica Birykova. Same mother, different fathers. They came in on March 5, at five p.m. They're from the Meshkovo-Pogorelovo village, Shevchenko Street." Nikolai Chan-Chu-Mila is an orderly here. He doesn't look at me when he speaks. "I'm their godfather. . . . I did their baptisms. We're old friends. They brought the girls in during my shift. Of course I recognized them straightaway. I can't describe what I went through when I first saw them."

Dmitry Butym is the girls' father. He waits on the other side of the fence, he's taking their bodies home today. Deep red folds rim his eyes. "Vera was heating up food in the kitchen. Arina had gone out to play in the yard. They didn't have a chance, either of them. The little one died instantly, a piece of shrapnel went through her heart. The older one, they got her heart going for two minutes, but it wouldn't beat on its own. Their mother is in the Dubki hospital, she has shrapnel in her thigh—it damaged things as it went through. You have to excuse me, all I can think about right now is burying my children."

There's a new body being brought in. The attendants are unwinding a striped bedsheet. It's a man, the breathing tube still in his throat and his body flayed. Somebody tried to save him but couldn't. He is left to lie in the yard.

Four men with dark roses are waiting for their colleague to be released to them. Igor was a security guard, a civilian. "That goddamn Tornado comes down, and that's it."

A body in camo trousers is carried out from the shed. The body is purple, with a wide gash where a face should be. Two men from the investigations unit bend over him. They take down a description of his clothes, remove his trousers, take a DNA sample by dipping a piece of gauze in his blood. One of them pokes his fingers into the crushed mess of the man's mouth—they need to establish which of the skull bones are broken.

A light-haired woman swathed in a black headscarf speaks, "My mother lived on the fifth floor. She couldn't get down to the bomb shelter in the cellar. Her next door neighbors, they helped her, they were like family. She died in the morning, peacefully. As much as you can call it peaceful—she was on the bathroom floor, hiding from all this horror. The next day, at exactly the same time, a rocket hit the building next door and blew out all of her windows. But she was already gone by then. I think it was some kind of miracle, that she died peacefully on the Sunday. The next day she would have died in a state of terror. She was seventy-seven. I have a photo of the apartment, what was left of it, from the neighbors. This is the view from her window, the building next door that was hit. It was the next day, she wouldn't have survived it. She died on Forgiveness Sunday. And on the 7th all of her windows burst. She would have been so frightened. If it had to happen, I'm glad it was on the 6th and not on the 7th. I'm so grateful. My mother was named Svetlana Nikolayevna. She was half Russian. Her husband, my dad, was born in Russia, in Krasnoyarsk. He was stationed here, that's how they met. My maternal grandfather was from Kursk. We were a Russian-speaking family. We're going to the cemetery now. My son is in Kyiv. My name is Oksana."

Army base A0224 is one of the two military installations at Mykolaiv that was hit by artillery fire. On March 7, at 5:15 a.m., the barracks were struck by a Kalibr missile. Nine dead, including five conscripts who had not yet seen fighting. Fourteen wounded. Two of the conscripts initially presumed missing in action were found several hours later—they had fled and hidden.

A chunk of a three-story building has been reduced to rubble. There's a bunk bed still sitting on an intact bit of floor. Emergency responders dig through the rubble by hand. They work with the military personnel, passing the pieces up a human chain. They are searching for the body of the last missing man. His name was Stas. He was a native of Western Ukraine and had been drafted eight months ago.

Yaroslav, the press officer, had a lucky escape that night. He is squinting at the sun, his hands never not on his rifle. "They sounded the alarm at about 5:15. I shot up and shouted, 'Boys, everyone out!' We were the first ones out of the barracks, we didn't even put our boots on. . . . There were guys standing outside, and I told them to get inside. God forbid that they hit us with something, the shrapnel would go everywhere. . . . I started to go back inside. I ran back in and when I got to the second floor, maybe seven meters from me, I saw the tiles flying up, then a flash—fire. I saw fire. At 5:17 they hit us.

"I was knocked back by the blast. I covered my head with my arms. There was glass raining down on me. I try to turn on my . . . Fifteen seconds pass and I turn my flashlight on and I'm crawling. I can hear people screaming, a woman was screaming. I'm crawling and crawling, but I can't feel the ground under me anymore. There is no ground. I hear the sergeant shouting, 'Everybody outside!' I managed to get back and started to run out. I had my rifle with me. Everybody I saw, whoever was left, I told them, 'We have to get down to the shelter.' And that's how we made it out. Taras, Danila, some of the other guys, they were all buried under the rubble. There had been twenty-nine of us in the sleeping quarters.

"I don't want to start cursing . . . but I'm not taking prisoners, not after this. And I don't care about their parents or wives. I don't feel any pity. I'm twenty years old, I was training to be a veterinarian, but I don't have any pity left for anyone."

Somewhere up at the front lines, the Ukrainians have shot up a Tiger infantry mobility vehicle. Its Russian crew of four has surrendered. At HQ, they think that the Russians were doing reconnaissance, but those who were actually there think the Tiger was probably just lost.

Arthur has a black bandanna over his face. In his former life, he was a specialist in economic cybernetics. "There was a car driving up from the direction of Kherson. When it got here, I saw it was armored. They rolled down a window. I look inside: Russians, in uniform. I say, 'Surrender.' I cursed them out too. The guy rolls the window back up before I could shoot. I started shooting out their tires. The car rolled for maybe another twenty seconds. Somebody threw a grenade and the car burst into flames. They didn't want to come out at first. We smashed the windows in, and then they began to surrender."

"Did you talk to them?"

"We tried not to. These terrifying warriors. All our guys were laughing their asses off. It was the usual bullshit: they thought that they were just doing military exercises, all of that crap. 'I don't even know where I am.' Total bullshit, of course they know."

They handed the prisoners over to the Security Service.

Someone has graffitied "Death to the enemies" on the dividing line in the middle of the road. The soldiers are warming up by the wood-burning stove. "Those Russians fucked up our spring."

"I heard that it came from those towers," says a soldier nicknamed the Actor. "A sniper or a machine gunner, I don't know for sure. One bullet hit forty centimeters from my foot. After the third bullet, I finally clocked that they were aiming right at me."

"Are you waiting for them to storm the city?"

"I'm waiting for all this fuckery to fuck back off. And I hope that the residents of the occupied territories are making plenty of Molotov cocktails. And I'd like to wish my daughter happiness. She's three. I named her Maria.

"My family stayed. My brother's house is a little bigger than mine. We all live in the same village—my brother, our mother, and me. My brother is older, so he's the head of the family, you know how it goes. His job is protecting the women and children, my job is to be here. I was in Varvarovka when they shelled the Kulbakino air base, working at a shipbuilding plant. My uncle woke me up at 6:30, and we could hear the air base being shelled. I was at the central recruiting office by 8:20. They gave me my enlistment papers and said to come back at six o'clock the next morning, all packed. I only told my wife after I got back. She knew, though—she knew I would do that."

"Where could we evacuate to? This is our land," says another soldier. "My family is in Odesa. They won't touch Odesa while Mykolaiv is standing. That's why I'm here.

"We keep saying: 'Russians, go home! Just go home, that's it. We didn't ask you to come here. You don't have to die here.'

"Why won't they collect their corpses? They're just fertilizer for our fields. So sorry, but your son will come here and you'll never see him again, no neat little grave for you to visit. Something happens to me, though, my mom will grieve for me and bury me herself.

"People who used to be like brothers to us are our enemies now, because they attacked us—that's not what brothers do. We have to defend our land, we have to stand our ground. We didn't want this war, we didn't see it coming.

"I'm from Mykolaiv myself. Am I supposed to just sit home and wait? I went down to the recruitment office on the very first day.

"We don't want to wage war against Russia. So don't you come and wage war against us.

"They think Ukraine is weak. No. Ukraine is really good. We know every hole and every burrow here. This is our land you've come to.

"We don't want war. We want you to leave us alone."

So far, twenty-two babies have been born at the Mykolaiv maternity hospital during the war, two of them in the makeshift bomb shelter in the basement. All of the babies survived.

There are almost no C-sections anymore, because the stitches need rest, peace, and quiet, and there's no peace now, not with the air raids. A maternity ward has been set up in the basement, but the operating rooms are still on the third floors. This is very dangerous. A siren blares. Expectant mothers walk down to the basement, step by step, holding on to the walls, their descent slow and ponderous. The midwives carry the babies down.

Lena Sylvestrova lies on a metal gurney under a woolen blanket. Her husband, Aleksei, is trying to soothe her. The palm of his hand is on her neck. Lena gave birth at 4:30 a.m. by C-section. She had tried for a natural birth, she labored for almost twenty-four hours. She is twenty-eight and her husband is twenty-six. This is their first child. She went into labor early in the morning, after curfew. Aleksei drove her to the hospital himself.

"My due date was just around the corner when the war started. I was so worried, waiting for it all to kick off. I was constantly on edge, waiting. Worrying that we'd get caught in an air raid or shelling in town. I was lucky—they managed to do my C-section between two air raid sirens. Imagine, you are in labor, all you want is some peace and quiet for your baby, but instead, your city is being endlessly bombed!"

Aleksei strokes her cheek.

"I'd love to remember what it's like, walking around without worrying about getting shot."

The light in the basement is dim, the women sit along the walls. The chief physician takes Aleksei to the archive department and quietly opens the door. Inside, a midwife sits on a pile of mattresses cradling a white bundle. She holds the bundle out toward Aleksei. "I don't want to hold her, I'm scared," he tells her.

"Better get used to it. Don't be scared, nothing to be afraid of."

Aleksei takes Masha into his arms. It's his first time. The midwife gently adjusts his hands.

"She's so tiny," Aleksei says. He falls silent, his face dipping ever closer to his daughter's. "My little girl. Hello there! Are you sticking your tongue out at me? Really, Masha? We're going to be together every day, every single day, deal?"

"We only want peace. Please write that," says a woman in a white lab coat. "My name is Nadezhda Sherstova. I'm a senior nurse anesthetist. I've been doing this job thirty years. Since the war started, whenever a baby is born, there's no joy in the parents' eyes. You worry about the mothers, their milk coming in. That's what scares me. There is no joy for the parents."

"She was a real pain," Aleksei tells the chief physician. "Constantly kicking. She'd hear my voice and start in on her dancing in there. Wouldn't let her mom sleep at night. She's kicking a little right now. I thought she would look like me. When we did the ultrasound, they said she looked like me, but look how pretty she is."

The next shelling of Mykolaiv began at 8 p.m. on March 11 and lasted most of the night, with brief pauses. According to Mayor Oleksandr Senkievich's official statement, more than 167 residential buildings sustained damage, including City Hospital No. 3 (which was filled with wounded civilians), a prepared-food plant, eleven schools and day cares, and an orphanage. Eleven private homes were completely destroyed. Shrapnel shredded the yard of the cancer ward and the emergency department. Kuzya, the beloved hospital guard dog, was killed. They covered him up with a towel. The cemetery was shelled, too. Fires have broken out all over the city.

CONCLUSION

NOVAYA AND I (WE WERE A CULT)

GO STRAIGHT FROM THE SUBWAY, follow the weaving boulevard, then you turn down Arkhangelskiy Alley, go past the pink church (they say it's haunted), then left on Potapovskiy. Go past the garden with the lilacs (it used to be filled with homeless people, now there are just statues), past the abandoned, boarded-up building (it's always been boarded up, which is strange, because we are right in the center of Moscow), past that, and there, on your left, are our editorial offices. The building used to be a printers'; it's old, painted warm gray.

It has dark and deep basements. I remember how R. brought some weed once and we went down there to smoke it and then convinced ourselves that somebody was looking for us, and so we climbed out extremely slowly, holding on to the walls, whispering, Quiet, shhhhhhhh!

There's a roof that you can sort of access. There's usually a lock on the door but you can just take the fire escape. Lena Racheva once climbed up there and then got caught by security, and then the newspaper had to apologize to the building owner. But if you talk to the owner, they'll open the door for you. One time, we had an anniversary party up there on the roof. It was April 1, 2006, sunny and cold. I got drunk very quickly and stopped being able to hear anything. The editor in chief, Dmitry Muratov, kept calling my name. When I finally heard him, he handed me my new ID—I would now be a staff writer at *Novaya Gazeta*. I was instantly sober. For three days, no matter how much I drank, I couldn't get drunk. I was so filled with joy, there was no room for anything else.

The security guards are on the ground floor. They're always changing. It's a tough job. People leave rams' heads in front of our office (it's supposed to be threatening), live sheep (it's supposed to be funny), protest in front of the building ("You're traitors to the motherland"). One time, someone sprayed the front door with an acrid-smelling liquid, so they had to call in chemists to test it, then tear out the asphalt in front of the building and put in a new sidewalk there. The security guards don't like us so much. We used to have to show our IDs at the door, but now we have key cards, you just tap and go. The stairs. On the second floor are HR, distribution, advertising, legal, and the director's office. More stairs. I'm going to the third floor.

Tap your key card again. Open the door and the first thing you see is a glass box, the smoking room—we call it the gas chamber. It can barely fit three. It feels like being on the tram during rush hour, blowing smoke in each other's faces. When I first started working at *Novaya*, you could smoke anywhere. But then the law changed, and the editor in chief quit smoking and said we couldn't, either. But they still smoke in two of the offices! And in the news department, they just climb out onto the roof of the addition and smoke out there. Lucky.

In summer, we would eat strawberries on that roof and drink rosé. In the winter, there's snow and you can go stand in it, lie in it, leave your mark.

The front hall has a small exhibition on the history of our newspaper. Politkovskaya's computer, an issue that traveled to space (one of our columnists is a cosmonaut), a shard of shrapnel that nearly killed Muratov in Chechnya (back then he wasn't the editor in chief, he was a war reporter), a bow belonging to my first editor, Nugzar Mikeladze (before he was a journalist, he was an archer and competed on the national level). I walk past it, I know all of it so well. Take a turn, five steps, and you're face to face with the target board. That's where people hang up announcements. You can read about who filed the best piece and who fumbled. I always look for my name. Sometimes I'm praised (and in that case, the phrasing matters, I always memorize it); sometimes I'm chastised. One time, my computer froze—it was old, very old—and while I was restarting it, it deleted the piece I had written for the New Year's issue. I never turned it in. I was reprimanded, and they hung the reprimand up on the board. I went to yell at our finance director, who kept not getting us new computers. He goes, Why don't you just write a new piece? You're supposed to be talented, you can pull it off. Can you believe that jerk? I still remember that.

They also hang up the photos of people who have been killed or who've died. They put a little table in front of the photos with a bouquet. The photos and flowers remain there until the funerals. And then the photos get moved to the round room, where they are hung over the table where we hold our editorial meetings, next to the photos just like them.

So far there are six.

To the right of the bulletin board is the bathroom. One time, I went to the ladies' room to find a man painting the building, just hanging there right in front of the window, with an impenetrable face. Another time, a drunken Babchenko shot up the door with a BB gun and then Nikita Girin took the door off the men's room and hung it on ours as a replacement. They fired Babchenko. He was fired and rehired maybe three times, he was too much one of us to really let go of, until one day, they fired him for good. He would come back to the offices bearing champagne and ask all the girls if they wanted to feel his pecs. Bald, tall, and awkward, a really good guy. Now he lives abroad, considers himself a Ukrainian, and writes about how the Russians are orcs and Russia is Mordor.

In front of the bathroom, the bar. It's actually the cafeteria, but we call it the bar because it sounds cooler. It used to have wood-paneled walls, heavy, lacquered wood furniture, but then Muratov went to Hemingway's favorite café and decided that we should have what they have. The walls were whitewashed, we got simpler tables and chairs, and they were carelessly painted in blue and green. In the old cafeteria, writers' funniest excuses hung on the walls ("I didn't come to work because I wasn't inspired and I refuse to work without inspiration") alongside the covers of the best issues. Now it's just nothing, blank space. That's where we eat. You can get free bread and soup, it's practically communism.

Farther down the hall, that's where the guard ladies sit. There are three guard ladies, they're these old ladies, they spend the night at the offices. Their job is getting you out before ten. But I would stay late all the time, begging them for permission, telling them anything I could think of, and they eventually came to terms with me. I love to work in the office at night. It's all dark and quiet, the silence itself feels alive. It's a bit scary to walk down the halls in the middle of the night, it feels like at any moment someone might call your name. Writing feels good, it's just you and the piece, nothing else. In the mornings, before anybody comes in, I ride through the halls on the scooter that my editor Mikeladze once rode. I know my way around perfectly and can lean into all of the turns. I'll never fall.

Then there's my office, room 305. I've been in there seventeen years, holy shit. It used to have tattered linoleum and dirty walls, a cracked leather easy chair that was amazing to sleep in if you curled up in it. But recently, they remodeled and threw my favorite chair out, replaced everything with furniture from IKEA. Now there's a red fabric love seat. It's good for sleeping on, too. We take turns.

Our office has six desks and a small editorial suite with two more. When I first came to work here, that was where Nugzar Mikeladze and lead staff writer Lena Milashina sat. I was very afraid of them both. Mikeladze had blue eyes and black hair with gray streaks. He was tall, never hurried, talked slowly, walked slowly, but thought very fast. He had a deeper knowledge of Russian than anyone. He taught me everything that I know. When he read through my pieces, he'd raise his eyebrows at the bad sections and I would run out of the office and hide, catch my breath—it was way too scary to watch. Milashina was petite, volatile, always extremely direct. Sometimes she and Mikeladze would argue—they'd yell at each other, Milashina would throw papers at him, one time it was an ashtray. I'd squeeze my head into my shoulders and wait out the storm. Then they would go out for coffee and come back laughing together.

When Mikeladze died, we hung up his portrait over his desk. His languid smile. When I am eaten up by anxiety, I press my forehead against the photo and plead: Nugzar Kobayevich, help me, please.

It always works.

My department is called the reporter group. That's my family. Two Lenas, Pasha, Olya, Nikita, Katya, Irina. Only now, when I'm so adult, have I learned to distance myself from them a little bit. I used to be sure that they'd always understand me and I'd understand them. That I was never alone. There were some years when I didn't have friends outside the office at all—why would I need to, there were so many people I loved right here.

My desk is the messiest (Lena Milashina's is a close second). A mound of papers, books, letters, pens, tea bags. I'm cozy amid this chaos. Under my desk, I keep extra clothes—a T-shirt, a pair of jeans, socks, underwear, sneakers. I can take off for the field any moment. I have a piggy bank with spring feet next to my keyboard, that's where I keep my change. The walls of my cubicle have reproductions of paintings by Munch and other Norwegian artists, a photograph from a Pussy Riot action in which the girls ran up to cops and French-kissed them, some cards people sent me. On top of my monitor, I kept three bullets and two pieces of shrapnel—things that had just barely missed me. That's how I warded off death.

This is where I was when I found out that Politkovskaya had been killed. It was a Saturday, I will never forget it. This is where I would leave for my trips out into the field. This is where I would read out my typeset pieces, printed out on large white sheets of paper. You read through them word by word, following along with your finger, drawing special symbols on them with your pen. After my head injury, I lost the ability to write and spent hours sitting at my desk, crying in horror, worried that it would never come back. We celebrated so many birthdays, cut so many cakes, drank wine, and discussed the future, which would, of course, be completely unbelievable and amazing.

Outside, fascism was descending on our country. We were describing the process as well as we could. Our paper came out three times a week, across the whole country, our website was updated 24/7. We did our job well, we really tried. It was terrifying and disgusting and heartbreaking outside. Inside, it was warm.

I wasn't friends with my colleagues from other media outlets. I didn't go to the big media parties. Actually, sometimes I would—and every time, I would be disappointed. It felt like they were all talking about bullshit and not real work, and then gossip—who was getting married, who was getting fired. Other journalists didn't respect *Novaya* much—they said that we were too activist, that we were allowed to be because we never wrote anything actually important, that we got paid nothing (that part was true). I wouldn't even bother standing up for us. I knew that I was working at the best newspaper on earth. More and more often, other writers talked about censorship, about the pieces that got taken down. Their publications were being shut down, one after the other, there were fewer and fewer places to work.

Novaya lived on. We weren't that easy to get rid of. We owned the majority of our shares, we chose our editors in chief ourselves, as well as the editorial board and council. We held elections every two years. Campaigns, debates, a special newsletter, a ballot committee. They'd stopped having real elections outside, but we kept it up. We thought that was funny.

Most often, we would elect Muratov to be editor in chief. He's big and bearded, blue eyes, looks like Hemingway. Always wears ratty T-shirts. He has a strange and special gift: the ideas that he comes up with always land, even when they initially seem insane. He once studied to be a folklorist. He loves grand gestures and making big plans. He loves me and I love him back. Whenever we fought, which happened several times, I'd cry inconsolably. Who else has the power to hurt me like that? When my mother was facing a potential cancer diagnosis, he was able to get her examined with lighting speed, overnight, and gave us the money for it. She was in the clear; that meant I could live. He always had a bottle in his office. Piled up by the wall, his collection of valuable hockey jerseys, which he was slowly selling off, donating the money toward treatment for sick children, the most hopeless cases. When Muratov was given the Nobel Peace Prize, I got really excited. My thought was, Now they won't kill him. I was excited that people would finally see how great he truly was—I mean everyone else, the people outside our office. He split up the prize money among a handful of charities, not leaving anything for himself.

In his Nobel speech, he spoke about war. He saw it was drawing nearer and he was trying to stop it.

He couldn't do it.

We continued our work for thirty-two days from the first day of the war. Then *Novaya* was issued two warnings from the censorship agency; after that, they would revoke our media license. Without the license, we couldn't publish. Our collective voted to stop putting the paper out, hoping to save it that way. I didn't vote. I was at war.

They revoked our license anyway, five months later. *Novaya* sued. It lost the case in every court.

Novaya Gazeta no longer exists.

Now, when we are not here anymore: no more editorial meetings, no pitch meetings, no fucking closing the issues, no running or swearing or crying reporters, no small victories or enormous and terrifying events that need to be compressed into stories. After everything I was ever afraid of actually happened, and I am empty, and I have nothing left to hold on to, I can think.

The motto for *Novaya Gazeta* was "Same Letters, New Words."

How much does the word weigh?

(sometimes, an entire living life)
Can the word stand up to armed tyranny?
(no)
Can the word stop a war?
(no)
Can the word save a country?
(no)
Can the word save the person who says it?
It saved me.
But just me.

Acknowledgments

This book was made possible by:

My mother Galina Kostyuchenko

My sister Svetlana Vidanova

My partner and my first reader Iana Kuchina

My fearless protagonists and sources

My colleagues, photographers Anna Artemyeva and Yuri Kozyrev

My editors Nugzar Mikeladze and Olga Bobrova

My editor in chief, Dmitry Muratov

My second family, *Novaya Gazeta*

My readers, who believed in me and believed me

My agent Chris Parris-Lamb

My translators Bela Shayevich and Ilona Yazhbin Chavasse

I wrote this book having lost my home and country. I lived in apartments provided by Prague Civil Society, Jan Michalski Foundation, and Château de Lavigny.

I would also like to thank Lina Egorova, Ulyana Dobrova, Ivan Kolpakov, Masha Gessen, and Roman Anin, whose careful questions made me think and accept that I can and must go on living.

Translators' Acknowledgments

To my parents, who took a leap of faith and changed our fates, with love and gratitude.

—Ilona Yazhbin Chavasse

With the deepest love and gratitude to *moi kumir* and Mark Krotov. And to Lena herself.

—Bela Shayevich

Index

INDEX

INDEX